Seeing the Myth in Human Rights

PENNSYLVANIA STUDIES IN HUMAN RIGHTS

Bert B. Lockwood, Jr., Series Editor

A comlete list of books in the series
is available from the publisher.

to J + I + E

CONTENTS

Preface   ix

Introduction   1

Chapter 1. Sacred Myth, Political Myth   21

Chapter 2. The Sacred Center of Human Rights   36

Chapter 3. The Sacred and the Social   62

Chapter 4. The Legal Personality and a New World Order   92

Conclusion. Making and Unmaking Political Myth   117

Appendix. The Universal Declaration of Human Rights   133

Notes   139

Bibliography   173

Index   185

Acknowledgments   193

PREFACE

The state is invisible; it must be personified before it can be seen, symbolized before it can be loved, imagined before it can be conceived.
—Michael Walzer, "On the Role of Symbolism in Political Thought," 194

There are any number of reasons why one might object to seeing the myth in human rights—why one might object, in other words, to the work of conceiving of contemporary human rights as a powerful form of modern myth. One might argue that such a conception ties contemporary human rights to a religious logic that such rights were specifically designed to supersede. One might argue that such a conception, in addition to undermining the avowed secularity of such rights, also threatens to undermine their universality—to portray human rights as intractably indebted to culturally specific values and languages and thus to reinforce the perception of human rights as a mechanism for a subtle form of cultural imperialism. More generally, one might argue that the word myth by definition serves to call into question the very legitimacy or viability of human rights. All of these potential objections are valid insofar as they presuppose a definition of myth as a vehicle for, on the one hand, particular religious dogma or, on the other, erroneous or even duplicitous discourse. The central premise of this book, however, is that such presuppositions about myth are unfaithful to contemporary scholarship in the field of religious studies, and that they are therefore blind to a series of important insights that the academic study of religion has to offer into the unique logic, authority, and history of universal human rights.

Contemporary scholarship on religion has converged upon an understanding of myth not merely as a mode of doctrinaire or duplicitous discourse, but as a mode of human labor that serves the broad, enduring function of generating meaning, solidarity, and order within all manner of human communities. This definition does not merely hearken to today's most prominent scholarship on myth; as I will argue, it dovetails in unexpected ways with a prominent body of scholarship on the origin and function of contemporary human rights. Ultimately, I will argue, the framework of myth furnishes a means for making sense of a series of crucial yet paradoxical dynamics within the creation and broadcast of human rights in the twentieth and twenty-first centuries. These paradoxes become particularly visible within the creation and afterlife of the founding document of contemporary human rights: the 1948 Universal Declaration of Human Rights. In the course of negotiating this document over a two-year period, members of the First Commission on Human Rights vaunted the secular credentials of the Declaration even as their descriptions of the logic of human rights were permeated by discourses of sacredness, veneration, and teleology. Even as the Commission came to recognize the impossibility of negotiating a binding and enforceable document and thus committed itself to a conception of the Declaration as educational, it nevertheless placed heavy emphasis upon the Declaration's capacity to fundamentally transform the ethical and even the metaphysical landscape of international and domestic law. Finally, even as the Declaration ultimately remains a nonbinding and unenforceable prelude to the numerous official conventions that now define the landscape of human rights law, this document is nevertheless recognized by many theorists as a text commanding a moral and political authority distinct from the more straightforward legal authority of the subsequent conventions that have emerged from it.

Such human rights paradoxes have been acknowledged and speculated upon by theorists ranging from Jacques Derrida to Jürgen Habermas. Yet, while it is not unheard of for commentators to attribute such paradoxes to a religious or quasi-religious logic lurking somewhere within the Declaration, rarely have human rights theorists drawn systematically upon the wealth of scholarship on myth and religion to substantiate such suspicions. In other words, while it is not at all uncommon within today's flourishing field of human rights scholarship to encounter references to the manner in which human rights appear in some way to partake of a religious logic—appear to escape the purely secular bounds conventionally ascribed to international law—such references are almost always marked by a surprising paucity of efforts to set the resources of religious studies to the work of elucidating these interpenetrations of religion and secularity. Such will be the task of this book. Centering upon the 1948 Universal Declaration of Human Rights, *Seeing the*

Myth in Human Rights draws upon a breadth of historical and theoretical materials to highlight the manner in which this document ultimately functions as one of today's preeminent exemplars of modern political mythmaking. In presenting an analysis of the Declaration through the lens of myth, this book will mobilize and expand upon a variety of important insights and texts from within the field of religious studies, and it will put these insights and texts into conversation with thinkers from within the realms of, among other things, political philosophy, critical legal studies, and human rights historiography. Such, I will argue, is the nature of myth as understood by today's most prominent scholars of religion: myth is a phenomenon that is not merely germane to the exploration of specific religious narratives but is key to a broader understanding of the nature of political authority in the modern world.

Introduction

On December 10, 1998, the United States Information Agency released a special edition of its *Issues of Democracy* to commemorate the fiftieth anniversary of the adoption of the Universal Declaration of Human Rights. President William Jefferson Clinton headed up this special edition with his own commemoration of the Declaration, which he described as "one of the most important documents in the twentieth century, indeed of human history."[1] The Declaration, he asserted,

> represents the first time men and women sought to articulate
> the core aspirations of all the world's people. The authors of the
> Universal Declaration struggled to understand and harmonize their
> differing cultural traditions and convictions during a three-year
> debate that culminated in a set of rights recognized by all as
> transcending national, social, and cultural boundaries. . . . On
> December 10, 1948, the United Nations General Assembly adopted
> the Universal Declaration without a single dissenting vote. Over the
> past half century, the Declaration's thirty articles have entered the
> consciousness of people around the world. They are now invoked
> routinely in constitutions and courts. They set a standard against
> which we must all now measure ourselves.[2]

Clinton's description of the Declaration exemplifies the manner in which people across the globe have come to understand this document, its core principles, and its place within the historico-political landscape of the twentieth and early twenty-first centuries. In the decades following its adoption, the Declaration has been depicted as the product of a monumental, unprecedented struggle culminating in its unanimous adoption by the General Assembly and its gradual incorporation into the consciousness of people, constitutions, and courts around the world.[3] In such depictions, the universal scope of the Declaration is emphasized even as its nebulous legal status is downplayed. Clinton sums up the Declaration's enumerated rights as emblematic of "a standard" rather than as a set of rights the infraction of which would be punishable by law. In keeping with this sense that the Declaration conveys standards rather than concrete rules, Clinton admonishes us to measure ourselves against the tenets of this document—an admonition that stands in tension with his initial assertion that this document articulates innate values that have *already* shaped human societies around the globe, irrespective of national, social, and cultural boundaries. This tension between the prescriptive and the descriptive logics of the Declaration brings to light a striking ambiguity within the narrative of universal human rights: a logical, chronological, and ontological circularity in which, as Jack Donnelly puts it, "Human rights shape political society, so as to shape human beings, so as to realize the possibilities of human nature, which provided the basis for these rights in the first place."[4]

This circular logic is discernible within the Declaration on many levels. On the one hand, this is a legal document that not only lays out a series of important rights but that has served as one of the foundations upon which the edifice of contemporary international law has been erected. It features centrally among the seminal documents comprising the "juridical revolution" of the 1940s: documents including key texts such as the UN Charter of 1945, the Genocide Convention of 1948, and the Geneva Convention revisions of 1949.[5] As Michael Ignatieff points out, "The U.S. State Department's annual report for 1999 on human rights practice around the world describes the constellation of human rights and democracy—along with 'money and the Internet'—as one of the three universal languages of globalization."[6] Far from merely contributing to the human rights language of globalization, the Declaration is in fact widely perceived to be its fount. As such, it commands a political capital far exceeding that of other international legal documents. Today, the mere charge of human rights violations, even when leveled independently of the more concrete articles of subsequent rights documents, has the power to cow political leaders and rile the international community.

The indisputable authority of the Declaration, however, stands in dramatic contrast to its negligible enforcement capabilities. A nonbinding document designed to subvert the very state-centered international order upon which it depends for its implementation, the Declaration proves to be a remarkably "weak" document when it comes to the important matters of "regulatory effect [and] systems of compulsion."[7] As Joseph Slaughter puts it, "from an institutional standpoint, international human rights law has little formal immediacy, lacking administrative formations, social structures, and enforcement instruments comparable to those of the modern nation-state."[8] These regulatory weaknesses originate and retain their most striking form within the Declaration itself. This document is and has always been innately "extrajudicial"—dependent, as Slaughter puts it, "upon processes of personal and global incorporation and consumption" that operate beyond (or, more accurately, *beneath*) the conventional trappings of law.[9] The Declaration, in other words, occupies a space within the corpus of international law that is quite different from, though intimately tied to, the enforceable conventions and treaties that have grown from it.

The history of the creation of the Declaration, moreover, reveals that its nebulous legal status was only partly a concession to the complex and conflictual geopolitical landscape of the 1940s; its unconventional logic was also the product of a broader vision on the part of its framers. As the First Commission on Human Rights came together over the course of two years to do their work of generating a declaration, it quickly became clear that the creation of a legally binding document such as an international "bill of rights," though certainly crucial, would involve a level of political specificity that would likely make international consensus impossible in 1948. Far from quelling the aspirations of the Commission, however, this political reality fueled a conviction on the part of many of the framers that the path to international consensus must run through the articulation of a set of fundamental principles capable of transforming the international political landscape itself. The key to achieving the political consensus necessary for a legally binding covenant, in other words, lay in formulating a set of principles that could "immediately strike public opinion and serve as a guide for the future policies of the State"—a set of principles imbued with a level of "emotional appeal, conviction, and provocative language" that would render it capable of sounding "a bugle call" not only to states but, first and foremost, to the individuals living within those states.[10] Even as it maintained its commitment to the eventual creation of an enforceable covenant, the Commission quickly came to see the Declaration as a document that, if properly formulated, could become capable of wielding "considerable moral weight" even in the absence of specific enforcement mechanisms.[11] Thus, while the political obstacles of the late 1940s certainly cannot be gainsaid, the Commission's deliberations over the two-year period culminating in December 1948 are replete with testaments to the idea that, as Lebanese delegate Charles Malik put it, "the morally disturbing or judging is far more important than the legally binding," and that the key to human rights would therefore be to make them a matter of internal orientation rather than external coercion.[12] Malik's attentiveness to the power of moral outrage and judgment was mirrored by Commission Chair Eleanor Roosevelt's unflagging commitment to human rights as an institution of "soft power," and her insistence that the implementation of human rights must begin "In small places, close to home—so close and so small that they cannot be seen on any map of the world."[13] Prominent framers such as Malik and Roosevelt acknowledged throughout the Commission's negotiations that the extrajudicial logic of the Declaration was bound to imbue this document with an unconventional legal and political authority. Today, a growing number of commentators have come to embrace this conclusion and have, in response, infused the field of human rights theory with a vein of scholarship geared toward an exploration of the ways in which conventional frameworks of law and legal regulation only partially capture the unique logic and authoritativeness of the Declaration.[14]

Theorists who give serious consideration to the Declaration's extrajudicial logic have tended to fall into two broad camps. In one camp are human rights "pragmatists," content to set aside the philosophical and metaphysical elusiveness of this document and focus their energies upon "the application of human rights instruments, that is, their interpretation, administration, and enforcement."[15] The other camp consists of human rights "philosophers" convinced that deliberations over human rights' applications must be preceded by a reckoning with the constitutive peculiarities of human rights that I have been discussing here. For human rights pragmatists, an understanding and application of human rights as "pragmatic instruments" is sufficient for the cultivation of a global human rights regime.[16] Such pragmatists profess to be clear-eyed about the Declaration's legal and enforcement weaknesses while nevertheless insisting on the capacity of such rights to serve as a centerpiece for a healthy global political order. As Ignatieff asserts in his own version of this human rights pragmatism, "People may not agree why we have rights, but they can agree that we need them."[17] In the same breath with which he gives voice to human rights' lack of universal coherence, Ignatieff disclaims the necessity of engaging such incoherence. In fact, a preoccupation with the fact of human rights' fundamental ambiguities is, in this view, one of the surest ways of *undermining* the cultivation and deployment of human rights values. Ignatieff's approach carries the benefit of sidestepping what many perceive as intractable and even debilitating philosophical questions. Other theorists, however, disagree with pragmatists' claims to be able to evade such questions. Pauline Tseng captures the mandate of the latter, "philosophical"

camp of human rights theorists in her assertion that "practical questions concerning the meaning and scope of specific human rights provisions, and their
application, cannot be separated from underlying questions of what we mean
when we speak of 'human rights.'"[18]

Within the camp of human rights theorists willing to take up this imperative of giving serious consideration to the question of what we mean when we
speak of human rights, we find a series of interrelated approaches to making
sense of the Declaration and its unique combination of authoritativeness and
legal weakness. Taking a primarily historical approach, Mary Ann Glendon
emphasizes its framers' commitment to the principle that a human rights
declaration must function as a "cultural" or a "moral" document before it
could function as a legal document—that the fundamental mandate of the
Declaration was always to build up better human beings rather than to punish those who violate human rights.[19] This endeavor on the part of the framers of the Declaration inevitably lent itself to a different type of document
than one focused upon the practicalities of enforcement. Donnelly, for his
part, offers up an unapologetic embrace of the circularity of the Declaration,
describing it as a document designed to generate a universalizable vision of
"human nature" out of the combination of "a moral posit" (in contrast to an
empirical fact) and "a social project rooted in the implementation of human
rights."[20] Slaughter and Lynn Hunt, for their part, both assert that the authority of this document can only be understood as a product of the interaction
between the Declaration and extrajudicial "cultural" realms such as that of
modern literature. As Slaughter puts it,

> the absence of fully effective administrative and enforcement
> institutions and the lack of a tangible international community
> do not mean that contemporary human rights are devoid of
> regulatory effect or systems of compulsion. If law, like power more
> generally, operates through a combination of coercion and consent
> (what Antonio Gramsci theorized as hegemony), then part of its
> force comes from the cooperation of extrajudicial institutions
> and discourses. That is, the effective jurisdiction of the law is not
> restricted to, and its instruments of compliance are not housed solely
> in, those institutions that bear its name—legislatures, the judiciary,
> law enforcement, etc. In contrast to the weakness of legal appara-
> tuses, cultural forms like the novel have cooperated with human
> rights to naturalize their common sense.[21]

Slaughter, in fact, does not ultimately limit his claims about the extrajudicial edifice of human rights to the Declaration or even to human rights law
more generally. Rather, he embarks upon the presumption, common within
the field of critical legal theory, that *all* legal institutions, practices, and discourses ultimately rely upon extrajudicial supplements. In casting this much
broader net, Slaughter aligns himself not only with Gramsci but with theorists such as Peter Fitzpatrick and Jacques Derrida, theorists who have proposed a number of ways in which modern law sits uneasily within the secular,
positivist parameters it regularly claims to have set for itself.[22] When assessed
in this light, the Declaration is actually not unique among legal documents;
rather, it might more accurately be described as a document that brings into
high relief the extrajudicial logic resting at the heart of all legal institutions.

Human rights philosophers such as Slaughter and Derrida allow us to see
the manner in which declarations in general are particularly suited to the task
of highlighting law's extrajudicial logic. By their very nature, such documents
erect themselves not merely as paradigms for future legal rules but as dis-
ruptors of the status quo, as vehicles of novel juridico-political orientations.
They aspire to the decidedly utopian task of "taking something that does not
exist and, as it were, forcing it into existence."[23] Such a task necessarily compels the creators of such documents to reach beyond the confines of existing
legal and political institutions. This reaching beyond can take the form of an
imbrication with broader cultural products such as art and literature, but it
also typically takes the form of an appeal to extrajudicial authorities imagined to be capable of definitively legitimizing one political vision over other
possibilities. The Universal Declaration of Human Rights is no different from
other declarations in this respect; like the famous American and French declarations that preceded it, this document presents itself as a vehicle of both
rupture and political novelty, and, even as it professes to speak for everyone, it pointedly reaches beyond the confines of positive law and popular
sovereignty to legitimize its prescriptions. In grounding its disruptive vision
within an appeal to the extrajudicial, the Universal Declaration mirrors other
declarations in its blurring of the line between the "constantive" and the "performative"—in its dramatic creation of a novel political paradigm through an
appeal to facts that exist only by virtue of its own narrative.[24]

The Declaration, however, makes a significant departure from its predecessors—indeed, from all preceding declarations—in its refusal to enlist
a deity in the service of its prescription for political novelty. Such deities,
whether articulated in the form of "God" or the French "Être suprême," have

played a fundamental role in securing the legitimacy of human endeavors to disrupt and reinvent existing political realities—in guaranteeing, as Derrida famously put it, "the rectitude of popular intentions [and] the unity and goodness of the people."[25] The Declaration, by contrast, endeavors to lay the same type of extrajudicial groundwork for its claims, but it does so without the slightest recourse to a transhuman agent—not even to the secular standby of "Nature." If declarations in general serve as sites at which the extrajudicial comes into particular visibility, the Universal Declaration of Human Rights thus brings a new dimension to this, embodying an endeavor to transcend the bounds of positive law through a narrative that is radically secularized. This endeavor, the first of its kind, is fraught with a complexity that belies the dogged straightforwardness of human rights pragmatism.

In the spirit of the "philosophical" approach of Derrida and his ilk, this book will insist that an interrogation of human rights must reach beyond questions of pragmatism, administration, and enforcement and, first and foremost, must plumb the depths of what we mean when we speak of human rights. I will argue that the Declaration's unique configuration of characteristics—its particular tenets, paradoxes, and historico-political repercussions—can be very fruitfully explored from within the framework of political myth. The notion of political myth derives from the theorization of the "sacred myths" of institutionalized religions such as Christianity, yet it ventures beyond such religiosity to encompass broader, "postmodern" or "extra-institutional" conceptions of religious language, belief, and behavior.[26] Explicitly political phenomena have come to receive attention from theorists of myth for a number of reasons, not the least of which is the fact that political actors have assumed increasingly conspicuous and authoritative roles as mythmakers in what Robert Bellah calls the "post-traditional" world.[27] The fact that most such post-traditional societies are professedly secular has not, according to many theorists of religion, diminished political leaders' roles as providers of elements that Bronisław Malinowski described as fundamental to all myth: "charters, warrants, validations, legitimations, and authoritative precedents for beliefs, attitudes, and practices."[28] I will argue that this is nowhere truer than within the field of universal human rights, a field that has sought to fuse, on a global scale, "a utopian ideal and a realistic practice for implementation," and has thus exemplified the interpenetration of ethics, ontology, mythmaking, and modern secular politics.[29]

In deploying the framework of political myth, I do not by any means speak pejoratively of the Declaration or its prescriptions; rather, I shall speak of mythmaking in the broadly sociofunctionalist sense of a dense, evocative narrative designed to generate meaning, solidarity, and order for a particular audience. To invoke such things for their audience, myths must command an indisputable authority, and mythopoeic narratives are therefore distinguished by the manner in which they eschew conventional modes of argumentation in favor of the deployment of unequivocal assertions. These assertions can be grounded within a number of different logics, but the key to myth is that the logics within which they are grounded aim in various ways to locate themselves "beyond questioning." Of course, the question whether a given narrative proves successful in this endeavor to locate its prescriptions beyond questioning presents a somewhat different point of focus, and it is for this reason that many theorists distinguish the study of the production of myth—the question of a narrative's *mythopoeic* character—from the study of the reception of a given myth by the audience for which it was intended—the question of a narrative's *mythic* character.[30] My analysis of the Declaration will center upon the mythopoeic: the deliberate, often painstaking work that Commission members undertook to produce an ethico-political narrative capable of commanding a "uniquely realistic" status.[31]

It should be obvious, however, that distinctions between production and reception are always somewhat artificial, particularly in the case of an analysis of a myth whose origins are ancient or otherwise unknowable. The Declaration, of course, presents no such problem of obscurity of origin, but my emphasis upon its mythopoeic qualities will still occasionally blur the lines between the dynamics of production and reception by making forays into the question of how this document has been received by its intended audience. I would argue, for example, that the very project of exploring the mythopoeic nature of the Declaration rests upon the reality that this document has achieved something of a mythic status over the past six decades. Thus, while this book is predominantly an inquiry into the mythopoeic nature of the Declaration, it unquestionably ventures on occasion, primarily in its final chapter, into an analysis of human rights' mythic dynamics as well.

The sociofunctionalist definition of myth at the heart of this analysis hearkens strongly, but by no means exclusively, to the work of Émile Durkheim. For a number of reasons, Durkheim is an invaluable resource for an analysis of the Declaration as an exemplar of myth. In the first place, Durkheim is widely appreciated for the manner in which he insisted upon the relevance of the study of religion to modernity—even to those areas of life that seemed to be undergoing a shift away from the dominance of institutional forms of religiosity. Durkheim, in fact, offered a series of observations about the manner in which human rights values in particular exhibit a religious function in a world marked by increasing religious pluralism and even secularization. Human rights values, Durkheim was convinced, retain what he understood to be the decidedly religious role of serving as "a system of collective beliefs and practices that have a special authority."[32] Though he offered his prognosis prior to the creation of the Universal Declaration—hearkening instead to the eighteenth-century rights declarations of the United States and particularly of France—and though he did not flesh out these observations in anywhere near the depth with which he explored other religious phenomena, his observations offer an important entrée into an exploration of the mythopoeic logic of the 1948 Declaration. The theoretical groundwork that he laid for approaching religion as a human phenomenon designed to suffuse our world with sacredness, solidarity, and order furnishes a crucial foundation for an appreciation of the Declaration as a document designed to do much more than codify particular rights, but ultimately designed to invoke and enshrine "a shared moral basis taken to be universally common to all people."[33]

Durkheim is relevant to the work of understanding the Declaration for an additional important reason: as I shall show throughout this book, the Declaration's most prominent framers harbored decidedly "Durkheimian" notions about human rights and their capacity to command a particular moral weight within the blossoming international landscape of the twentieth century. Many of their postulations about the justification and the propagation of human rights bear a striking affinity to Durkheim's own descriptions of the social logics of religion, particularly as such logics play out in societies where political life has to some extent become unmoored from the influence of traditional religious institutions. This is not to say that the Declaration's framers were either forthright or systematic in their deployment of this religious logic; on the whole, they were not. Indeed, the very legitimacy of their project hinged (and often continues to hinge) on a *disavowal* of the Declaration's entanglement with any particular religious logics. An understanding of the Durkheimian orientation of the First Commission on Human Rights thus requires a willingness to reenvision the phenomenon of religion—to push this category beyond the bounds within which it is so frequently and so readily sequestered, particularly within the social sciences.[34] Far from a new mandate, this reenvisioning and broadening of the category of religion is a project that has unfolded within the field of religious studies over the past three decades, inspired in no small measure by Durkheim himself and his insistence on what is often articulated as "the persistence of the sacred": the existence of "something eternal in religion that is destined to outlive the succession of particular symbols in which religious thought has clothed itself."[35] Commission members' own descriptions of religion indicate that they (quite understandably) harbored only a vague inkling of Durkheim's more expansive understanding of religion. On the whole, their more conventional understanding of religion led them to articulate the Declaration's strong "moral" logic as something emphatically distinguishable from the logic of religion. A central undertaking of this book will be to problematize this distinction: to highlight the manner in which the Declaration's success as a shared moral basis—its success in "establish[ing] powerful, pervasive, and long-lasting moods and motivations in men"—was understood by Commission members to depend in no small way upon their success in charging this document with an affectivity and authority capable of transforming its audience into a cohesive community united in its veneration of a particular sacred item.[36] This endeavor, I will argue, is the stuff of religion, whether or not it is acknowledged as such.

The sociofunctionalist approach of Durkheim and his successors presents an indispensable lens through which to view this broader logic of religion that transcends the bounds of particular religious traditions. The sociofunctionalist methodology approaches religion first and foremost as a human-generated phenomenon—as an "ordinary" rather than an "exotic" category of human activity.[37] The fact that most myths have foregrounded transcendent agents, forces, and timeframes should not, according to this approach, eclipse the human labor that always goes into the creation and maintenance of authoritative narratives of this sort, and it should certainly not eclipse the recognition that such narratives serve specific human purposes. Moreover, and more significant to the present work of seeing the myth in human rights, myth's historical embeddedness in the transcendent should by no means relegate the study of myth to narratives focused upon deities and other transhuman forces. The human-centered logic of the sociofunctionalist approach has steadily and insistently propelled the study of religion beyond the realm of the supernatural where, prior to the nineteenth century, it was almost universally presumed to reside. This broader approach has inspired theorists of religion to be attentive to the mythopoeic dynamics of a variety of authoritative secular or quasi-secular narratives—narratives united in their endeavor to fulfill human cravings for meaning, cohesiveness, and order but nevertheless markedly different in substance from the myths at the heart of most of the world's religious traditions. Durkheim is widely recognized as a father of this sociofunctionalist approach and as a pioneer in the endeavor to broaden the study of religion. His nearly lifelong effort to sever the tie between the religious and the supernatural points to another way in which he is indispensable to an exploration of the mythopoeic logic of the Declaration. The Declaration, as I will show, is an avowedly secular document that is nevertheless painstakingly designed to do the mythopoeic work of encapsulating a prescription for human meaning, morality, and solidarity within an evocative, highly authoritative narrative—within a narrative functioning not merely as a framework for law but, in the words of Chilean delegate Hernán Santa Cruz, as "a true spiritual guide for humanity."[38] For various reasons that I shall highlight in upcoming chapters, the framers of the Declaration refrained from using the language of myth to describe their work. The mythopoeic logic of this document, however, is apparent throughout the extensive records surrounding its negotiation, and throughout its framers' public broadcast, in sundry speeches and essays, of the purpose and the promise of this document.

Though I will insist, in line with a host of contemporary theorists, that myth cannot be defined in any way that commands universal scholarly consensus, I have structured my analysis around three aspects of the Declaration that are not only key to the logic of this document but that, I will argue, strongly resonate with Durkheim's own sociofunctionalist formulation of myth. Ultimately, the First Commission on Human Rights endeavored to do much more than simply enumerate a set of rights to which all humans might lay claim; instead, they endeavored to narrate into existence both a moral and a legal landscape centered upon the sacredness of the human being. This endeavor, I will argue, is thoroughly mythopoeic in nature, despite the fact that the religious logic of this endeavor appears on the whole to have escaped the notice the Declaration's framers. For two important methodological reasons, then, I deploy the framework of myth somewhat flexibly: I do not claim that the Declaration's mythopoeic aspects are concrete indices common to all instances of mythmaking, and I do not claim that Commission members were conscious of the mythopoeic nature of their work. This approach is important in the first place because even the framers' relatively frequent use of religious terms such as "sacredness" fail to translate neatly into academic conceptions of religion and myth, so it would be methodologically inaccurate as well as unfaithful to the history of the Declaration to imply that the Commission attributed an overtly religious meaning to their efforts. The religious logic in which I am interested operates much more subtly within the creation of this document.

In the second place, this more flexible approach to myth within the Declaration allows me to take account of the fact that scholars of religion have achieved no consensus on a canon of elementary indices of myth—nor even of religion more broadly. Jonathan Z. Smith is well known for having embraced this impasse, ultimately insisting that the designation of a phenomenon as "religious" is a more or less imaginary act undertaken by scholars.[39] This claim that the study of religion ultimately rests upon an act of imagination is not to claim that this field is spurious; rather, ongoing scholarship in this field has shown the phenomenon of religion to be much more variable, and much less secure, than has often been recognized. As we shall see in the following chapter, early theorists of religion often strove to couch their analyses of religion and myth in clear, stable formulations later revealed to be oversimplified or even downright imperialistic. In the midst of his critique of such early modes of religious studies scholarship, Smith formulates an approach more conducive to an appreciation of the complex, fluid world of religion: essentially, one should be capable of bringing "some central element in the academic imagination of religion" explicitly and systematically to bear upon a designated phenomenon.[40] The mythopoeic framework that I bring to bear on the Declaration is deployed very much in this spirit.

Chapter 1 locates my analysis of the Declaration within the broader academic theorization of myth. I explore the question of how we might define "political myth" in light of recent trends within the contemporary study of myth and religion, and I broach a definition for its examination with respect to the Declaration. In the course of staking out a definition, I address the negative connotations inhering for many people within the word "myth" itself. The widespread assumption that myth refers to narratives in some way fanciful or untrue poses a particular problem for an examination of the mythopoeic nature of human rights since the fundamental tenets of universal human rights remain, in certain important contexts, contested. To invoke the notion of myth with respect to the status of the Declaration therefore runs the risk of appearing dismissive of human rights' truth or integrity. Needless to say, such is not my intention in embarking upon this analysis, though this very predisposition to envision myth as something fundamentally fictitious or inaccurate presents an entrée into my interrogation of the sociofunctionalist definition of myth—a definition that by its very nature avoids identification of mythopoeic narratives in terms of substantive claims that can ultimately be proven "true" or "false." Rather, the sociofunctionalist approach focuses upon the claims that mythmakers attempt to make to their audiences, and the peculiar authoritativeness with which they endeavor to imbue such claims.

Ultimately, I show that the framers of the Declaration aspired to create a narrative with the power to transition its global audience from an epoch of, as the Preamble puts it, "barbarous acts which have outraged the conscience of mankind" to an epoch of "freedom, justice, and peace in the world." In doing so, they endeavored to do what mythmakers have aspired to do for millennia: to narrate into existence a world that is less capricious, less cruel, and more humane than it frequently appears to be.

In the course of its negotiations, the Commission on Human Rights faced a crisis that was considerably more subtle than that of the "barbarous acts" referenced within the Preamble of the Declaration: it faced the problem of articulating a set of evocative, universalizable principles in the absence of shared ontological and metaphysical foundations. Commission members quickly recognized that a human rights vision geared toward a global audience could not ground its claims within any culturally specific framework of human flourishing. Chapter 2 demonstrates the manner in which, in lieu of a quest for a common foundation for human rights, the framers of the Declaration simply and axiomatically "set apart" a human characteristic designed to emblemize and secure human rights. I propose that the Commission's enshrinement of "inherent human dignity" within the Preamble of the Declaration embodies a logic of sacralization. Inherent human dignity, in other words, stands within the Declaration as a characteristic which, as human rights scholar Johannes Morsink puts it, "no person and no political or social body or organ gave us" and which no such person or body can take away without charge of profound transgression.[41] By this logic, the inherent dignity of each individual is located beyond questioning by the framers of the Declaration—a gesture that a variety of theorists have identified as exemplary of the overlap of religious and secular meaning making within post-traditional social and political contexts.

Within the Declaration, this sacralization of human dignity stands in direct and ongoing tension with the previous epoch of the wartime period, particularly as embodied in the politics of Germany's Third Reich. This previous epoch is marked, in the minds of the Commission on Human Rights and in the minds of many contemporary theorists, by the sacralization of what has come to be called the "organic state" or *Volksgemeinschaft*. There is little doubt that the *Volksgemeinschaft* served as a key emblem of sociopolitical orderliness within the discourse of the Third Reich and that such a formulation stands starkly opposed to that of the inherently dignified individual aspired to by the Commission. In the course of my analysis of the Commission's sacralization of human dignity, I therefore trace the crucial role of the barbarous acts of World War II and the Holocaust in shaping the Declaration's own formulation of sacredness.

The logic of sacralization is not self-contained; as the brief definition above implies, items unequivocally set apart in this manner always partake of broader human imperatives of orderliness and community building. Chapter 3 focuses upon this social radius of mythmaking: upon the manner in which a particular logic of sacralization serves simultaneously to constitute and to validate the communitarian identities and practices of those in its thrall. The sociofunctionalist approach—with its emphasis upon the intrinsically social thrust of all religious belief and practice—proves crucial for a thorough understanding of human dignity as an item of sacredness within the Declaration, for the Commission members' negotiations, writings, and speeches give every indication that they perceived the setting apart of human dignity to be dispositive of a particular social identity as well as of the cultivation of the beliefs and practices conducive to such an identity. The particular social identity toward which the Commission aspired is articulated within the Declaration's Preamble as "the human family." In Chapter 3, I trace the role of this concept within the negotiation and the propagation of the Declaration. In the course of exploring its role, I highlight the mythopoeic logic of the Declaration's vision of human family: the manner in which this concept functions to push the logic of sacralization toward a communitarian vision intended to span the entire globe.

Notwithstanding the Commission's concerted endeavor to align the tenets of the Declaration with preexisting value systems across the globe, the human rights narrative ultimately conveys more than a simple consolidation of certain basic values endemic to the majority of the world's cultures; it delineates "minimum conditions for a dignified life, a life worthy of a human being."[42] Just as importantly, it designates a specific venue for the codification, regulation, and enforcement of these conditions. This framework of regulation proves intricately bound up with the sacralization of inherent human dignity and with the violation of this dignity witnessed during the wartime era. In Chapter 4, I address the Declaration's invocation of "the rule of law," ultimately highlighting the manner in which this invocation functions to translate human dignity into the realm of orderly political practice. While the notion of the rule of law is not necessarily in itself dispositive of a mythopoeic logic, I argue that it functions as such within the Declaration.[43] Within this document, the rule of law furnishes a powerful vision of political orderliness that serves first and foremost to secure the sanctity of human dignity and to concretize or, in Durkheim's terms, to "organize," the community drawn together by this sacred item. This chapter thus endeavors toward more than a simple delineation of the legal logic of the Declaration; rather, it emphasizes the very particular incarnation of "law" envisioned by the Commission, and it reveals the profound interdependence of the Declaration's logic of sacredness with its logic of legal orderliness.

An attentiveness to the mythopoeic dimensions of the Declaration proves valuable not merely for the manner in which it allows us to better understand the unique nature of this document, but also for the insights it affords into a variety of broader human rights issues, many of which have arisen in defiance of all expectations of the Commission on Human Rights itself. For this reason, my concluding chapter moves beyond the specific context and logic of the Declaration to consider some of the wide-ranging implications of its particular narrative within our contemporary era of human rights. If we understand mythmaking to encompass not only the production but also the reception of certain types of narratives, can we indeed imagine that the Declaration has come to command a mythic status today? My central assertion is that the Declaration has successfully entrenched itself in the imaginations of a very broad swath of communities across the globe. Serving now as the bedrock for a variety of subsequent conventions as well as for many global and local vernaculars of justice and injustice, the Declaration has, as one human rights scholar puts it, blossomed from "a 'mere' statement of principle with no legally binding authority at all" to a document with "growing moral, political, and even legal force."[44] Given this success, can the framework of myth help us to grapple with ongoing shortcomings in the deployment and the acceptance of human rights principles? In my final chapter, I touch upon a series of such shortcomings, each of which sheds further light on the mythopoeic logic of the Declaration and the implications of this mythopoeic logic for today's international human rights landscape. These issues furnish an opportunity to broaden my theorization of human rights and myth beyond the specific context of the creation and propagation of the Declaration.

My interrogation of the particular complexities that continue to plague the reception of the Declaration—and indeed my interrogation in Chapters 1 through 4 of the Declaration's mythopoeic elements—raise an interesting contradiction: ultimately, such analyses necessarily enact a certain "unmaking" of the mythopoeic narrative that the Declaration's framers constructed over the years of 1947 and 1948. If, as we see in the proceeding chapter, the peculiar authoritativeness of myth derives in part from its ability to efface the contingency of its origins and its assertions, then it is bound to be the case that an exploration of the origins and aspirations of a given mythopoeic narrative results in a certain undermining or unraveling of its axiomatic presentation of information. This unmaking of myth can serve the ultimate goal of a debunking, or it can serve the somewhat less extreme goal of a type of reappropriation such as we see in the case of the Commission's unmaking of the Nazi myth of the organic state in the course of its work of solidifying the authority of the Declaration.

My intention in this project of unmaking is neither of these things; rather, it is much more akin to Samuel Moyn's goal of treating human rights "as a human cause, rather than one with the long term inevitability and moral self-evidence that common sense assumes."[45] In embarking upon his own project of unmaking, Moyn takes aim at a pervasive feature of contemporary human rights scholarship: namely, at the manner in which many contemporary historians of human rights have effectively mythologized what was actually a highly contingent process of human rights ascendency in the second half of the twentieth century:

> Historians in the United States started writing the history of human rights a decade ago. Since that time, a new field has crystallized and burgeoned. Almost unanimously, contemporary historians have adopted a celebratory attitude toward the emergence and progress of human rights, providing recent enthusiasms and uplifting back-stories, and differing primarily about whether to locate the true breakthrough with the Greeks or the Jews, medieval Christians or early modern philosophers, democratic revolutionaries or abolitionist heroes, American internationalists or antiracist visionaries. In recasting world history as raw material for the progressive ascent of international human rights, they have rarely conceded that earlier history left open diverse paths unto the future, rather than paving a single road toward current ways of thinking and acting. And in studying human rights more recently, once they did come on the scene, historians have been loathe to regard them as only one appealing ideology among others. Instead, they have used history to confirm their inevitable rise rather than register the choices that were made and the accidents that did happen.[46]

My project is undertaken in a spirit similar to that of Moyn, but to quite a different effect: like Moyn, I seek to lend clarity to the human labor involved in the creation of modern human rights. Unlike Moyn, however, I assert that we cannot fully understand this human labor without appreciating the Commission's concerted endeavors to imbue the Declaration with a powerful, affective authoritativeness—an authoritativeness that, ironically, depends in no small way upon an *effacement* of the human labor involved in the creation of this document. The sociofunctionalist framework of myth furnishes an invaluable tool for navigating this paradox.

The complex array of actors, sources, and negotiations that gave rise to the Declaration has been well documented by historians, particularly over the past twenty years. The drafting of this document at the hands of the Commission on Human Rights took place over the course of nearly two years, but this drafting was preceded not only by important framing discussions dating back to the 1945 formation of the United Nations but also by a much longer history of human rights politics dating back at least to the eighteenth century. Though, as Moyn has pointed out, it would be inaccurate to depict the long history of human rights politics as a quasi-teleological process culminating inevitably in the Declaration, there is little question that this longer trajectory has borne in important ways upon the creation of this document. This book considers some of the aspects and ramifications of this longer history of human rights, but it does not aspire to undertake a comprehensive history of the Declaration; it aspires neither to thoroughly map the permutations of prior human rights ideals within the Declaration nor to exhaustively enumerate the particular contributions or reservations of the Commission's various members. Ultimately, I aim in this book to do something at once more modest and more ambitious: I aim to tease out a certain pervasive, under-examined logic discernible throughout the text of the Declaration, the Commission's negotiations of this text, and the writings and speeches whereby the Declaration's most prominent framers gave public articulation of this document's tenets and aspirations. These various materials come together to create what Wendy Doniger has described in other contexts as a "continuum of narratives" designed to entrench human rights values permanently in the minds and practices of people around the world.[47] The Commission's vision and strategies to this effect ventured far beyond a straightforward pragmatic or utilitarian endeavor to "build support for human rights on the basis of what such rights actually *do* for human beings."[48] Rather, the Commission's multifaceted narration of human rights endeavors to accomplish nothing short of the construction of "a new moral order of international relations"—a moral order dependent, Commission members were convinced, on its ability to inspire much more than a merely pragmatic commitment from its audience.[49]

Contemporary scholarship on religion offers a singular contribution to the theorization of this central mandate of universal human rights. Such scholarship invites us to recognize the obvious mythopoeic qualities of the Declaration's narrative while resisting the tendency to conflate myth with either religious dogma or with outright falsity. Ultimately, neither of these more conventional formulations of myth do justice to the Commission's particular human rights project.

At many points, this book ventures beyond the text of the Declaration and the words of its framers, ultimately rallying a wide ranging body of human rights scholarship that, often unintentionally, lends further clarification to the mythopoeic logic of the Declaration. My emphasis, however, rests primarily upon the words and the aspirations of some of the most prominent members of the First Commission on Human Rights within the postwar context of the mid to late 1940s. My emphasis upon this population and this time period is not intended to downplay the variety of actors who have made important contributions to the drafting and the continuing propagation of the Declaration; it is rather an acknowledgment of the fact that this document's mythopoeic logic becomes particularly (though certainly not exclusively) salient in the discourses of those figures who, for various reasons, became tasked with the job of publicly advertising and legitimizing it: figures such as chairwoman Eleanor Roosevelt, vice-chairman P. C. Chang, rapporteur and career human rights spokesperson Charles Malik, and early drafter René Cassin.[50] I remain aware, however, of the manner in which my emphasis upon the words of the Declaration's most prominent advertisers runs the risk of reproducing a version of the human rights triumphalism that Moyn finds so problematic—the triumphalism exhibited, for example, in Clinton's depiction of the Declaration as a product of an unequivocal global consensus. The question of the potential harms and inaccuracies of "universalizing" the often tenuous moments of consensus among the Declaration's main spokespeople warrants serious engagement, and my own interrogation of the Declaration is undertaken in full recognition of the value of the recent work of "historical demystification" proposed by scholars such as Moyn.[51] However, as I make clear over the course of the following chapters, certain key features of the Declaration's logic only become clear when we *pull back* to some extent from the recent focus on human rights demystification and give serious consideration to the Commission's concerted endeavor to mythologize and, in effect, to reify the Declaration's most fundamental tenets.

This approach to human rights is by no means an attempt to ignore or obscure the constellation of complex, conflictual dynamics that underlay the creation of the Declaration and its entrenchment within today's international legal landscape. Such dynamics include the stark differences of opinion among various Commission members (particularly the differences between Malik and the various Soviet bloc representatives, who ultimately abstained from the final vote); the irony of ongoing colonial and racist practices within the domestic jurisdictions of many UN member states; the harsh reality of certain prominent member states' unwillingness to tolerate infringements upon their national sovereignty; and, moving into today, the ongoing debates over the Eurocentrism of universal human rights. Far from endeavoring to obscure such dynamics, my analysis of the Declaration hinges upon a claim that both acknowledges and, ultimately, stands in tension with the project of historical demystification: to comprehend the history and the enduring authority of human rights, we must retain an appreciation of the ways in which Commission members worked diligently to *mystify* the Declaration—worked not merely to legitimize but to "naturalize" the origins and the basic tenets of this document. To retain an appreciation of this fact is not to endorse it; it is merely to recognize the fact that we cannot thoroughly understand the Declaration and its ongoing permeations within today's matrices of human rights without an awareness of the work Commission members did to imbue the history and the tenets of the Declaration with an intuitiveness and an affectivity that, in no small way, pushes against the clear-eyed debunking of many of today's critical theorists of human rights.

Ultimately, while the central focus of this book is the Declaration and its mythopoeic logic—along with some of the most prominent events, people, and discourses that gave life to this logic—*Seeing the Myth* is also necessarily a book about how we understand and theorize myth, and particularly how we do so within certain contemporary contexts. The history of the creation of the Declaration and the subsequent dissemination of its tenets reveals an aversion on the part of its framers, at least in their public pronouncements,[52] to the vocabulary of institutional religion—with the notable exception of their references to the way the tenets of the Declaration should be understood to incorporate the basic values of *all* institutional religions. Even in the midst of this aversion to conventional discourses of religion, however, the Declaration exhibits characteristics that fit uneasily within the purely "immanent" framework of modern positive law.[53] As Slaughter observes, [the Declaration's] preamble emerges without citing the traditional natural law pretext (the extratextual warrants of Nature and Nature's God), but it also comes without any executive force other than its appeal to common, "brotherly" sense. Contemporary human rights law is hybrid because it appropriates formal aspects of both eighteenth-century natural and nineteenth-century positive law without conscripting their substantiating metaphysics or institutionalizing the social, civil, and political force that underwrote those legal regimes.[54]

In coming together to create this document, the Commission made a concerted effort to simultaneously incorporate and sidestep the logics of each of these preeminent legal approaches. The Commission ultimately offered up a forceful assertion of human sacredness and a prescription for the cultivation of this sacredness, but it did so with reference neither to transcendent extrajudicial foundations nor to the practical mechanisms of legitimation and enforcement upon which secular legal systems inherently depend. The framework of myth presents a novel means for understanding how they accomplished this paradoxical feat. In so doing, the framework of myth also provides us with an opportunity to wrestle with a phenomenon that has been of recent concern to scholars of both religion and law: namely, the persistence of certain powerful religious logics within even our most avowedly secular institutions. While it is not uncommon to encounter references within the field of human rights theory to the Declaration's unique moral and even metaphysical logics—even to human rights' status as, in the words of José Casanova, "a truly modern sacralization"—this book draws upon a rich body of theory from within the study of religion to lend depth and systematicity to such references.[55] Such an approach stands to improve our understanding of religion within the modern world, but it also promises to deepen our understanding of human rights, international law, and even secularity itself. Moreover, it presents a means of furthering the ongoing scholarly project of pushing the study of religion into the realm of the extra-institutional, where, today, it so clearly persists in so many interesting ways. The Declaration, a document whose language is simultaneously religious and vehemently secular, presents what is perhaps one of history's most compelling cases for the extension of the theoretical framework of myth into the territory of secular politics.

CHAPTER 1

Sacred Myth, Political Myth

In her history of the creation of the Universal Declaration, Mary Ann Glendon describes a sculpture that stands on the plaza outside the United Nations headquarters in New York City:

> A gift from the government of Italy, it consists of an enormous sphere of burnished bronze, suggesting a globe. The sphere is pleasing to behold, even though it startles with its imperfection. There are deep, jagged cracks in its golden-hued surface, cracks too large ever to be repaired. Perhaps it's cracked because it's defective (like the broken world), one thinks. Or maybe (like an egg) it has to break in order for something else to emerge. Perhaps both. Sure enough, when one peers into the gashes on its surface, there is another brightly shining sphere coming along inside. But this one is already cracked too!
>
> Whatever is going on inside those spheres, it does not seem to be all chance and accident. There is a tremendous sense of motion, of dynamism, of potency, of emergent possibilities.[1]

This sculpture embodies a logic of woundedness and rectification that, while relevant to the development of human rights in the twentieth and early twenty-first centuries, also speaks to the more general human endeavor to create order and meaning within a world marked by all variety of imperfection: the imperfections of war and conflict, of human knowledge, of biological finitude. This connection between the work of the Commission on Human Rights and the broader work of meaning making within a broken world is not speculative; the Commission's members were overt in their assertions that they were involved in the work of rejuvenating a world rent not only by statism and war, but also rent by a moral orientation that had facilitated the profanation of that which, according to many, should be most scared to us: human life. The task that such members envisioned for the Declaration, then, was not merely to delineate particular rights, but also to recalibrate both the legal and the moral landscapes of the twentieth century—to reorient people's sensibilities and commitments such that, as Roosevelt put it, the people of the world could be inspired and enabled to "progress inwardly."[2] Furthermore, the Committee worked very self-consciously under the imperative that this recalibration should avoid any appearance of cultural or ideological bias— under the imperative that, to a large extent, this vehicle of recalibration efface its own constructedness and contingency. Only through such an effacement could the Commission claim to be articulating a set of principles aligned not with imperialist ambitions or elitist predilections but with the proper, albeit recently undermined, order of things.

How does one accomplish such moral recalibration? For the greater part of human history, throughout the past and into today, this type of moral calibration has fallen within the purview of myth. Though frequently grounded within specific religious traditions and practices, and though very often identified as a narrative concerned with gods or other supernatural beings, myth in its broadest sense consists of narratives designed to dictate a world to its audience that is simultaneously factual and moral—simultaneously descriptive and prescriptive—and to do so in a manner that brokers no counterargument. Myths distinguish themselves by the "extraordinary authority" with which they speak: they do not "argue" or "induce discussion" but instead *present* their descriptions of the world and the moral imperatives stemming from these descriptions.[3] They accomplish this authoritative presentation of information in a variety of ways: by describing the prescriptions of supernatural beings, by narrating the feats of exemplary figures from earlier times, by explicating the origin of the world or of a given people, or by drawing connections between the present and a paradigmatic epoch in the past. For all their potential variation, though, such narratives partake of an important common logic: they enable narrators to set language to the task of "lending an historical intention a natural justification, and making contingency appear eternal."[4]

Notwithstanding the tendency to think of myth as primarily concerned with supernatural beings and cosmic (or at least prehistoric) timeframes— and notwithstanding myth's strong historical ties to precisely such matters— mythopoeic narratives need not hinge upon such particularities. We witness the cultivation of authoritative, evocative narratives within all types of societies, including societies that lack a strong orientation toward the supernatural. Such "post-traditional" societies, distinguishable in part by their efforts to forgo appeals to controversial sources of authority in the course of prescribing social and political norms, nevertheless share with all human societies the need to cultivate authoritative narratives aimed at morally (re)orienting their members. The Declaration offers its prescriptions within precisely such a post-traditional context: in the face of an evident and intractable pluralism of beliefs regarding the supernatural, this document pursues its goal of moral recalibration in an emphatically secular language. The Declaration's secular discourse, however, is not the rationalist discourse of Enlightenment philosophy or the empiricist discourse of positive law; indeed, it is a discourse that pointedly aims to locate its claims beyond the realms of realms of both rationalism and argumentation. Instead, the Declaration presents a formulation for social and political life that is simultaneously mythopoeic and secularized—a striking example of what theorists frequently refer to as political myth. Given the lack of scholarly consensus on the basic parameters of myth, however, the definition of political myth is far from a settled matter. This chapter will trace a definition of myth that is both germane to a theorization of a secular narrative such as the Declaration and is simultaneously faithful to the sociofunctionalist formulation of religion.

Toward a Theory of Political Myth

One of the most significant trends within the theorization of religion in the twentieth century—and one of the most important refinements that contemporary theorists have made within this field—has been an increasing emphasis on the political nature of all forms of religious meaning making. Prior to the second half of the twentieth century, the scientific study of religion was marked by a tendency to frame religious beliefs and practices as apolitical and basically consensual—as the almost inevitable products of human encounters with such things as the unexplainable facets of the world,[5] the mystery of death,[6] the numinous,[7] or some other transcendent experience. The study of myth has lent itself particularly well to this approach, dealing as it does with timeframes, figures, and archetypes that are often avowedly ahistorical, and with narratives that by definition function to naturalize the ontological and normative claims that they impart to their audiences. The same "'always-already-given' quality" that lends mythic narratives their power is the very same quality that has led many theorists to neglect the strategic human labor that inevitably goes into the construction and maintenance of such powerful narratives.[8] However, as theorists beginning in the 1970s point out, when such political work is neglected, we run the risk of separating the events, characters, and ideals described in a given myth from the variable, politically charged events, characters, and ideals of the everyday world; we run the risk, in other words, of separating myth from its constitutive "political, historical, and cultural contexts."[9]

Scholars of religion over the past forty years have endeavored in a variety of ways to take account of the fact that, whether they ultimately work to broadcast or to obscure such contexts, myths "are always context-sensitive"—are always "a tool in the hands of human beings."[10] The study of myth over the intervening years has been marked by multifaceted efforts to ground analyses of such narratives within equally robust analyses of the particular contexts in which they are created, reiterated, and revised. In highlighting myth's "labors," "strains," and "achievements," the analyst of a given myth seeks to understand not merely the content of the narrative but its contribution and indebtedness to broader systems of meaning within a particular society.[11] Given the manner in which such narratives endeavor to efface the very social, political and historical contingencies that underlie their creation and their preservation, it is no small irony that this approach entails a certain unmaking of the very myth that one seeks to understand. This tendency toward unmaking has often had the effect of entrenching sociofunctionalist scholars of religion within a camp of theorists accused of "reducing" mythopoeic narratives to little more than socio-political ideologies.[12]

Yet, this endeavor to bring together the (often apolitical) content and the (always political) context of myth has important and far-reaching implications. The tendency among nineteenth- and early twentieth-century theorists to divorce the contents of mythopoeic narratives from the contexts of such narratives has not merely influenced the development of the study of myth, it has infused the broader study of religion with presumptions from which scholars continue to endeavor to extricate themselves. One of the trickiest of these is the presumption that "religious" beliefs and practices are clearly and universally distinguishable from "nonreligious" beliefs and practices—that the logic of religion is sufficiently distinct from other areas of human life to warrant a markedly different framework of analysis. This presumption is deeply implicated within the presumption that, as Talal Asad puts it, "religion has an autonomous essence not to be confused with the essence of science, or of politics, or of common sense."[13] The fact that such essentialism lends itself nicely to comparative analysis has helped to endear this approach to religious studies scholars of all sorts. Whether one favors a phenomenological, a psychological, or a structuralist approach to the study of religion, such study is rendered much less complicated when one assumes that all religions are comprised of certain elementary features that operate independently of the historical and social dynamics of the societies that gave birth to them, and that can therefore be cross-culturally compared with near impunity. Indeed, the allure of this approach is hardly limited to academia; the popular successes of Mircea Eliade and Joseph Campbell, both comparative scholars of religion and of myth in particular, attest to the pleasure inherent in imagining that the category of religion fundamentally transcends our myriad historical, cultural, and political differences.[14] However, as scholars in the late twentieth and early twenty-first centuries have turned a critical eye upon the presumptions of their progenitors, this legacy of religious essentialism has generated particularly passionate soul-searching. If one erects a theory of religion upon the presumption that religion is "delimite[d], and therefore definable," does one run the risk of favoring particular religious traditions over others?[15] Yes, claim theorists ranging from Asad to Bruce Lincoln.[16] If in fact religion should not or cannot be so delineated, precisely what object of study resides at the center of religious studies? In pushing this critical spirit to its limit, Smith claims that the object at the center of religious studies is ultimately an "imaginary" one:

> while there is a staggering amount of data, of phenomena, of human experiences and expressions that might be characterized in one culture or another, by one criterion or another, as religion—*there is no data for religion*. Religion is solely the creation of the scholar's study. It is created for the scholar's analytic purposes by his imaginative acts of comparison and generalization.[17]

Smith's admonition is crucial: it articulates a fundamental shift in the scholarly approach to religion that reaches back to the nineteenth century but has achieved particular traction only in the past thirty to forty years. An infusion of new data—predominately, but not entirely, non-western—has forced scholars to recognize the parochialism of the longstanding presumption that religion is a phenomenon readily distinguishable from other aspects of human life. As Brent Nongbri puts it, "The very idea of 'being religious' requires a companion notion of what it would mean to be 'not religious,' and this dichotomy was not part of the ancient world."[18] Nor is it intrinsic to much of the so-called Islamic world, argue Asad and Lincoln.[19] Nor to Hinduism or even to much of Christianity, as the likes of Diana Eck and Robert Orsi have pointed out.[20] Ultimately, it seems that what such a presumption is intrinsic to is a particular brand of "Western secular modernity," and, by extension, to the history of colonial expansion, the Protestant Reformation, and the European Enlightenment.[21] This interpenetration of histories, and their bearing upon contemporary conceptions of religion both within and outside the academy, has been the focus of extensive inquiry and critique in recent years, and has been a central preoccupation within the burgeoning study of secularization and secularity.[22] Even outside of the field of secular studies, however, such inquiries have inspired a generation of scholars to work in various ways to complicate the distinctions we tend to draw between the religious and other realms of human life.

The shift away from a conception of religion as something clearly distinguishable from other human institutions has gone hand-in-hand with a rejection of the conception of religion as a force that impresses itself upon more or less passive individuals and communities—a force that impedes upon human life from "beyond the sphere of the usual, the intelligible, the familiar."[23] Myth, by its very nature a phenomenon evocative of various modes of "beyond," has proven a particularly difficult phenomenon to extricate from this presumption. However, a number of influential scholars of religion have pushed for precisely such a reconceptualization, and have laid the groundwork for thinking about mythmaking as an enterprise that is deeply political and, simultaneously, deeply invested in the effacement of its own politics.

Lincoln, for example, is well known for his aversion to the reification of myth and of religion more broadly, and has insisted upon a rejection of simplistic distinctions between myth and mere social or political "ideology." A mythopoeic narrative, asserts Lincoln, "packages a specific, contingent system of discrimination in a particularly attractive and memorable form. What is more, it naturalizes and legitimates it." [24] In his endeavor to foreground the "anthropologic"—that is, the human-centered logic—of mythmaking, Lincoln ultimately makes little distinction between myth and ideology.[25] His formulation of myth draws upon a deep vein of Durkheimian logic, although, as Chapters 3 and 4 reveal, Durkheim himself was consistently inattentive to many of the power dynamics inherent in the production and maintenance of ideological discourses.[26]

Lincoln's neo-Durkheimian approach focuses on the sociopolitical work done by myth rather than on the particular subject matter presumed to reside at the center of such narratives. Myths, in other words, are distinguishable "not by their content but by the claims that are made by their narrators and the way in which those claims are received by their audience(s)."[27] As Doniger somewhat more bluntly puts it, "myth is above all a story that is *believed*, believed to be true, and that people continue to believe despite sometimes massive evidence that it is, in fact, a lie."[28] Mythmakers deploy narrative in a variety of ways to generate and maintain this brand of audience commitment, but such variations are undergirded by the common socio-political labor of articulating "normative judgments which would be impossible without presuming a knowledge of what is right and wrong for society and its members."[29] In this manner, myths are always intimately linked to "value-laden interpretations" not merely of the past but of the present and the future.[30]

In addition to the way this politically oriented approach compels an attentiveness to context and human agency in the construction and maintenance of mythopoeic narratives, it offers another important advantage: in broadening the definition of myth beyond the contents of certain conventional religious narratives, this formulation runs less risk of tying myth to the fate of any particular religious tradition(s) than if one presumes that mythopoeic narratives must by definition involve gods, sacred places, or prehistoric timeframes. This advantage is important not only for reasons of sound methodology, but for the way the definition pushes against the presumption that human mythmaking will decline or depreciate as the world's religious traditions change. This conclusion is a mistake not unlike that made by proponents of the so-called secularization thesis, who have long mistaken declines in church attendance in the United States and Western Europe for a global decline in religion. This not only erects western sociopolitical developments as the barometer of the trajectories of other regions of the world, but it overlooks the astounding variety of religious identities and practices that continue to flourish within the "secularized" countries of Europe and the United States.[31] Ultimately, such presumptions threaten to stifle our understanding of human meaning making in the modern world. Moreover, they threaten to exacerbate dichotomous thinking about "western" versus "non-western," or "modern" versus "premodern," societies. Perhaps nowhere is this phenomenon clearer than in the approach to myth famously formulated by Ernst Cassirer. In *The*

Myth of the State, Cassirer is renowned, though not by any means unique, for having fallen into an understanding of modern myth as a reversion to "the first rudimentary stages of human culture," and as an indication of "the defeat of rational thought."[32] Presumptions such as these, which associate myth with nonrational or, less generously, irrational thought, are difficult to avoid when one relies upon a definition of myth that emphasizes particular prescientific motifs and modes of meaning making.

On the other hand, Lincoln's effacement of the boundary between myth and ideology begs the question of what precisely distinguishes a mythopoeic narrative from other authoritative social or political narratives. If we insist that the function served by a narrative is a more accurate index of its mythopoeic nature than is its particular content, we might well deprive ourselves of the simplest means of distinguishing myth from "mere" politics: namely, the designation of myth as concerned with beings, accomplishments, or chronologies that transcend the secular world. While there is little question that many myths concern themselves with precisely such things, the sociofunctionalist approach refuses to posit such items as lodestars for the study of myth or of religion more generally.

Taken to its limit, then, this approach potentially brokers no definitive distinction between myth and any other narrative conveying an aspiration, as Kim Dovey puts it, "to depoliticize speech" and to "transform history into nature."[33] Lincoln, indeed, sees no distinction. In his conceptualization of the term, it is the narrative endeavor toward depoliticization and naturalization that marks such a narrative as mythopoeic. Myth, Lincoln asserts, aspires "not only to the status of truth, but, what is more, to the status of *paradigmatic* truth."[34] Mythopoeic narratives convey information, but they do so in the service of a very particular human enterprise: they "evoke the sentiments out of which society is actively constructed."[35] The particular devices deployed by narrators to evoke these powerful sentiments can vary dramatically, but whatever their particular substance, myths, according to Lincoln and his ilk, are distinguishable by the way they package "a 'model of' and a 'model for' reality" into an attractive, memorable, and highly authoritative narrative, a narrative that asserts rather than argues its claims.[36]

Ultimately, this expansive approach leaves us with scant means of distinguishing political myth from what we might call the "sacred myths" of institutionalized religions such as Judaism, Hinduism, or Christianity.[37] To the extent that all such narratives function to capture a particular prescription for human belief and behavior within an attractive, memorable, and authoritative narrative, isn't *all* myth to some extent "political myth"? While the likes of Lincoln might answer in the affirmative, it may nevertheless be useful in some circumstances to draw a substantive distinction between narratives that pointedly hearken to supernatural figures, locations, and time-frames and those that pointedly do not. From among the variety of possible reasons for drawing such a distinction, one will prove particularly important to an analysis of the mythopoeic logic of the Declaration: in the case of the Declaration, the creators of this document clearly aspired to imbue it with the unequivocal authority that we have seen to be a marker of myth, but the very authority of this narrative hinged in no small way upon the claim that the realm of religion can be distinguished in some coherent way from the realm of politics. Its authority hinged, ironically, upon the very distinction that theorists of myth and religion have become increasingly committed to effacing.

The importance of this claim to be able to separate religion from politics within the Declaration will become clear in upcoming chapters, but suffice it here to say that the framers of the Declaration undertook their work within a context that both presumed and demanded a realm of political meaning making cleansed of the potentially conflict-ridden logics of religion—a Rawlsian realm that, while not hostile to religion per se, clearly envisioned overt religious language to be an impediment to the achievement of a universal consensus regarding the basic tenets of universal human rights.[38] To fully understand the human rights project undertaken by the Commission, it will be important to take seriously its claim to have met this demand for separation. However, to take seriously *various political actors' claims* to have cleansed the contents of a narrative of the religious is not tantamount to asserting that the realms of religion and politics can be so cleanly separated; it is, rather, to recognize the Declaration's embeddedness within a historical context in which it had become feasible and even desirable to envision a distinction between religion and nonreligion.

Herein lies a definition of political myth that, while perhaps not helpful in all cases, proves indispensable for an understanding of the Declaration: a political myth is a highly authoritative narrative that "presents" rather than argues its claims, and that does so while avowing to have divested itself of a particular religion, or, as in the case of the Declaration, of religion in general. In their own extensive work on the subject of political myth, Chiara Bottici and Benoît Challand propose a similar contextual point of orientation for the exploration of political myth:

it is only in modern societies that the specifically *political* role played
by myth has been recognized. In ancient societies, political myths
and religious myths coincide most of the time in both their contents
and their functions. Indeed, the appearance of purely political myths
is a typically modern phenomenon—a consequence of both the
modern separation of politics from its religious anchorage and of its
democratization.[39]

Ultimately, of course, even the contextual distinction between political
myth and religious myth is not as simple as it might seem, given that the
transition from "ancient" to "modern" modes of legitimation and meaning
making is anything but a straightforward affair. Many of history's most ardent
secularists—the revolutionaries of eighteenth-century France, for example—
have drawn both overtly and covertly upon the religious logics of the culture
against which they pitted themselves. In his thick description of the process
he terms "reoccupation," Hans Blumenberg highlights the manner in which
all progenitors of heterodox sociopolitical movements remain parasitic upon
"consecrated" cultural elements even as they claim to be transcending or dis-
rupting them, a phenomenon that profoundly blurs the boundary between
premodern and modern as well as the boundary between religion and secularity.[40] Blumenberg—not himself a theorist of religion, but nevertheless a
scholar acutely attuned to the role of religion in the construction and cultivation of modern societies—utilizes the term "ritualization" to describe what is
in fact a mythopoeic logic at the heart of this process of reoccupation:

> An ingrained traditional mode of activity has lost its motivating
> content of ideas and thus also its intelligibility, so that the schema
> of the activity is available for a retrospective interpretation and
> integration into a new context of meaning, which in the process
> makes use of and secures, above all, its sanctioned status as
> something that is beyond questioning. In the same way the persistent
> linguistic element stemming from the sacral sphere also marks a
> position as one that is not to be disturbed and that possesses both
> familiarity and consecration for consciousness.[41]

The Declaration unfolded within a context suffused with the various dynamics described by Blumenberg. As the Commission on Human Rights endeavored simultaneously to disrupt and to "reoccupy" certain ingrained modes

of thought and governance, they took tremendous pains to frame the novel tenets of the Declaration in terms that would look deeply familiar to potential audience members, and they strove to locate the Declaration's fundamental claims beyond questioning. All this they worked to do while pointedly forgoing any appeal to the transcendent sources of authority—God, l'Être Suprême, Nature—that have so readily served as means of grounding political declarations of the past.

Myth and the Human Condition?

When theorized in terms of function, myths can be understood to accomplish a variety of things: furnishing an explanation for bewildering or frightening phenomena, entrenching social hierarchies, legitimizing particular moral or ethical ideals, contextualizing and grounding ritual practices. Theorists who have pushed back against the tendency to link myth with supernatural phenomena or prescientific modes of knowledge have done so in part out of a recognition that, even in contexts marked by rising skepticism regarding the supernatural, or rising levels of available empirical information about the world and universe, people continue to gravitate toward authoritative, affective narratives, and, furthermore, that political actors continue to seek to create and deploy such narratives.[42] At the risk of essentializing, is it possible to posit a fundamental human need that myths, in all their variety, function to address? As an array of twentieth-century theorists have endeavored to transport myth out of the realm of the "exotic"—to conceptualize myth as an ordinary category of human expression and activity—they have persistently located one function in particular at the heart of mythmaking: namely, the function of humanizing a world that might otherwise appear inscrutable, hostile, or capricious.[43] Blumenberg captures this most fundamental function in his designation of myth as "a system for the elimination of arbitrariness . . . . In one sentence: the world ceases to contain as many monsters. In a sense that initially is not ethical at all, but more nearly physiognomic, the world becomes 'friendlier.' It approaches what the man who listens to myth needs: to be at home on the world."[44] Even Smith, who understandably hesitates to offer a universalist definition of myth, echoes Blumenberg's definition in his insistence that the mythopoeic narratives at the center of his analysis "are best described neither in terms of repetition of the past nor in terms of future fulfillment," but rather in terms of "a difficult and incongruous present" and an attempt at "rectification" of that incongruity.[45]

In propounding this "anthropological" definition of myth—a definition in which authoritative, evocative narratives are deployed for the ultimate purpose of serving the human need to reduce anxiety about our world—Blumenberg and Smith tread upon ground broken by Rudolf Bultmann, Hans Jonas, and the teacher they held in common: Martin Heidegger. Both Bultmann and Jonas pushed against the tendency of many of their contemporaries to define myth as a tool for explaining phenomena that could not (yet) be explained by other means. Rather than tying myth solely to the function of explaining the mysteries of the world—a maneuver that effectively locks myth into a losing evolutionary battle with science—these theorists laid the groundwork for thinking about myth not merely as a means of presenting an objective picture of the world, but as a means, as Bultmann puts it, to "express man's understanding of himself in the world in which he lives."[46] Whether a given mythopoeic narrative functions to explain an aspect of the universe, legitimize social hierarchies, ground particular moral ideals, or bolster ritual practices, it functions most fundamentally, according to this approach, "as an expression not of the nature of the world but of the nature of the human experience of the world."[47] In a manner that only sometimes involves the acquisition and securing of specific items of information, myth undergirds the human enterprise of "achieving intelligibility" within the world.[48]

Speculative or empirical information about how the world works is merely one facet of this intelligibility, and it is not, according to such theorists, the most important function of myth.[49] Rather, it is simply one of a variety of ways in which myth performs its most elemental function: the articulation and naturalization of our "most important meanings."[50] And, while this phenomenon of wrestling with and overcoming fundamental experiences of human anxiety can appear to unfold as a private or individualized enterprise, this appearance is deceiving. As Doniger stipulates, very much in line with the sociofunctionalist approach, myth is ultimately "public in its effect and reception."[51] Mythopoeic narratives work in the service of the health and solidarity of the societies to which they speak and, in so doing, they endeavor to ensure the security and wellbeing of both society and individual. The fact that many societies have entered into what Charles Taylor calls a "secular age"—an age in which "belief in God [or the transcendent] is no longer axiomatic"—has abolished neither human anxiety nor our need to narrate ourselves into cohesive, purposeful communities.[52] It has merely altered the narratives that we cultivate to contend with these needs.

Ultimately, of course, there is no denying the fact that this understanding of myth as a vehicle for the rectification of human anxiety borders upon a certain essentialism—an essentialism of function rather than of content, but an essentialism nonetheless. In speaking of the phenomenon of sacredness in the modern world, Gordon Lynch refers to such qualified essentialism as a "neo-ontological theor[y]," a theory that allows scholars the luxury of staking out a critical distance from conventional categories of religion while retaining the luxury of presuming "universal ontological phenomena to which this culturally specific term points."[53] Lynch's critique along these lines is legitimate: if the contemporary critique of essentialism is to be taken at its word, theorists of religion should perhaps shy away from any presumption of common experiences underlying our mythopoeic endeavors. Yet most theorists of religion are unwilling to go quite this far—unwilling to abandon all presumption of what Stephen K. White, in a somewhat different context, refers to as common "existential realities."[54] Indeed, Doniger and Laurie L. Patton pointedly argue against such an approach within the study of myth:

> Late twentieth-century discourse on myth finds itself positioned between two temptations—academic arcanity and blatant commercialization. Responding to the legitimate critiques of deconstruction and the new historicism, scholars can bind themselves even closer to their texts and ethnographies, emerging only occasionally to suggest timidly some possible new meanings. Or scholars can take the other extreme—wresting mythic narratives from their political, historical, and cultural contexts in order to make unfounded comparisons and to market new forms of enlightenment to unsuspecting consumers.[55]

Patton and Doniger advocate a "methodological middle course" between these approaches—between a "reductive contextualization" that would resist positing any underlying commonalities between the myths of various communities and an "acontextual mystification" that would imply that all mythmakers are ultimately doing the same thing.[56] The phenomenon of human anxiety, with the attendant drive to deploy narrative to the task of eliminating arbitrariness, furnishes precisely such a middle course: it commands a nearly universal relevance as a basic human experience even as it simultaneously remains implicated within specific contexts that beg to be historicized, interrogated, and otherwise "unpacked" by the theorist of myth. As White depicts such existential realities, they are "in some brute sense universal constitutives of human being" even as their meaning "is irreparably underdetermined" and thus always in need of contextualization.[57]

The international legal realm that the Commission navigated in the late 1940s was marked by a daunting array of crises clamoring for material and existential rectification. The Commission on Human Rights undertook its project in the face of the physical catastrophes of an across-the-globe war, the humanitarian catastrophes of widespread civilian deaths, and the philosophical catastrophe of the implosion of a European framework of human rights that many had upheld as a beacon to the rest of the world. They worked under the shadow of the potential absurdity of proclaiming the universality of human rights in the face of massive human rights violations, and the uncomplimentary charges of "nonsense upon stilts" that have long been leveled at such projects.[58] They worked under the pressure of articulating a vision of human rights that could be recognized as valid in every society across the globe—a task that forced Commission members to unmoor the Declaration from the transhuman extrajudicial sources that had secured the legitimacy of all previous declarations.

In the face of their awareness that many representative states would be unwilling to support a legally binding covenant, Commission members worked under the pressure of formulating a vision of human rights entailing more than a simple enumeration of (unenforceable) regulations, aspiring instead to imbue the Declaration with an authoritativeness capable of, as one framer put it, "plac[ing] a moral obligation on the different countries to find a way and means of giving effect to the rights proclaimed therein."[59] This constellation of difficulties, coupled with the conspicuous international scrutiny under which the Commission operated, rendered the stakes of the Declaration's narrative frighteningly high. These high stakes permeate the text of this document as well as the speeches and testaments disseminated by Commission members in support of it. Most important, these high stakes lurk in the background of the Commission's endeavor to infuse the Declaration with a mythopoeic authority: to make this document capable of asserting rather than merely arguing its vision of the human and the moral imperatives stemming from this vision. Only by virtue of such authority could the Commission hope to fulfill its mandate to, in the words of Haitian delegate Emile Saint-Lot, "give society new legal and moral foundations."[60] Even in the midst of what would turn out to be his abiding skepticism about the Commission's focus on an unenforceable declaration rather than a covenant, Soviet delegate Vladimir Koretsky avowed that the Commission would never succeed in its charge "if it presented as a Bill of Rights a document full of legal complications and reservations."[61] Rather, he asserted, the Declaration "should be as simple and as clear as the Decalogue."[62] The particular strategies whereby the framers of the Declaration enabled this document to present itself and its mandates in this forceful way will be the subject of the following chapters.

CHAPTER 2

The Sacred Center of Human Rights

It is something of a truism to say that human rights, or some facet thereof, command a sacred status in the contemporary world. What does such a claim really mean? This claim might refer to the manner in which human rights reiterate or replicate a Judeo-Christian logic of human value,[1] or it might refer to human rights' indebtedness to Enlightenment principles of intrinsic human worth.[2] Yet the history of the creation of the Declaration reveals that Commission members systematically shied away from both of these conceptions of sacredness when undertaking their negotiations and their public advocacy of this document. The Declaration makes no reference to God or other transcendent forces, no reference to human reason or human capacity as epistemic foundations for human rights' inviolability, and instead offers up the following opening lines:

> Whereas recognition of the inherent dignity and of the equal
> and inalienable rights of all members of the human family is the
> foundation of freedom, justice and peace in the world,
>   Whereas disregard and contempt for human rights have resulted
> in barbarous acts which have outraged the conscience of mankind,
> and the advent of a world in which human beings shall enjoy
> freedom of speech and belief and freedom from fear and want has
> been proclaimed as the highest aspiration of the common people, . . .

Following its invocation of, on the one hand, inherent human dignity and inalienable rights and, on the other, the necessity of recognizing the existence of such human qualities for the preservation of justice and peace in the world, the Preamble unfolds a series of goods that the Declaration is intended to effect: the advent of a world in which human beings shall enjoy basic freedoms, the neutralization of potential sources of popular rebellion, the development of friendly relations between nations, the promotion of social progress and better standards of life, and the cultivation of universal respect for human rights and fundamental freedoms:

> Whereas it is essential, if man is not to be compelled to have recourse, as a last resort, to rebellion against tyranny and oppression, that human rights should be protected by the rule of law,
> Whereas it is essential to promote the development of friendly relations between nations,
> Whereas the peoples of the United Nations have in the Charter reaffirmed their faith in fundamental human rights, in the dignity and worth of the human person and in the equal rights of men and women and have determined to promote social progress and better standards of life in larger freedom,
> Whereas Member States have pledged themselves to achieve, in cooperation with the United Nations, the promotion of universal respect for and observance of human rights and fundamental freedoms,
> Whereas a common understanding of these rights and freedoms is of the greatest importance for the full realization of this pledge, . . .

Finally, immediately before embarking upon the enumeration of its thirty articles, the Declaration offers itself up as the vehicle by which all people and all nations might propagate these goods. In the closing lines of its Preamble, the Declaration proclaims its role as a preeminent vehicle for the generation of

> a common standard of achievement for all peoples and all nations, to the end that every individual and every organ of society, keeping this Declaration constantly in mind, shall strive by teaching and education to promote respect for these rights and freedoms and by progressive measures, national and international, to secure their universal and effective recognition and observance, both among the peoples of Member States themselves and among the peoples of territories under their jurisdiction.

It is important to note that, notwithstanding the prominence of a certain consequentialist language in the narrative of the Preamble, the Declaration's

opening words do not enact a simple utilitarianism; to reduce this document
to a mere mechanism for the prevention of violence would be no more faithful to the logic of the Declaration than it would be to attribute human rights'
sacredness to the agency of a divinity. Rather, both the consequentialist logic
of the Preamble and the specific articles comprising the Declaration's body
are preceded by an assertive invocation of "inherent human dignity." These
words, the very first proclaimed in the Declaration, mark one of the most
elemental discursive gestures enacted by the Commission on Human Rights.[3]
Embodying much more than a rhetorical flourish or even a widely accepted
ontological foundation, the placement of inherent human dignity at the commencement of the Declaration establishes the fulcrum of what Malik termed
the "right scale of values" instituted by the United Nations at this crucial historical transition.[4] This historical transition is depicted in the Preamble's second recital as an emphatic rupture with a previous era of barbarous acts that
have outraged the conscience of mankind, and the Declaration is proffered
as the instantiation of this rupture—a rupture accomplished through its reiteration of a human characteristic that it claims from the outset is inherent.

The Preamble simultaneously presumes and performs its fundamental
premise of inherent human dignity. Very much in the vein of what Derrida
terms the "fabulous"—that is, fable-like—quality of all political declarations,
the Universal Declaration "deduces the need for a speech act of recognition that publicly identifies human rights as inherent and inalienable, and
it declares *this* declaration to mean *that* speech act of common recognition
and understanding."[5] Yet, unlike the paradigmatic eighteenth-century declarations that preceded it, the Universal Declaration makes no endeavor to
ground its most basic premise within any particular worldview or shared
system of belief. Even as it designates itself as the embodiment of a common standard of achievement for all peoples and all nations, it offers no substantive evidence—no "strong foundational arguments"—for the existence of
human dignity.[6] To the contrary, as Slaughter observes,

> The textual life of contemporary human rights law began in 1948
> with a technically invalid syllogism in the preamble of the Universal
> Declaration. Simplified, that syllogism reads: (major premise:)
> The "recognition" of inherent human rights "is the foundation
> of freedom, justice and peace in the world"; (minor premise:)
> "A common understanding of these rights and freedoms is of the
> greatest importance" to realize that recognition; (conclusion:)

"*Therefore*, the General Assembly proclaims this *Universal Declaration of Human Rights* as a common standard of achievement for all peoples and all nations."[7]

In the face of its acknowledgment of the need for a common understanding of our basic rights and freedoms, the Declaration refrains from offering up any epistemological foundation for the human dignity that it locates at the forefront of its Preamble. The reason for this is clear: the Declaration offers no common understanding of human dignity because there is almost certainly no such common understanding available once the question of foundations is shifted to a universal scale. Given that the Commission aspired to make precisely this shift to a universal scale, it immediately faced the problem of having no recourse to a foundation for human rights capable of commanding global consensus. Indeed, the Declaration's philosophical paucity along these lines has been recognized as one of the distinguishing features of this document.

Ultimately, in lieu of a common recognition and understanding of the foundations of human rights, Commission members invoked inherent human dignity axiomatically, without metaphysical, ontological, or empirical argumentation. Throughout the course of their negotiation and broadcast of the Declaration, the Commission designated this human characteristic to be both the justification for, and the inviolable core of, the emerging global community that they sought to engender. Presented not merely as an elementary human characteristic but as, in the words of Lebanese delegate Karim Azkoul, "an absolute and general principl[e] which [is] independent of the United Nations" itself, inherent human dignity ultimately functions as much more than a basic human trait, it functions as the sacred center of the Declaration.[8] Within the narrative of the Preamble, human dignity stands as an item unequivocally set apart and designated for veneration as both an emblem of the ethos of human rights and as a guarantor of the faithful observance of the Declaration's prescriptions.

That inherent human dignity serves as a sacred center of human rights is indubitable. However, it would be a mischaracterization of the Declaration to link its vision of the sacredness of human dignity solely to a particular theological or philosophical genealogy. In fact, even a formulation of sacredness that shies away from specific theological or philosophical tenets and instead equates sacredness with a more general vision of a universe suffused with "transcendent meaning" fails to do justice to the logic of the Declaration.[9]

Short of its invocation of inherent human dignity itself, this document point-edly disclaims any allegiance to an overarching vision of transcendent mean-ing—any allegiance to what Michael Perry has famously described as "the finally or ultimately meaningful nature of the world and of our place in it."[10] Rather, the logic of sacredness that permeates the Declaration is of a different sort. Even as it furnished the Commission with its most elemental means of grounding the tenets of universal human rights, the Declaration's sacral-ization of human dignity was and remains an overtly secular endeavor. In their public roles as delegates and advocates for the Declaration, Commission members were emphatic in their avoidance of language with specific religious resonances, just as they were consistent in their identification of specific reli-gious doctrines as potential impediments to their universalist project. Thus, while Commission members' negotiations and commentaries are peppered with both subtle and overt references to the sacred, it would be a mistake to assume that these framers had, unconsciously or not, failed or betrayed their secular mandate through their use of such language. Instead, the framers' invocations of the sacred work very much in the service of what Asad, hear-kening to Durkheim, calls a "secular morality."[11] Critical to an understanding of this unique conjunction between sacredness and secularity is an appreci-ation of the way in which the notion of sacredness has been approached in recent years within the field of religious studies.

The "Situational" Sacred

The notion of the sacred has long played a central role in the theorization of both myth and religion more generally. Perhaps more than any other com-parative category, the sacred has served as a key designator and decipherer of religion itself—as a verification of the "religiousness" of a particular set of beliefs and/or practices. Since the nineteenth century in particular, the category of the sacred has served as a focal point for the consolidation and categorization of the world's dazzling array of beliefs and practices. This pre-eminence has had both positive and negative implications. While discourses and practices of sacralization can furnish a compelling and perhaps even a universal point of orientation for the interpretation of religion, the category of the sacred has also served as a key means whereby theorists have "rendered a variety of overlapping social usages rooted in changing and heterogeneous

forms of life into a single immutable essence"—into "a universal human experience called 'religious.'"[12]

Asad, among others, is rightly skeptical of this maneuver. While it carries
the benefit, discussed in a related context in Chapter 1, of universal applicability, this particular index of religion has frequently attained this universal
applicability by conceiving of the sacred as a force or a substance existing
and operating independently of human will and action. The sacred, in other
words, can quite easily slip from a helpful focal point for the study of religion
to a "mythic thing"—to "a universal quality hidden in things and an objective limit to mundane action."[13] Not surprisingly, as theorists have become
increasingly attentive to the role of human agency and action in the cultivation of religious beliefs and practices, this essentialization of the sacred
has faced significant scrutiny. In recent years, scholars have endeavored to
imbue the study of the sacred with the same dynamic of human agency and
political labor that has come to inform the study of religion more broadly.
Durkheim and his progeny in the sociofunctionalist tradition have played
a crucial role in this development. Thus, while Durkheim is certainly guilty
of equating religion with sacralization—he famously defined religion in
The Elementary Forms of Religious Life as "a unified system of beliefs and
practices relative to sacred things"—his approach to the sacred has also furnished a broader foundation for a more politically oriented definition of
both sacredness and religion.[14]

David Chidester and Edward T. Linenthal deftly capture this shift in the
scholarly approach to the sacred in their synopsis of two predominant yet contrasting approaches, which they term the "substantial" and the "situational":

> In the first instance, some definitions of the sacred presume to have
> penetrated and reported its essential character. Familiar substantial
> definitions—Rudolph Otto's "holy," Gerardus van der Leew's "power,"
> or Mircea Eliade's "real"—might be regarded as attempts to replicate
> an insider's evocation of certain experiential qualities that can be
> associated with the sacred. . . . By contrast, however, a situational
> analysis, which can be traced back to the work of Emile Durkheim,
> has located the sacred as the nexus of human practices and social
> projects. Following Arnold van Gennep's insight into the "pivoting
> of the sacred," situational approaches have recognized that nothing
> is inherently sacred. Not full of meaning, the sacred, from this

perspective, is an empty signifier. As Claude Lévi-Strauss proposed, the sacred is "a value of indeterminate signification, in itself empty of meaning and therefore susceptible to the reception of any meaning whatsoever."[15]

Chidester and Linenthal advocate for a theorization of the sacred as "an adjectival or verbal form" rather than as something resembling a noun— as "a sign of difference that can be assigned to virtually anything through the human labor of consecration."[16] They vaunt the situational conceptualization of the sacred for its attentiveness to "the relations of meaning and power that are at stake in the formation of a larger social reality."[17] After all, a definition of the sacred as "of indeterminate signification" and therefore as "susceptible to the reception of any meaning whatsoever" points naturally toward the crucial political and ideological acts of "choosing, setting aside, consecrating, venerating, protecting, defending, and redefining."[18] As Peter Berger, another situational theorist, puts it, "Whatever else constellations of the sacred may be 'ultimately,' empirically they are products of human activity and human signification."[19] While this approach to the sacred is not immune to the risk of a certain kind of reification,[20] its constitutive emphasis upon human activity and human signification renders it an invaluable point of orientation for a politically oriented interpretation of a wide array of authoritative narratives.

The scholarly shift toward the situational definition of the sacred proves highly relevant to the study of religion in modernity; indeed, it is one of the key means by which theorists have pursued the logic of religion into post-traditional realms of discourse and practice. The category of the sacred presents a particularly compelling entrée into a variety of extra-institutional religious logics, as the recent rise of treatments of the topic attest.[21] The situational definition offers a framework for making sense of the discourses and actions of ostensibly secular actors who might partake of the logic of sacralization even as they eschew overtly religious terminologies of "sacredness" and "veneration" to describe their endeavors. The creation of the Declaration involves a somewhat different set of actors: actors who in many cases made frequent use of such terminology but who simultaneously denied that, in doing so, they were drawing upon or instantiating any particular religious logic. In either case, the situational definition provides a framework for making sense of actors who endeavor to invest particular ideas or items with an "acquired objectivity"—with an authoritativeness that looks "as if it had always been built into [such] objects and was ready-made"—but who do so while pointedly eschewing references to particular religious traditions.[22]

The relevance of the category of the sacred to such extra-institutional phenomena was directly broached by Durkheim at a number of points in his scholarship. Writing before the creation of the Declaration, he noted that the human rights discourse of France in the late nineteenth century already disclosed a certain logic of sacralization—a logic marked by an endeavor to invest the human person with "something of that transcendental majesty which the churches of all times have given to their Gods."[23] Though his extrapolations on modern religious life never attained the methodological rigor of his work on so-called primitive religions—and though his analysis of the human rights discourse of his day was more than a little aspirational[24]— his schematic observations hinted even in the late nineteenth century at the compelling connection that might be drawn between the logic of sacralization and certain secular political projects.

In the spirit of Chidester and Linenthal's situational approach, and with a particular eye toward Durkheim, the phenomenon of sacralization will be defined herein as follows: the narration of an unequivocal "setting apart," be it within a self-proclaimed religious or secular milieu, for the purpose of engendering a particular moral orientation and, more generally, a social world informed by this moral orientation. This definition hearkens not only to Chidester and Linenthal but also to the etymological roots of the word "sacred," which, in the words of Asad "generally referred to individual things, persons, and occasions that were set apart and entitled to veneration."[25] As Morgan Marietta synopsizes, "Sacredness is the invocation of an absoluteness, or the adherence to specific values about which there is little or no question."[26] Such gestures of setting apart serve, when they are successful, to create "symbols, objects, sentiments, and practices that are experienced as expressions of a normative, absolute reality."[27] It is important to recognize the manner in which this situational definition ruptures a dyad that for many years structured scholarly engagements with the sacred: namely, the dyad of "the sacred and the profane."[28] When we approach the sacred not as a thing with an essential character but as the product of a setting apart whose only real "substance" is the normative, absolute authoritativeness it seeks to generate, the profane also becomes indeterminate; it also becomes situational. Rather than an independent quality or a generic realm of human life, the phenomenon of profanation becomes determinable only in relation to specific gestures of sacralization.[29] For this reason, this chapter does not put forth a definition of profanation in tandem with this definition of sacralization. As will become clear below, profanation can look quite different within differing contexts of sacralization.

There is little question that the Commission on Human Rights endeavored to imbue the Declaration with a sacredness of the sort described above, even as it repeatedly attested to the secularism of this document. Inherent human dignity is posited within the Preamble of the Declaration—and at various other moments in its body—in a manner that invites no argument and brokers no disagreement.[30] This document enshrines inherent human dignity as a characteristic that no person and no political or social body or organ gave us and that, therefore, no person or institution can violate without charge of profound transgression. As an item presumed to transcend the machinations of all political and social institutions, human dignity is set apart within the Declaration as something philosophically and practically beyond questioning. The Declaration's framers accomplished this unequivocal setting apart of human dignity in large measure by simply invoking it within the Preamble, pointedly unaccompanied by any ontological or metaphysical underpinnings. Far from endeavoring to couch the reality of human dignity within a universe structured by some brand of transcendent meaning, the Declaration simply places it beyond negotiation or dispute—ultimately situating it, in the words of Werner Hamacher, as "an elucidation of human essence as it has always existed."[31] From this location, human dignity immediately serves as the undisputed foundation of the rights enumerated in the rest of this document.

This straightforward presentation of the fact of inherent human dignity, however, cannot be disentangled from yet another important invocation within the Preamble: namely, the "barbarous acts which have outraged the conscience of mankind" and that have, by a somewhat paradoxical logic, provided the inspiration for the Declaration's very reaffirmation of human dignity. Within the Preamble, in other words, human dignity is presented simultaneously as inherent and as recently compromised—profaned at the hands of those very political and social machinations that it is postulated to transcend. This intimate link between inherent human dignity and the barbarous acts of World War II and the Holocaust (unquestionably the epoch to which the Declaration is referring) lends an additional nuance to the sacredness of this item. Within the narrative of the Preamble, human dignity remains "haunted" by this epoch, much in the way that the likes of Michael Taussig and Georges Bataille understand the sacred always to be haunted by—and in fact bolstered by—actual and potential threats of profanation.[32]

The work that the wartime epoch performs in simultaneously threatening and highlighting the sacredness of human dignity is crucial, and it is a primary focus of this chapter.

Yet it would be an overstatement to contend that the atrocities of the wartime period were invoked within this document as a definitive antithesis to human dignity, as the substantial definition often postulates in relation to the phenomenon of profanation. Rather, as this chapter shows, the framers of the Declaration strove throughout the negotiation and broadcast of this document to broaden their extrapolations of the threats to human dignity well beyond the specific outrages of the wartime period, even as they repeatedly utilized this period as a point of reference. Moreover, while there is no question that human dignity was intended to serve within the Declaration as a vehicle for the prevention of violence, to reduce it entirely to this function would be to ignore the Declaration's multifaceted assertion that such dignity is *inherent*—intrinsic to human beings, independent of their social and political location within the world. Ultimately, the human dignity of the Declaration is tied to, yet irreducible to, the barbarous acts that furnished the occasion for its reaffirmation.

The wartime period provided Commission members with an "anchor in experience"—with a concrete point of reference for their negotiation of many of the Declaration's particular rights. But its role as a historical anchor is ultimately secondary to its broader and more enduring role as a conceptual foil for the Commission's formulation of the proper sacred center of human rights.[33] The barbarous acts of the wartime period, in other words, furnished a striking example of an alternative object of sacralization, an example perceived to be both historical and ever-possible. Hamacher hints at this logical link even as he pushes his own examination of human rights in a very different direction:

> [The Declaration] proclaims nothing new, but only makes explicit
> and public what implicitly has determined human nature for as long
> as the being called man has existed. The goal of this reminder, this
> explication and publication of the rights of man, this opening up of
> something that, as such, is already revealed and accessible to all, is to
> eradicate the "sole cause of public calamities and of the corruption of
> governments."[34]

The recent atrocities of World War II and the Holocaust provided not so much a justification as an illustration—simultaneously empirical and potential—of the necessity of the Declaration's enshrinement of human dignity as the sacred center of human rights.[35] In the course of their negotiations, Commission members drew repeatedly upon this illustration even as they understood human dignity itself to transcend the particular context of these atrocities.

Sacredness in the Epoch of "Barbarous Acts"

State sovereignty exists in perpetual tension with human rights, even when such tensions remain hidden from the view of the citizens of a given state. The rise of the Third Reich brought this ever-present tension between the state and the human being into dramatic relief. Though there are many human rights lessons to be derived from the history of the rise of German fascism, two insights are of particular importance to an understanding of the Commission's endeavor to enshrine human dignity within the Declaration. In the first place, the ascendance of the Nazi Party revealed that the human rights enshrined in the renowned declarations of the eighteenth century were, in practice, simply another form of civil right, fundamentally dependent upon the mechanisms of the state for their implementation. More disturbingly, it revealed the manner in which, under certain circumstances, the sovereignty of the state becomes expressed through the very act of expelling certain individuals from the embrace of these protective state mechanisms.

Perhaps no theorist has more famously explored these matters, and the implications of these matters for human rights, than Hannah Arendt. In the course of documenting the origins of totalitarianism in Germany and Eastern Europe, Arendt ultimately credited such movements with having laid bare the underside of the human rights frameworks of her time. Central to Arendt's conclusion is her assertion that "in the sphere of international law, it has always been true that sovereignty is nowhere more absolute than in matters of 'immigration, naturalization, nationality, and expulsion.'"[36] The implications of this proposition are dire: in moments of dramatic social, political, and economic crisis, claims Arendt, states become more likely to function in a manner directly contrary to the indiscriminate, inclusivist logic of human rights. Nowhere was this proposition more clearly demonstrated than in the logic of the German *Volksgemeinschaft* or "organic state," described by Hitler as "the organization of a community of physically and psychologically similar living beings [coexisting] for the better facilitation of the maintenance of their species."[37]

Though the ideal of the organic state, guided by the enlightened will of a ruler attuned to the guiding spirit of the age, has pervaded the political theorizing of figures from Plato to Hegel, Arendt and others in her wake have mapped the confluence of historical events that, for the first time, propelled this vision of the organic state to the political forefront in Germany and that ultimately set the mechanisms of the state into deadly opposition to the logic of human rights.[38] One of the driving forces within this confluence was a phenomenon with which Arendt wrestled throughout *The Origins of Totalitarianism*, and which Michel Foucault eventually captured in the term "biopolitics": namely, the manner in which Nazi leaders transformed particular human populations into tools for the legitimation of the state.[39] If it was the innovation of the American and French declarations of the eighteenth century to have posited the sovereign individual as the locus of political legitimacy, the Reich accomplished the opposite, deploying its human populations in much the same way that a state might deploy its other material resources. In the case of the Reich, the larger goal toward which it directed its various human populations was the cultivation of a quasi-biological ideal of a "perfect society."[40] The Reich embarked upon this biopolitical project very much in spite of existing human rights mechanisms, quickly discovering that supposedly inalienable rights become nonexistent if a person has no nation to appeal to for their implementation. As Arendt puts it, "The Rights of Man, supposedly inalienable, proved to be unenforceable—even in countries whose constitutions were based upon them—whenever people appeared who were no longer citizens of any sovereign state."[41] It is in this manner that, in the words of Giorgio Agamben, "the very figure who should have embodied the rights of man par excellence—the refugee—signals instead the concept's radical crisis."[42]

As the population of minorities and stateless people exploded throughout Europe in the interwar years, Nazi propagandists were furnished with a vast pool of effectively superfluous beings who could readily be portrayed as threats to what Himmler described as the "organically indivisible national community."[43] The paralysis of surrounding nation-states in the face of the stateless—the "constitutional inability of nation-states to guarantee human rights to those who were not its citizens"—furnished an important foundation for Germany's escalation of measures against such individuals.[44] Moreover, this demonstration of the practical nonexistence of basic human rights for those without claim to a state furnished a precedent for the Reich's production of additional superfluous people through the legal disenfranchisement of its own "non-Aryan" citizens.[45] Jews in particular came to embody what Agamben has described as the Reich's "privileged negative referent of the new biopolitical sovereignty."[46]

The logic of biopolitics is intricately tied to a logic of sacralization. Agamben has famously explored this link, though his own exploration has focused upon a particular etymology of the term "sacred" and has thus propelled him down a quite specific path originating in ancient Rome, culminating in the Holocaust, and persisting even into the western liberal democracies of today. Agamben draws upon a situational notion of the sacred to the extent that he foregrounds the highly political act of setting apart as a key feature in the production of sacredness, but he ultimately attributes a decidedly more substantial quality to this phenomenon. Originally, claims Agamben, sacralization referred to a very specific political maneuver whereby an unlucky individual becomes forcibly excluded from the protections of both the political and the religious realms—a maneuver wherein a sovereign places an individual beyond "the sanctioned forms of both human and divine law" and thereby leaves that individual radically exposed to violence at the hands of other humans.[47] An individual subtracted from the realms of human comity in this way is reduced to "bare life," stripped of the political personhood that not only elevates us above other animals but that imbues us with identity and agency vis-à-vis all other humans. Such acts of exclusion—and, more important, the *threat* of such acts—serve as a mechanism for intimidating and constraining all members of a political body, and thus ultimately for creating and securing the power of the sovereign.[48] This manner of generating sovereign power dates back at least to the politics of ancient Rome, but Agamben claims that it has achieved both a subtlety and a ubiquity today within the liberal democracies of the west that makes it difficult for most citizens to recognize.[49] Much less difficult to recognize is the manner in which the totalitarian regimes of the mid-twentieth century embodied such a biopolitical logic, and it is for this reason that Agamben credits these regimes—and the life of the concentration camp in particular— with having laid bare the link between a particular logic of sacralization and the production of political sovereignty.

The Nazis did not, of course, refer to the recipients of their political aggressions as sacred; to the extent that sacredness was ascribed to any item within the context of German fascism, it was to the German *Volk* and the *Volksgemeinschaft* that brought it into political life. Thus, notwithstanding the importance of Agamben's historical and political insights (including their value for a thorough understanding of today's human rights frameworks, which will be touched upon below), the manner in which the *Volksgemein-schaft* itself functioned as a particular item of sacredness in this period simply cannot be ignored.

Ultimately, the situational definition as proposed in this chapter has the potential to orient in a somewhat different way to the sacred logic of Nazism. As Nazi propagandists and policymakers struggled to create order and meaning out of the crises of World War I and its aftermath—an endeavor unquestionably suffused with its own broader mythopoeic logic[50]—they enshrined the *Volksgemeinschaft* as the central, perpetually embattled emblem of the health and integrity of the German nation. This emblem could hardly have been better suited to the logic of sacralization: the racial and evolutionary science of the day could be interpreted to quite literally "naturalize" the ideal of the *Volk*, thus allowing advocates of the *Volksgemeinschaft* to frame their work of legal, social, and physical discrimination as human iterations of objective "laws of Nature or of History" rather than merely as contingent or utilitarian measures of political self-defense.[51] This selfsame racial/evolutionary science laid the groundwork for a powerful logic of profanation focused firmly upon particular individuals and communities and the capacity of such individuals and communities to compromise the integrity of the *Volksgemeinschaft*—to compromise it not merely through their acts of political mischief but, much more fundamentally, by virtue of their very biology.[52] The threat of biological/racial contamination, dovetailing almost perfectly with the political imperative of sovereignty-through-expulsion, gave rise to the constellation of legal, discursive, and physical gestures of setting apart that have come to epitomize the Nazi era.[53] Ultimately, the story of the European Holocaust can be told as an unfolding of efforts to cordon off and bolster the *Volksgemeinschaft* through the rhetorical villainization of European Jews and other minorities, through their systematic legal disenfranchisement, and through their physical ghettoization, expulsion, and extermination. This transformation of vulnerable individuals into instruments for the sacralization of the state is precisely the logic against which Commission on Human Rights pitted itself.

For Agamben (and for Arendt as well, though she does not use the term "biopolitical"), universal human rights are inextricably bound up with the very biopolitical logic that perpetually threatens to turn humans into mere vehicles for the generation of political sovereignty. This interconnectedness becomes apparent only when human rights exit the realm of solemn proclamations and become "a practical political issue," as they did in the face of Germany's treatment of its "impure" populations.[54] In such contexts, the human rights frameworks of Europe accomplished little more than to occlude the radical vulnerability of humans existing outside the protections of a state—to occlude the ease with which an individual who is "nothing but a human being" can be transformed into a means to a political end.[55] This demonstration of the interconnectedness of human rights and biopolitics led Arendt to evince a deep skepticism toward human rights and, eventually, to call for a retheorization of the very foundations of these rights. Agamben comes to much the same conclusion, ultimately calling for an overhaul of the very fundaments of modern international politics.[56]

The framers of the Declaration, however, took quite a different tack when faced with the humanitarian catastrophes of World War II and the Holocaust. Far from evincing a skepticism of the sort conveyed by Arendt, and far from embarking upon a radical critique of the sort proposed by Agamben, the Commission on Human Rights committed itself to a reaffirmation of the logic of human rights and a reappropriation of the discourse of sacralization. This reaffirmation and reappropriation function in creative conjunction with the wartime period, ultimately building upon rather than rupturing the troubling trajectory traced by Agamben and Arendt. To accomplish this, the Commission made frequent reference to the events and the consequences of the wartime period, and they pointedly tied these references the more general, ever-present threat of political abuses of vulnerable individuals and groups.

As previously asserted, however, such references did not ultimately work in service of a utilitarian justification for the Declaration's most fundamental tenets, even if they did furnish a utilitarian argument for many of the specific rights enumerated in the body of the Declaration.[57] Rather, the wartime veneration of the *Volksgemeinschaft* was repeatedly depicted by the Commission's most prominent spokespeople as a symptom of a broader tendency to prioritize states over people—as a violation of a human integrity that, within the narrative of the Declaration, always already exists. The specter of state violence, of which the barbarous acts of the wartime period are merely one possible example, ultimately furnished a crucial occasion for a global reaffirmation of human dignity even as the Commission refused to allow it to furnish the foundation for such dignity.

Enshrining the Sacred Within the Declaration

The Nazi *Volksgemeinschaft* represents an important item for consideration not merely for the way in which it sheds light upon the broad scope of the situational definition of the sacred but, much more importantly, because it served as the primary referent by which the Commission solidified its own notion of that which required unequivocal setting apart—that which should serve as both an emblem and a guarantor of a rejuvenated international political landscape. The self-destructiveness of the organic state began to disclose itself to the international community as World War II came to a close and appalling details of the Nazi reign began to come to light. Photos and narratives emerging from wartorn Europe contributed to an inchoate atmosphere of human rights activism in the 1940s, and to the shift among Allied leaders from a position of relative ambivalence regarding the promotion of fundamental human rights and freedoms to a position of advocating for an invocation of such rights in the very Charter of the United Nations in 1945.[58] Shocking photos of the Nazi concentration camps offered a striking, if incomplete, vision of the ultimate implications of a politics in which individuals are perceived not as entities of inherent and irreducible worth but rather as a means to "the care of the nation's biological body."[59] This early evidence served to fuel one of the central preoccupations of the Commission: the creation of an international juridico-political mechanism that would make it impossible for individuals to fall victim to a human economy of the sort exemplified by Nazi Germany. Commission members eventually converged upon the conviction that such a mechanism required the establishment of a criterion by virtue of which people become bearers of rights independently of their connection to "governments, courts, legislatures, or international assemblies."[60] This criterion is human dignity, posited in the Declaration as a characteristic inherent to all humans and thus primary to all other characteristics imbued through the instruments of religion, politics, or society, *including* the instruments of the United Nations itself.[61] Malik lays out the importance of articulating a quality inherent to human beings as such, a consideration that he claims "was not always present to the mind of the Commission [but] was nevertheless there, at the base of every defense and decision":

It is the question of the nature and the origin of [human rights]. By *what title* does man possess them? Are they *conferred* upon him by the State, or by Society, or by the United Nations? Or do they

belong to his nature so that apart from them he simply ceases to
be man? Now if they simply originate in the State or Society or the
United Nations, it is clear that what the State now *grants* it might
one day *withdraw* without thereby violating any higher law. But if
these rights and freedoms belong to man as man, then the State
or the United Nations, far from conferring them upon him, must
recognize and respect them, or else it would be violating the higher
law of his being.[62]

The Commission's negotiations were permeated, according to Malik, with a
shared conviction that the Declaration must function as "an original document deriving from the essence of man."[63]

Malik's forceful articulation of the centrality of inherent dignity to the
human rights project should not eclipse the fact that Commission members
held differing and even contentious views about the most effective way to
ensure the realization of such dignity. Indeed, one of the primary sources of
conflict among Commission members—particularly between the six Communist delegates and most other framers—was the practical question of *how*
human dignity was to be effected and upheld. Contrary to the positions of
most other members of the Commission, the Communist delegates almost
uniformly asserted that human dignity and basic human rights could not be
made a reality independently of the empowerment of states—states harbor-
ing "the framework of a democratic and progressive legislation," but states
nevertheless.[64] Byelorussian delegate Leonid Kaminsky captured this sentiment in his lament before the UN General Assembly that the Declaration as
conceived by most Commission members tended toward a neglect of "the
material conditions without which effective respect for the rights of individual could not be guaranteed," and thus risked ignoring "the existence of
the individual as being outside his own *milieu*."[65] The result of ignoring this
broader milieu would inevitably be to locate man in opposition not only to
the governments upon which he must rely for protection; as Soviet delegate
Koretsky admonished, it would inevitably end up positioning man "in opposition to his own people."[66]

These contrasting approaches are embodied within two Draft Preambles
submitted for consideration during the Commission's Third Session. The
first draft, submitted by the USSR, reflected an abiding concern voiced by
Communist delegates that a conception of human dignity operating independently of, or even in opposition to, the mechanisms of the state was not

only fundamentally illusory but an unacceptable threat to the stability of the governments upon which all individuals must ultimately depend for their well-being. In the interest of upholding the rights of individuals while maintaining the sovereignty and integrity of the political bodies upon which such individuals depend in practice, the Soviet Draft Preamble afforded considerable latitude to UN member states in their implementation of basic human rights, ultimately offering up the Declaration to be used "at their discretion in taking appropriate legislative and other measures . . . for the dissemination of [its] provisions."[67] A second Draft Preamble under consideration at this time, compiled from an assortment of drafts that had been submitted piecemeal to the Commission by France, Belgium, Lebanon, and the American Federation of Labor, conceived of human dignity in language substantially similar to the Declaration as it would eventually be adopted. This draft highlighted in its opening lines the need for recognition of the inherent dignity of all members of the human family, and it significantly downplayed the role of state discretion in actually operationalizing this dignity.[68]

The deep-seated differences between these two approaches were never resolved among Commission members, and, indeed, the matter of state sovereignty remained an enduring point of dispute between Communist delegates and most of the rest of the Commission. This dispute ultimately contributed in no small way to six of the eight abstentions in the General Assembly's final vote.[69] As became clear early in the work of the Commission, however, the majority of the Declaration's framers operated under the presumption that human dignity must serve, as Malik put it early on, as "the basic woof of the Preamble."[70] The abuses of the wartime period inspired most Commission members to cohere upon the conviction that the key to both the universalism and the effectiveness of the Declaration lay in grounding it upon what Azkoul described as a broadly held "conception of the human person."[71] Long before the Commission had arrived at its negotiation of the particular language of the Preamble, this conception of the person was presumed by most Commission members to exist in distinction from—if not, as Koretsky lamented, in direct opposition to—the state. Malik, who would eventually become a lifelong spokesperson for the Declaration, was instrumental, though by no means alone, in the consolidation and narration of this particular logic of inherent human dignity.

It is difficult to overstate the influence of the wartime era upon this line of thought, notwithstanding the fact that historians of human rights vary in their assessment of the extent to which the Nazi regime directly influenced the Commission's formulations of the basic tenets of the Declaration. Morsink, as we have seen, has asserted that we cannot understand the creation of this document without an appreciation of the role played by the Nazi regime as a negative point of reference.[72] Glendon has taken issue with claims of an unequivocal connection such as that laid out by Morsink and others. Even in the course of her denial, however, Glendon has acknowledged that one of the core imperatives of the Declaration was to reject the positivist approach to law that had dominated theories of international relations prior to World War II, and thus to clear a space for an alternative logic to undergird the international legal regimes of the future. The notion of inherent human dignity was indispensable to this task of articulating a vision of the human that would bear rights independently of the world's various political institutions. The specter of Nazi Germany, however, is almost impossible to disentangle from this equation:

> Prior to World War II, legal positivism (the view that there are no rights other than those granted by the laws of the state) flourished in the United States and Europe and was dogma in the Soviet Union. But legally sanctioned atrocities committed in Nazi Germany had caused many people to reevaluate the proposition that there is no higher law by which the laws of nation-states can be judged. The Declaration implicitly rejected the positivist position by stating that fundamental rights are recognized, rather than conferred.[73]

Ultimately, even as Commission members worked to remain consistent with their mandate of articulating the Declaration in universalizable terms, their conflation of the Declaration's vision of the human with the larger project of correcting the arbitrary exercise of state or other governmental power and of curtailing any such future instances discloses a heavy investment in the barbarous acts of the wartime era as a point of reference for the setting apart of human dignity as both emblematic and inviolable. Nowhere is this clearer than in the speeches of Malik. In his numerous proclamations locating human dignity at the heart of his description of the right scale of values necessary for the cultivation of peace and human flourishing, Malik rarely ventured far from the bogey of powerful, overreaching governments:

> In this age of advancing governmental control, of national consciousness and sovereignty, it is difficult to convince man that

he is not meant to be the slave of his Government; it is difficult to establish in his mind the right scale of values whereby he can see clearly that the State exists ultimately for his sake and in his service and not conversely. But unless we reject the total subordination of man to the State; unless, that is, we succeed not only in limiting the claims of the State on man, but also ensuring the State's recognition of his claims on it, the battle for the fundamental rights and freedoms will have been virtually lost.[74]

Malik's treatment of these issues frequently borders upon the utilitarian; yet, notwithstanding the importance of World War II and the Holocaust to the negotiation of the Declaration, the Commission's investment in this period is more complicated than a straightforward utilitarian deduction from the example of the Nazis. In the first place, as Malik intimates in the quote above, the menace of state sovereignty is ultimately a common feature of modern life, hardly unique to the wartime context. Malik in fact had little trouble maneuvering between the historical and the universal, clearly perceiving the universal potential for the subordination of the individual to the state. And while Communist delegates such as Pavlov and Koretsky took regular issue with the Commission's prevailing presumptions about the generic dangerousness of the state, even these framers recognized and agitated against the ongoing threat of state violence to which, in their understanding, all humans in the modern world were capable of falling victim. The predominant difference between these factions of the Commission was the Communist attribution of this threat specifically to fascist systems of governance.[75] For the great majority of Commission members, though, the wartime era served as a powerful focal point that nevertheless readily pointed beyond itself and the specific fascist regimes of the twentieth century, and this expansiveness was crucial to the framers' universalist mandate—to their ongoing refusal, as René Cassin put it, "to lower the Declaration to the rank of an act of resentment turned toward the past."[76]

Yet, to take this deliberate expansiveness as an indication that the Commission was ultimately content to embrace a broader utilitarian argument for human dignity—one grounded upon the general fact of violence rather than upon the specifics of 1940s Europe—would also be a mistake.[77] While the specter of state violence unquestionably served to highlight the need for an unequivocal index of human worth, this ever-present fact of violence does not itself *engender* this index of human worth. Malik and his colleagues' many indictments of the oppressive state were undergirded by an insistence, mirrored in the Declaration itself, that this index of human worth exists prior to the machinations of the state—requiring reaffirmation, certainly, but pointedly not requiring the underpinning of utilitarian or other modes of argument:

> It is this reaffirmation, if only he heeds it, that might still save
> [man] from being dehumanized. For society and the state under
> our modern conditions can take perfect care of themselves: have
> advocates and sponsors on every side: their rights are in good
> hands. It is man, the real, existing, anxious, laughing, free and dying
> man, who is in danger of becoming extinct. It is man who is the
> unprotected orphan, the neglected ward, the forgotten treasure.
> And therefore it is good that the Declaration has not lost sight of its
> main objective: to proclaim man's irreducible humanity, to the end
> that he might yet recover his . . . sense of dignity and reestablish his
> faith in himself.[78]

Inherent human dignity serves within the Declaration to both articulate and enshrine our irreducible humanity—to set it apart as an unquestioned premise of law and politics in the postwar era. As a feature that is always-already-given, inherent human dignity is not the product of an argument but the referent to which all arguments within the new international arena become beholden. As Roosevelt put it, inherent human dignity is not a right; rather, it is the reason "why we have rights to begin with."[79]

The sacralization of human dignity—its enshrinement as an axiomatic index of human entitlement to the rights in the Declaration—ultimately *precedes* the logic of peacemaking, even as it also ultimately draws upon this logic. Morsink reminds us that

> while the drafters surely thought that proclaiming this Declaration
> would serve the cause of world peace, they did not think of the
> human rights they proclaimed as only or merely a means to that end.
> Regardless of the consequences for world peace, these rights have
> an independent grounding in the members of the human family
> to whom they belong and who possess them as birthrights. If this
> were not so, a government could torture people (or violate any other
> right) as long as it was thought or shown to serve the cause of world

peace. This is precisely how most governments rationalize and justify their human rights violations, but it flies in the face of the truth about the Declaration and about human rights generally.[80]

The language of the Preamble pointedly suggests that the rights of the Declaration "*already exist* and now need to be more firmly implemented to avoid the scourges of future wars."[81] By what logic do these rights exist? They are rooted, in the words of New Zealand delegate Colin Aikman, not merely "in the structure and needs of the modern world" but "in the nature of man himself."[82] Far from describing human rights and the dignity from which they derive as "the original creation of 58 nations or their representatives meeting in a twentieth-century committee room," the Declaration proclaims them to be a preexisting reality, and, in so doing, effectively narrates them into existence.[83] This maneuver that then lays the foundation for a subsequent edifice of human rights law that, in the words of Slaughter, "legislates as if its common sense were already commonsensical, thereby transforming its tautological propositions into teleological projections of a time when everyone will know what everyone should know.[84]

We neglect a crucial facet of the Declaration's formulation of human dignity when we fail to recognize the way in which the logic of this document departs from conventional theological, philosophical, and historical modes of justification.[85] None of these modes of justification capture the logic of the Declaration's assertive, retroactive posit—a posit much more in keeping with what Slaughter, hearkening to the likes of Derrida and Frank Kermode, refers to as "'the establishment of an accepted freedom by magic.'"[86] Slaughter's attribution of this phenomenon to the advent of a particular trend within modern literature neglects the manner in which the Commission actively, if unconsciously, deployed a logic of sacralization to ground human dignity beyond all particular discourses of theology, philosophy, and even history.

Yet, to state that the Declaration locates human dignity beyond the bounds of theology, philosophy, and history is not to claim that human dignity *cannot* be justified from within the bounds of particular theological, philosophical, or historical frameworks. Malik, for example, is well known for his assertions to the effect that human dignity is a key feature within the "Platonic-Christian" tradition, and that its centrality within the Declaration is "a faint echo, on the international plane," of this tradition.[87] Such proclamations are problematic only if one presumes that inherent human dignity is a value endemic *only* to the Platonic-Christian tradition, and this, of course, is a claim that the framers of the Declaration worked to emphatically reject. The universalist mandate of the Declaration ultimately necessitated not only a refusal to ground the notion of human dignity within a "resentment" toward a particular history but also a refusal to link it to any particular worldview—a commitment, in other words, to divorce the language of human rights from any one parochial system of value. This preoccupation dominated the negotiation and broadcast of the Declaration, and it connects intimately to the Commission's sacralization of human dignity. Ultimately, Commission members gravitated to inherent human dignity not merely because it resonated with their own deeply held systems of value, but primarily out of their conviction that this notion embodies a value recognizable to human cultures across the globe.

This preoccupation with securing the cultural neutrality of the Declaration is particularly apparent in the Commission's navigation of the legacy of the European Enlightenment. As Morsink observes,

> Even a casual reader of the Universal Declaration will see that there is a similarity of language between this 1948 United Nations Document and the classical declarations of the eighteenth century. This similarity is especially strong toward the beginning of the document. The first recital of the 1948 Preamble speaks of "inherent dignity" and of "equal and inalienable rights," both of which recall Enlightenment ways of thinking. . . . In fact, the first sentence of Article 1 of the Universal Declaration is a virtual rewrite of the first article of [the French Declaration of 1789].[88]

Such similarities of language emerged in spite of Commission members' concerted efforts to curtail the inclusion of terms and points of reference with even a semblance of connection to the European tradition. The persistence of these similarities, however, is the product of a much more complicated phenomenon than mere "western" thoughtlessness or imperialism. The history of the negotiation of the Declaration reveals that the Commission on a whole was highly attentive to the potential charge of Eurocentrism, and this attentiveness merits recognition. Morsink, for example, has described the process resulting in what he calls a "bargain about God and Nature," in which Commission members opted to forgo a reference to "nature" as the foundation for human rights despite the fact that many of the framers—Malik most vocally—considered such a reference sufficiently agnostic to command global consensus.[89] Ultimately, the Commission concluded that the idea of nature as a nonmetaphysical foundation for inherent human dignity was too deeply implicated in "the single, natural, divine, and transcendent" ordering by which key Enlightenment figures had allowed the Christian God to "trickle down" into the ostensibly secular declarations of the eighteenth century.[90] Forced through the process of negotiation to take heed of the fact that "most of the drafters of the Universal Declaration did not share this Enlightenment belief in a single, transcendent source of value," even Enlightenment minded framers such as Malik and Cassin proved willing to vote for a document hearkening neither to God nor to nature.[91] As Roosevelt describes of her own experience of navigating the Declaration's universalist mandate,

> I happen to believe that we are born free and equal in dignity and rights because there is a divine Creator, and there is a divine spark in men. But, there were other [Commission members] who wanted it expressed in such a way that they could think in their particular way about this question, and, finally, these words were agreed upon because they stated the fact that all men were born free and equal, but they left each of us to put it in our own reason, as we say, for that end.[92]

As the Commission sought to disavow an indissoluble connection between the Declaration and the "Platonic-Christian" legacies of the west, they leaned heavily on inherent human dignity as an effectively empty, though universally resonant, category to be imbued with specific content as the proponents of particular worldviews came to embrace this document. Christopher McCrudden captures something of this distinction between dignity as an empty category and dignity as a culturally specific value in his discussion of the difference between "concept" and "conception": "whilst there is a *concept* of human dignity with a minimum core, there are several different *conceptions* of human dignity, and these differ significantly because there appears to be no consensus politically or philosophically" on the various underpinnings of this term.[93]

The capacity of human dignity to function as a "concept" proved invaluable to the Commission as it endeavored to make good on its universalist mandate. This mandate makes clear that inherent human dignity ultimately functions not only as an emblem of the human unencumbered from the state but also as a mechanism whereby the Commission becomes able to *translate* the world's myriad systems of value into the Declaration's prescription for human rights. Inherent dignity instantiates Malik's abstract idea of "irreducible humanity" even as it eschews substantive claims about the human—claims that our dignity hinges, for example, on our capacity for reason or on the fact of our creation in the image of God. The Commission's commitment to the sacralization of human dignity is inseparable from its preoccupation with such "translation," and the interplay of these preoccupations reveals a fascinating interpenetration of religious and secular logics. If we conceive of secularism, at least in its political sense, as something akin to Asad's influential definition of "an enactment by which a *political medium* . . . redefines and transcends particular and differentiating practices of the self that are articulated through class, gender, and religion," then inherent human dignity reveals itself, in its very capacity to be set apart as a concept, to be a secular mechanism par excellence.[94] Within the narrative of the Declaration, dignity's "secular" role as a mediator of difference and its "sacred" role as a locus of a normative, absolute reality converge to accomplish the Declaration's momentous task of combining "unity and universality with pluralism and differentiation."[95] To put this interplay of unity and pluralism, absoluteness and ecumenism, in the decidedly more poetic language of early drafter Jacques Maritain,

> Here we are no longer dealing with the mere enumeration of human rights, but with the principle of dynamic unification whereby they are brought into play, with the tone scale, with the specific key in which different kinds of music are played on the same keyboard, music which in the event is in tune with, or harmful to, human dignity.[96]

Amid clear evidence of the myriad social, theological, and philosophical differences of the world, Maritain, and eventually the Commission itself, imbued inherent human dignity with the capacity to furnish an enduring ballast for the negotiation of our deep-seated human variations.

In its promise to mediate, and thus ultimately to transcend, all parochial formulations of human worth, inherent dignity furnishes the most fundamental grounding for the Commission's claim that the Declaration is a document within which—"after the most careful, responsible, authoritative and joint consideration of every word, iota and meaning"—"The world as a whole has spoken."[97] The dual logics of sacralization and mediation allowed the Commission to enshrine a universal index of human worth within the

Declaration while simultaneously deflecting the charges of imperialism that might naturally stem from the vision of a cadre of elites prescribing values to the rest of the world. Malik in particular worked tirelessly to synchronize these logics:

> There may be a Greek or a Roman or a Jewish or a Christian or a Moslem or a Buddhist or a Marxist or a Chinese or a Russian or a Hindu or a German or a French or a Latin or an Anglo-American view of man and his dignity. Only the Universal Declaration, in the elaboration of which all these nations, cultures and religions participated, embodies such a view. At least this is the only document in history on which the whole world agreed, without a single State casting a vote against it as a whole. We may say then that in the Universal Declaration universal man himself is defining himself. We are not saying that this universal definition is "deeper" or more "correct" or more "true" than any of the particular definitions I enumerated above; we are only asserting that it is the first and only universal definition in history.[98]

Malik's description of the Declaration's universalism discloses a conviction, cultivated throughout the negotiations of the Declaration and articulated with increasing systematicity following its adoption, that the generation of a universalizable foundation for human rights simply could not be accomplished in any way other than through a twofold gesture of setting apart, a gesture that would not only sanctify human dignity but would also hollow it out, putting it forth as a "composite of many political, economic and sociological ideas, differing systems of law, and cultural traditions."[99] This setting apart of human dignity not merely as a marker of irreducible human worth but as an effectively empty category of ethical legitimacy was understood by framers such as Malik and Cassin "to bear directly upon [the Declaration's] universality" and thus upon its credibility as a synthesis, as opposed to a fabrication, of basic human values across the globe.[100]

CHAPTER 3

The Sacred and the Social

For all the Commission's aspirations to enshrine an item within the Declaration with sufficient "emptiness" to wield universal authority, inherent human dignity does contain one substantive characteristic: it unquestionably inheres in the human qua individual rather than in the human qua group member. This, we have seen, is most immediately a product of the wartime period and its broader portent of state oppression that served as such an important focal point for Commission members' formulation of human rights. The Commission's preoccupation with capturing an index of human worth and integrity firmly distinguishable from our status as citizens or group members permeated its articulations of the core tenets of universal human rights. Yet it can hardly escape notice that the formulation of dignity as a characteristic inhering most fundamentally within the individual, independently of this individual's membership in particular communities, resonates strongly with the very Enlightenment language from which the Commission worked so hard to extricate itself.

The resonance between the logic of the Declaration and the logic of a certain worldview that envisions individuals as "pristine and separate" monads who only secondarily participate in families, communities, and nations was repeatedly criticized by the Commission's Communist delegates, and it has since been highlighted by a wide variety of more contemporary critics.[1] Ultimately, this characteristic of the Declaration has furnished an important foundation for what has become known as the cultural relativist critique of human rights. Lee Kuan Yew, former prime minister of Singapore and a prominent deployer of the cultural relativist argument, is one among a host of critics who have singled out this axiom of the dignified individual as a "western" imposition, ultimately equating its enshrinement with a threat to communal values such as safety, stability, and shared morality.[2]

Yew is far from the only critic to have framed this veneration of the individual as an orientation that "has come at the expense of orderly society."[3] Perhaps worse for the legitimacy of a document such as the Declaration, it is, he claims, tantamount to the imposition of a "dogma" of western modernity upon more communalist cultures.[4] Indeed, none other than the American Anthropological Society voiced a warning to the Commission during the course of its negotiation of the Declaration that a document of this sort must "do more than just phrase respect for the individual as an individual," lest it risk creating "a statement of rights conceived only in terms of the values prevalent in the countries of West Europe and America."[5]

Given the Commission's attentiveness to the hazards of miring the Declaration within a particular ontology, particularly within the "dominant modern ontology" of the European Enlightenment, how legitimate are such concerns over the individualism of this document?[6] Is there a way of understanding the Enlightenment resonances of the Declaration's particular brand of individualism without presuming either a thoughtlessness or an outright disinguousness on the part of leading members of the Commission on Human Rights? One possible answer lies within today's burgeoning scholarship on the history and logic of secularity. Whether or not it engages overtly with the topic of universal human rights (it often does not), this body of scholarship provides a vantage point for formulating a tentative vision of the way in which the Commission's formulation of human dignity both does and does not remain subtly tied to a particular trajectory within early modern "Latin Christendom."[7] In his voluminous description of the secularization of Western Europe and the United States, Taylor traces an intricate constellation of developments within various Christian-dominated societies of Western Europe that eventually led to a widespread deterioration of the transcendent frames of reference that have undergirded so many (perhaps all) epochs and societies. Wherever in the history of Latin Christendom we locate it (Taylor and others trace the beginnings of this deterioration of such frames of reference to the very foundations of Christianity[8]), this shift produces at least two effects relevant to the question of the Declaration's Eurocentrism.

In the first place, the increasing emphasis upon "immanent" frames of reference gives rise to novel modes of juridico-political authority. As Marcel Gauchet puts it, this dethroning of "the beyond" resulted in a world in which

> we could no longer turn away from this inferior world toward
> eternal life, but had to devote ourselves to the fundamental hope

of attaining salvation through dedicating ourselves fully to terrestrial authority. The act of founding the world of equality was an
operation which, by reversing its ontological principle, destabilized
the hierarchical world's very basis, and was the decisive operation by
which, starting out from within religion, we left the religious logic of
dependency.[9]

Even without the analyses of thinkers such as Arendt, Foucault, and Agamben, it hardly requires a stretch of the imagination to perceive how this
increased dedication to terrestrial authority might sow the seeds of both the
Enlightenment conception of popular sovereignty and, simultaneously, the
organic state propagated by the Third Reich. The Declaration is unquestionably implicated within both of these political trajectories, and thus remains
intimately tied to the peculiar genealogy of European Christianity.

Moreover, this genealogy has contributed to more than just certain of the
political contexts in the background of the Declaration; it is largely responsible for the rise of a conception of the individual that looks very much like the
"pristine and separate" subject of Yew's cultural relativist critique. There is little question that a version of Yew's pristine and separate subject has featured
prominently within the deontological philosophical tradition of the modern
west. The "unencumbered self" posited within the philosophical systems of
figures such as Immanuel Kant and John Rawls—an idealized subject dis-
sociated from all situations that inhibit "rational reflection"—came into its
greatest prominence in the Enlightenment, though its origins reach back
at least to early modernity.[10] Brad S. Gregory, for example, has traced the
roots of this Enlightenment conception of the autonomous individual to the
immediate aftermath of the Protestant Reformation, a period in which widespread doctrinal disagreements among Christians facilitated the rise of one
of today's most easily recognizable secular notions: the notion that not only
Roman Catholicism but all revealed religion is fundamentally suspect as a
source of universal standards of meaning.[11] This period of religious conflict,
Gregory contends, furnished the background for a variety of philosophical
efforts to secure "a shared, supra-confessional basis for morality, social life,
politics, and human happiness, uncontentious because uncontroversially and
universally rational."[12] This quest for universalizable foundations has played
out for some of modernity's most influential philosophers as a radically individualistic endeavor—as an "austere project of detached, autonomous, rational reflection that defers to no received opinions or alleged authorities."[13]

To many critics, this radical individualism, which holds venerable communitarian institutions such as religion in profound suspicion, looks strikingly similar to the vision of the dignified individual enshrined at the heart of the Declaration.

Crucial to note here, however, is the fact that the modern philosophical project of autonomous rational reflection has functioned quite differently within the realm of *political* philosophy, and certainly differently within the realm of political *practice*. As Moyn reminds us,

> The universalism of the Enlightenment and revolutionary eras
> clearly does bear some affinity to contemporary forms of cosmo-
> politanism. Yet what is put forward as "the immortal rights of
> man" [in the eighteenth and nineteenth centuries] was nevertheless
> part of a political project strikingly distinct from contemporary
> human rights. . . . Unlike later human rights, [the rights of the
> eighteenth and nineteenth centuries] were deeply bound up with the
> construction, through revolution if necessary, of state and nation. It
> is now the order of the day to transcend that state forum for rights,
> but until recently the state was their essential crucible.[14]

Moyn's point here is essential: "the rights of the revolutionary era were very much embodied in the politics of the state, crystallizing in a scheme worlds away from the political meaning human rights would have later."[15] This state-centric scheme is the very one critiqued by Arendt in her description of the logic of the French Declaration of the Rights of Man and of the Citizen, and it is, ironically, a scheme from which today's human rights regime has not extricated itself. After all, as Asad reminds us, within today's human rights regime, "the universal character of the rights-bearing person is made the responsibility of sovereign states."[16] Notwithstanding its failure to extricate itself from such statist dynamics, the Commission on Human Rights' negotiations and articulations of the fundaments of human rights reveal that, in endeavoring to enshrine an index of "essential, irreducible moral worth and dignity," the Declaration's framers pointedly pitted themselves *against* this Enlightenment scheme of default state sovereignty just as surely as they pitted themselves against the trickle down of Christianity in the form of a foundational reference to nature.[17]

Thus, while the history of the framing of the Declaration leaves little question that this document is permeated with a particular socioreligious historical trajectory, these historical permeations are not by any means indicative of a straightforward emulation of the austere project of Enlightenment rationalism, and they are certainly not indicative of, in Ignatieff's words, "a triumphant expression of European imperial self-confidence."[18] As the previous chapter showed, the enshrinement of inherent human dignity within the Declaration involved an array of considerations on the part of the Commission, at the center of which stood the mandate to generate a universalizable document.

Ultimately, the most prevalent Enlightenment logic surfaces within this document not in the guise of the Commission's particular formulation of human dignity but in the guise of Commission members' conviction that a specific type of secularism would furnish the key to overcoming conflicting doctrines and ideas. As the previous chapter revealed, the secularism of the Declaration is manifest not merely in the Commission's effort to sacralize an immanent emblem of the irreducible worth of the human, but also in its endeavor to emplace a receptacle within the Declaration that could readily be filled with the parochial values held by differing peoples across the globe. While far from a mere reiteration of the state-oriented universalism of the Enlightenment, this brand of idealism concerning the capacity of a secular political device to mediate human pluralism—to serve as a lever to "pus[h] forward the transition toward a properly global system"—is, admittedly, deeply implicated within an Enlightenment quest to secure consensus through the renunciation of "any mention of divinity or of the divine origin of man."[19]

By many accounts, the Commission's effort to secure consensus through the sacralization of human dignity has ultimately been a success. Today, as Paolo G. Carozza points out, "the idea of human dignity serves as the single most widely recognized and invoked basis for grounding the ideas of human rights generally."[20] However, an appreciation of its hegemony as a mechanism for grounding the ideas of human rights should in no way obscure the fact that human dignity was never intended to be univocal. Rather, it was designed to provide the fulcrum for what Glendon describes as "a common standard that can be brought to life in different cultures in a legitimate variety of ways."[21] The enshrinement of inherent human dignity, in other words, represents one of the Commission's most elementary steps in building what Roosevelt described as "a bridge upon which [all people] can meet and talk."[22]

This endeavor toward bridge building is secular in the sense described above, but it is also thoroughly "religious" in the sociofunctionalist understanding of the term. After all, the role of the sacred within a mythopoeic narrative is never self-contained; rather, as Durkheim and his predecessors have famously postulated, items unequivocally set apart through the work of myth (and ritual) always unfold within broader contexts of deeply committed community building. Myth makers, in other words, always undertake their work with the aspiration to give birth to deeply held identities and cohesive, moral communities. As this chapter demonstrates, the Declaration's logic gives every indication that the Commission on Human Rights perceived the setting apart of human dignity very much in this spirit: that they perceived such dignity not merely as a locus of sacredness but as the generator of a particular social identity—as "a shorthand way of summing up how a complex, multi-faceted set of relationships involving Man is, or should be, governed."[23] The particular social identity toward which the Commission aspired is articulated within the Declaration's Preamble as "the human family."

The Human Family as Moral Community

In *The Elementary Forms of Religious Life*, Durkheim offers his well-known definition of religion as a system of beliefs and/or rites centered upon the classification and cultivation of sacred items: "A religion is a unified system of beliefs relative to sacred things, that is to say, things set apart and forbidden—beliefs and practices which unite into one single moral community called a Church, all those who adhere to them."[24] Myth, within this understanding of religion, is a narrative "that express[es] the nature of sacred things, the virtues and powers attributed to them, their history, and their relationship with another as well as with profane things."[25] Two important presumptions inform this definition: first, as we have seen, the sacred is not a sui generis phenomenon existing beyond the ken of human creators, and, second, the sacred does not exist independently of the beliefs and interests of a particular community. Religious beliefs, he asserts, "are always shared by a definite group that professes them."[26] Ultimately, the very function of religion, and the attendant work of sacralization, are to generate not just an individual orientation but a society—"A society whose members are united because they imagine the sacred world and its relations with the profane in the same way."[27]

In his emphasis on this social logic, Durkheim articulates a central mandate of the sociofunctionalist conceptualization of religion: theorists in this vein "sense that the true function of religion is not to make us think, enrich our knowledge, or add representations of a different sort to those we owe to science. Its true function is to make us act and to help us live."[28] A well chosen, well narrated sacred item provides the centerpiece for "a system of ideas by means of which individuals imagine the society of which they are members and the obscure yet intimate relations they have with it."[29] It inspires an individual not merely to acquiesce to the code of conduct of a particular community but to internalize that code of conduct, to take it on as an integral component of his or her identity. It functions, to use the words of Henri Bergson in a related context, to "induce a disposition of the soul."[30] Such dispositions push the individual toward more than a just a certain understanding of the world, though they certainly do this. In Durkheim's understanding of religion, the dispositions arising from the veneration of a given sacred item ultimately serve to elevate the individual above the intellectual and ethical limitations of animal life; they turn us toward something larger than ourselves and our individual interests—"toward ends that we share in common with other men"—and they thus furnish a path into a moral life that is impossible without the comity of others.[31]

Durkheim's definition and attendant caveats provide a valuable point of entry into the unique social logic of the Declaration. While it is not at all difficult to imagine how the Commission's endeavor at sacralization could be perceived as an effort to enshrine human dignity as an end in itself with no overt attention to the communal implications of this sacred item, this was far from the intention of the Commission on Human Rights. Admittedly, the Declaration itself is notoriously short on specific prescriptions for the social life of its audience—an understandable characteristic given the Commission's universalist aspirations. However, the fact of the relative paucity of social language within the Declaration should not eclipse the social language that is present in this document, particularly given that, as with the references to barbarous acts and inherent dignity, the Declaration's social references reside in large part within the important scene-setting Preamble of this document. Ultimately, neither the minimalism of communalist language nor the Commission's eagerness to frame the Declaration in universalist terms should occlude the fact that Commission members intended the sacralization of human dignity to inform and even to transform our social life—that they intended it to furnish the foundation for a unified, engaged "moral community" of the sort that Durkheim locates at the heart of all religious life.[32]

By "moral community," Durkheim means something quite specific, and this vision resonates strongly with the Commission's own aspirations for the community to be generated through the sacralization of human dignity.

Durkheim's moral community is pointedly not simply a group united by pragmatic concerns or, as he puts it, "utilitarian maxims."[33] Much less is it indicative
of a group brought together through mechanisms of overt coercion—corporal
punishment, for example, or legal sanction.[34] While Durkheim acknowledges
that all institutions aimed at human cooperation subject individuals to various "restraints, privations, and sacrifices," he identifies the moral community
as an entity that ultimately sustains itself through more than simple cajoling
or coercing; rather, this type of community inspires "genuine respect" in most
or, ideally, all of its members.[35] As he puts it, "An individual or collective subject is said to inspire respect when the representation that expresses it has
such power that it calls forth or inhibits conduct automatically, irrespective
of utilitarian calculation of helpful or harmful results."[36]

> When we obey someone out of respect for the moral authority that
> we have accorded to him, we do not follow his instructions because
> they seem wise but because a certain psychic energy intrinsic to
> the idea we have of that person bends our will and turns it in the
> direction indicated. . . . We are then moved not by the advantages
> or disadvantages of the conduct that is recommended to us or
> demanded of us but by the way we conceive of the one who recom-
> mends or demands that conduct.[37]

Ultimately, the greater part of Durkheim's scholarship on religion revolves
around the endeavor to capture the process whereby a particular person,
object, or idea comes to inspire desirable beliefs and behaviors "not by the
reality or threat of physical coercion but by the radiation of the mental energy
it contains."[38] This brand of genuine respect, he claims, is a hallmark of religion, and it is most effectively cultivated through the affective powers of,
among other things,[39] myth.

That the Commission on Human Rights aspired to the creation of a
moral community of the sort described by Durkheim is indubitable, though
perhaps not immediately obvious. Indeed, the manner in which the human
rights have been readily perceived by many critics as radically individualistic
attests to the ways in which the Declaration's communal logic is not immediately obvious. Notwithstanding the Commission's hesitation to be perceived
as imposing rather than simply reiterating human values, and notwithstanding most Commission members' clear suspicion of collectivities—their vocal
indictment of any scale of values that would prioritize the interest of groups

over the fundamental wellbeing of individuals—the Declaration itself point-edly erects inherent human dignity as the font and the guarantor of a par-ticular social orientation. This attentiveness to social orientation is hardly surprising given the basic understanding among Commission members that every individual is, as Glendon synopsizes, "constituted, in important ways, by and through relationships with others."[40] The Declaration takes account of this reality by embracing the fact of every human's situatedness "in a variety of specifically named, real life relationships of mutual dependency: families, communities, religious groups, workplaces, associations, societies, cultures, nations."[41] A number of features within the Declaration serve to articulate and anchor this basic reality of our social embeddedness: Article 1 calls upon us to "act toward one another in a spirit of brotherhood," Article 16 recog-nizes the family as "the natural and fundamental group unit of society," and Article 29 proclaims that it is within the community alone "that the free and full development of [one's] personality is possible." Far from promoting an unlicensed individualism, the Declaration is marked by the Commission's endeavor, as Indian delegate Hansa Mehta put it, to "pave the way to a new era of international solidarity" centered neither upon the state nor upon the isolated individual, but upon "the social human being, participating in social life, and striving for national and international co-operation."[42]

Not surprisingly, this attentiveness to the importance of the social embeddedness of every individual ultimately represented one of few points of enduring consensus between Communist delegates and most of the rest of the Commission. From the beginning of its negotiations, Koretsky and his colleagues had admonished fellow Drafting Committee members that a declaration "should not seek to separate man from his community; it should rather create a man who is free in the framework of a free society."[43] Even in the face of their disputes about the manner in which human dignity might be conceived to fit into this social vision, the Commission was in general agree-ment with this admonition; indeed, it permeated even the earliest iterations of the Declaration in the form of proclamations to the effect that humans are "essentially social" and thus "cannot live and develop themselves without the help and support of society."[44] This appreciation of our various modes of local situatedness, however, was emphatically qualified by the Commis-sion's insistence that both individual and civic agendas must "fit into [the] broader framework of respect for human rights, international goodwill, and the combating of intolerance and hatred."[45] To perceive the Declaration as offering an endorsement of "social life" per se would therefore be a grave misunderstanding; rather, the Commission envisioned the Declaration as a vehicle for the cultivation of a particular communal disposition, a disposition toward human dignity as an ultimate value. Quoting the German Constitutional Court, Glendon highlights the manner the rights enumerated in the Declaration are intended to function to "relat[e] and bin[d] the individual to society, but without detracting from the intrinsic value of the person."[46]

The Declaration's framers clearly appreciated that the enshrinement of human dignity could only unfold from within the bounds of preexisting communities such as families, religious organizations, and civil institutions. The general disposition of the Commission, however, was that all more localized relationships of mutual dependency, however central to the lives of individuals, should command our loyalty only insofar as they lend themselves toward respect for the sanctity of human dignity. As Malik puts it,

> It is true that I am told [in Article 29] I have duties to the community, but these duties are not simpliciter, they are not absolute: I have duties to the community in which *alone the free and full development of my personality is possible*. My duties are not to any community; they are only to the community in which my personality can be developed. Then also, it is not any development of my personality that is envisaged; even the full development of my personality is not enough: this full development must also be free. "Everyone has duties to the community in which alone the free and full development of his personality is possible." Thus in the one instance in which duties are mentioned the supremacy of man over all society and all social claims is perfectly recognized. Society, including its supreme organized form, the state, is for the sake of man—the full, free, personal man; and not conversely.[47]

It is from within this interplay of social life and ultimate value that the Commission formulated its vision of the unique moral community generated through universal human rights. The Declaration's invocation of the human family within the first recital of the Preamble embodies this endeavor to narrate into existence a community united in its genuine respect for the inviolable dignity of every individual. This vision of community pushes beyond a simple endorsement of preexisting forms of social life, aspiring instead to inform and, when necessary, *trans*form, our preexisting real life relationships of mutual dependency.

Precisely what vision of human social life does "the human family" con-
note? The Declaration, asserts Morsink, "looks at our world as one unified
ethical community."[48] Its text makes scant reference to what was then and
what continues to be the primary locus of international relations, the nation-
state, and instead aspires toward a "moral cosmopolitanism" among all individuals and local communities.[49]

> As a worldwide educational tool the Declaration has definite
> cosmopolitan aspirations, for the litany of the words "everyone"
> and "all" and the references to the "spirit of brotherhood" and "the
> human family" are clearly aimed beyond domestic contexts. They are
> imbued with the spirit of cosmopolitanism that we also find in [the
> Preamble's final paragraph], where the drafters express the hope that
> "every individual and every organ of society, keeping the Decla-
> ration constantly in mind, shall strive by teaching and education to
> promote respect for these rights and freedoms and by progressive
> measures, national and international, to secure their universal
> respect and effective recognition and observance, both among the
> peoples of the Member States and among peoples of territories
> under their jurisdiction." The individual human beings—who are the
> primary addressees and the subjects about whom the Declaration is
> being made—are not isolated, mutually disinterested, and possessive
> human beings. They are members of the family of humankind.[50]

The human family, coupled with the complementary mandate that we act
toward one another in a spirit of brotherhood, expresses this social logic
of inherent human dignity; it functions as a communal embodiment of the
sacred center of the Declaration. It articulates the Kantian imperative that
humans be treated as ends rather than as mere means, but it pointedly for-
goes Kant's elaborate rationalist argumentation. It also resists the more pragmatic manifestations of Kantian rationalism that have informed the work of
political theorists such as Rawls and Ignatieff—manifestations that typically
formulate human rights and the dignity at their core as basically prudential
measures designed to avert human injury and oppression. After all, while the
communitarian thrust of mythmaking might certainly be understood to be
utilitarian in a broad sociological sense, such narratives achieve their mythopoeic status largely by virtue of the way in which they aim to efface their own
sociopolitical utility even as they fulfill it.

Inherent human dignity, for example, hardly makes a convincing argument for its inherence by proclaiming the usefulness of treating human dignity as though it were inherent. Mythmakers by definition aspire to something more ambitious than a mere community of adherents united in their commitment to a pragmatic if ultimately unfounded ethical principle. In forgoing both rationalism and utilitarianism, the Commission's invocation of human family seeks instead to imbue the Declaration's social prescription with what Alexandre Lefebvre calls an "affective charge"—with a persuasive thrust that convinces and compels us independently of deliberate argumentation.[51] Though Lefebvre ultimately takes emphatic issue with Durkheim's applicability to universal human rights (a concern addressed below), he speaks to the Durkheimian logic of "respect" in his claim that argumentation of the Kantian or Rawlsian ilk is ultimately insufficient because such argumentation "*already* draws on the pressure of moral obligation."[52] Practical reason reinforces "moral pressure," Lefebvre reminds us, but it does not give birth to it.[53]

Of course, a moral community does not come into existence simply by virtue of being invoked, as the Commission was well aware. The creation and early advertisement of the Declaration is marked by an attentiveness to the manner in which the entrenchment of human rights would be dependent upon what Roosevelt called an "inward" human progress—would be dependent, in other words, upon the creation of a world in which people are strongly inclined to act towards one another in a spirit of brotherhood. Far from working in opposition to our more localized relationships of mutual dependency, Commission members imagined that this inward human progress would unfold from within the preexisting "intermediate" communities that always stand between the individual and the (ever untrustworthy) state.[54] The Commission, and Roosevelt in particular, couched the task of fostering inward human progress in the language of education; the Declaration, she asserted, "is an educational declaration, and the only way we can guarantee that these rights will be observed is by doing a good job educationally."[55] This understanding of the "educational" logic of human rights was echoed throughout the Commission's negotiations by many other members—in particular by Chinese delegate Peng Chun Chang, who played a crucial role in giving voice to the Commission's vision of the Declaration as not merely a mechanism for preserving international peace but for enabling "the full development of man."[56] Whatever mechanisms of enforcement the human rights community might eventually have at its disposal, framers such as Roosevelt and Chang were adamant that human rights would "carry no weight unless the people know them, unless the people understand them, unless the people demand that they be lived."[57]

With such admonitions, Roosevelt located the primary ethical thrust of human rights within the realm of what she called "public opinion," a realm that, she constantly reminded her audiences, predates the work of codification and enforcement.[58] Her words disclose the manner in which the educational thrust of the Declaration is clearly not of a straightforwardly rationalist or utilitarian bent. While the Preamble does enumerate a series of practical calamities that might be avoided through the protection of human rights (e.g., barbarous acts, rebellion against tyranny and oppression), the Declaration's posit of the human family is intended to do more than simply convey basic information, and it is certainly designed to do more than inaugurate a coercive legal-political regime; rather, to paraphrase Stephen K. White, the human family is a key element of the Commission's endeavor to provide a "broad cognitive and affective orientation"—to "disclose the world to us in such a way that we think *and* feel it differently than we might otherwise."[59]

Neither Roosevelt nor White makes reference to the framework of myth to describe this affective work, but Durkheim certainly does: he ties the cultivation of this brand of "public opinion" directly to the religious work of sacralization—of imbuing particular items with an authoritativeness capable of generating and sustaining "the ardor of shared conviction" within a given community.[60] Indeed, in his original French, Durkheim's terms are more or less identical to Roosevelt's: in the *Les formes élémentaires de la vie religieuse*, he attributes such communal ardor to the cultivation of, alternately, "l'opinion" and "l'opinion publique."[61] Both of these terms, Karen E. Fields points out, refer to widespread social sentiment and not merely to today's connotation of "discrete bits of 'opinion' that pollsters elicit through replies to questionnaires."[62]

The ardor that gives rise to moral cosmopolitanism is not something we argue our way into; rather, theorists such as Durkheim and Lefebvre (as well as Henri Bergson, in the background of Lefebvre) locate the genesis of such ethical orientations within the realm of what Richard Pritchard calls "unreflective consciousness."[63] Very much in keeping with Roosevelt and Durkheim's depiction of public opinion, Pritchard's notion of unreflective consciousness rests upon a conviction that human reason, while certainly an important contributor to our moral decisions, does not "enter on the ground floor where the fundamentals dwell."[64] Rather, as Chang put, it "The purpose of all social and political education [is] the *voluntary* recognition of the rights of others."[65] Indeed, Chang belabored this point concerning the voluntary nature of human rights cosmopolitanism: in the course of suggesting a revision during the Commission's Third Session to what was then Article 2 of the Declaration, Chang proposed that the article read "The exercise of these rights requires recognition of the rights of others and the welfare of all."[66] In the course of making his argument, he emphasized "the value of the voluntary element" in the word *recognition*:

> Emphasis should be placed not on restraining people, but on educating them. The purpose of all social and political education was the voluntary recognition of the rights of others. The Commission's ideal should not be the imposition of restrictions but rather the voluntary recognition by all of the rights of others. That [is] the ideal which the Declaration should express.[67]

The Commission wrestled openly with the task of imbuing the Declaration with an "unreflective" moral weight capable of enrolling people around the world into a voluntary comity of the sort described by Chang. The human family provides the fulcrum of the Commission's endeavor to infuse this vision of a global moral community with, as Durkheim puts it, "the warmth necessary to stir the heart and stimulate the mind."[68] The human family furnishes a resonant conceptual bridge between, on the one hand, our most intimate mode of social life and, on the other, the cosmopolitan social orientation appropriate to a world in which human dignity is held sacred.

René Cassin, the earliest proponent of the emplacement of the human family within the Declaration, asserted in the course of the Commission's negotiations that he had chosen this term in an effort "to convey the idea that the most humble of the most different races have among them the particular spark that distinguishes them from animals, and at the same time obligates them to more grandeur and to more duties than any other beings on earth."[69] Cassin acknowledged that this idea drew upon two important "juridical" concepts that, while crucial, were likely to prove uninspiring to most people: namely, "the concept of man as a reasonable being and the concept of reciprocal duties among men."[70] Rather than express these key concepts in the more rarefied language of law or philosophy, Cassin suggested that the Commission reach for a more accessible turn of phrase equating to the notion that "men are brothers."[71] Cassin's advocacy along these lines captures the role that he, and eventually the majority of the Commission, ascribed to the human family as a mediator of the local and the global—as an evocative and accessible embodiment of the social orientation demanded by universal human rights.

When Roosevelt described the Declaration as "frankly educational" in a 1948 speech, her assertion was easily misapprehended as a retreat from the Declaration's full potential as a regulatory mechanism.[72] While there is no question that Roosevelt's statement was made in the context of acknowledging the nonbinding nature of the Declaration, her commitment to the particular educational logic of human rights was not simply a concession to the reality of the international politics of her time; rather, Roosevelt was aligned with other Commission members in her conviction that, to be successful, human rights must permeate and inform the very fabric of social life in the postwar world. "Court decisions, and laws and government administration," she said, "are only the results of the way people progress inwardly."[73] Chang agreed: "Laws alone are not sufficient to bring about results by themselves"; the goal of the Declaration must be "to build up better human beings, and not merely to punish those who violate human rights."[74]

Ultimately, the Declaration's brand of education is far from a mere pragmatic compromise, and it is only partly a matter of conveying particular information about human rights. As the assertions of Chang and Roosevelt reveal, the primary educational mandate of the Declaration is the widespread internalization, at the local level of individuals and their real life relationships, of the notion that every individual is the rightful beneficiary of the entitlements and the protections of national and international law. It is, in Durkheimian terms, the cultivation of a sentiment capable of transforming all individuals, groups, and nations into a moral community—a community that such individuals, groups, and nations feel inspired to join out of genuine respect rather than out of utilitarian calculation. Though the Commission's commitment to the mechanisms of international law certainly cannot be gainsaid (indeed, such is the focus of the next chapter), the social language of the Declaration and its framers belies a straightforward legalism; rather, it reveals Commission members' deep-seated conviction that, as Cassin put it, the cultivation of human rights "depends primarily and above all on the mentalities of individuals and social groups."[75]

Thus, while the Declaration does contain a specific mandate for the provision of education in Article 26, its broader educational vision unquestionably points beyond the simple cultivation of knowledge and creation of pedagogical infrastructures; ultimately, it entails the cultivation of what Durkheim describes as a "state of consciousness."[76] Durkheim credits religious repre-sentations with the power to turn people away from their typical preoccupa-tions with their own wellbeing and to turn them toward higher, "collective" modes of existence—"impersonal" modes oriented toward "something that goes beyond us," something that we share in common with other people.[77] This shift to a more collective state of consciousness is rarely, if ever, accom-plished by way of a straightforward infusion of information; rather, it entails a dramatic transformation of "the nature of one's attachment to self and to others."[78] It entails, in other words, a conversion.

Lefebvre, hearkening to the work of Pierre Hadot, has highlighted the manner in which human rights aspire to convert human beings on multiple levels.[79] At the level of the nation, human rights—whether they are conceived as a means of inspiring constitution building or as a means of reforming problematic laws—"undertake a more or less complete transformation of the state. Following the etymology of *conversio*, human rights attempt to turn or redirect the state and send it in a different direction."[80] Given Commis-sion members' conviction that such transformations at the state level are ulti-mately driven by the opinions and the activism of citizens, it should come as no surprise that the human rights call to conversion is even more pressing at this local level.[81] As Lefebvre puts it,

> human rights are made *for me*. And by this I mean not only that
> the declarations identify me as a bearer of human rights but that
> they also singularize me as their primary guarantee. Or in other
> words, the message of [human rights declarations] is not only that
> they protect me, but just as importantly, they must also work on
> me. In this respect, [such documents] meet a basic requirement of
> discourses of conversion: they address the individual and seek his or
> her transformation.[82]

Though it is feasible, as we will see, to question the extent to which the Declaration's framers were ultimately willing to push this logic of conversion, there is no question that they operated within its purview. We witness the logic of conversion in the Commission's enduring conviction that compliance with the Declaration's articles would ultimately depend upon the extent to which the Declaration could broaden our moral lives beyond the confines of our realms of individual concern—the extent to which it could generate, in Cassin's words, "the solidarity of men."[83]

Thus, even as Article 26 proclaims the necessity of access to education, it does so only to the extent that such education functions in the spirit of pushing humankind toward a cosmopolitan solidarity of the sort described by Morsink. As a UNESCO representative put it during the course of the Commission's negotiations, under the Hitler regime "education had been admirably organized but had, nevertheless, produced disastrous results. It [is] absolutely necessary to make clear that education to which everyone [is] entitled should strengthen the respect of the rights set forth in the Declaration and combat the spirit of intolerance."[84] It is in light of this concern that Article 26 proclaims not merely the right to an education, but to an education "directed to the full development of the human personality and to the strengthening of respect for human rights and fundamental freedoms"—an education designed to "promote understanding, tolerance and friendship among all nations, racial or religious groups, and [to] further the activities of the United Nations for the maintenance of peace."

The human family expresses the Declaration's moral cosmopolitanism in a way that is designed to be universally resonant, even pithy. Yet, the human family also embodies a principle that is disconcerting on a number of levels: namely, the principle that we are all "duty-bearers."[85] This principle stems directly from the Declaration's enshrinement of the human individual as an item of ultimate concern. As Morsink puts it, "My having a human right entails that others (be they persons or institutions) have duties to make sure that I have whatever the right in question spells out that I ought to have."[86] This principle is disconcerting in the first place because it entails an inescapable logic of, as Arendt puts it, "common responsibility."[87] "The idea of humanity," she proclaims in *The Origins of Totalitarianism*, "has the very real consequence that in one form or another men must assume responsibility for all crimes committed by all men, and that eventually all nations will be forced to answer for the evil committed by all others."[88]

We need not look deep into the history of the early twenty-first century to find examples of the profound discomfort that such a principle inspires in political leaders—to say nothing of lawyers, judges, and multinational corporations.[89] Indeed, Arendt depicts this discomfort as a problem endemic to the project of human rights—as a clear demonstration of the very fundamental way in which human rights threaten the sovereignty of states, communities, and, in certain circumstances, those individuals whose desires or interests run counter to the dignity of others. The notion of the human family embodies this uncomfortable imperative of common responsibility, yet it also quite literally "domesticates" its radical logic, embedding it within an image that, for most of us, bespeaks our most proximate and familiar mode of social life. In invoking the human family, the Declaration endeavors to transport individuals across the ethical and cognitive chasm that frequently yawns between their most parochial interests and the interests of the whole of humankind.

The principle of common responsibility is disconcerting in another way as well: as numerous theorists have attested, the Declaration was created amid dramatic uncertainty about precisely *how* people and institutions are to fulfill its mandates—an uncertainty that endures to a large extent to this day, notwithstanding the elaborations of the two international covenants adopted in 1966.[90] Are we duty-bearers as individuals, as citizens, or as members of particular organizations? Am I a duty-bearer if I lack the means to help others? If I lack the will to help others? If I am not even aware of my role as a duty-bearer? "Since we have a human right by virtue of our humanity," asserts Morsink, "the fact that we have it is immediately clear. But in certain circumstances it may take a day, a year, or a decade for the rest of the world to decide who the duty-bearers in a particular case are and in what order they should step up to the plate."[91]

This uncertainty brings into high relief yet another aspect of the disjuncture between human rights' moral weight and their means of implementation. The Commission, as we have seen, opted early on to invest its energy in the construction of a document with a particular moral weight, and the notion of the human family furnishes an important means of envisioning the universal condition of dutifulness toward others independently of—or, more accurately, prior to—the fraught realm of implementation. This maneuver is crucial to the inherence of human dignity, for, as Morsink reminds us, the very idea of inherence undercuts the edifices of states and other regulatory bodies: "This entire system [of human rights law] is a man-made one; it therefore has difficulty embracing the inherent character of human rights that, according to the Declaration, accrue to us automatically at birth without the intervention of anything made or done by humans other than the acts of (natural or artificial) conception that brings us into the world."[92] Despite the indisputable fact that the human family is not a regulatory body in any conventional sense of the term—it contains none of the concreteness of the national governments to which later human rights conventions have specifically addressed themselves, nor any of the concreteness of the non-governmental entities to which human rights theorists have increasingly devoted their attentions—it plays a crucial role within the Declaration as a model of the only social formation truly consistent with the sacredness of all individuals. In this way, the notion of the human family enrolls us in a unified, affective ethical community even in the face of the tremendous practical uncertainties of the modern international legal landscape. To paraphrase an idea raised by Hent de Vries, the human family functions within the Declaration to generate a "*corpus mysticum*, as it were, in a new, post-secular guise."[93]

The Organic State and the Destruction of Common Life

The expansive yet intimate ethos of the human family could hardly be more different from the ethos against which the Commission so pointedly pitted itself. This difference is evident, in the first place, in the logic of sacralization and contamination outlined in the previous chapter: the Nazi notion of the *Volksgemeinschaft* sacralized a particular community at the emphatic expense of individuals perceived to fall outside of it. Ultimately, the sacralization of the *Volksgemeinschaft* endeavors to give rise to a community that is "closed" on multiple levels: on the political level, it includes some individuals while specifically excluding others; on the legal level, it suspends protections to certain individuals in light of "exceptional circumstances"; on the affective level, it maintains its social cohesiveness by systematically pitting itself "against all other men."[94] In the course of its negotiation of the Declaration, the Commission posited the human family in the first place as a straightforward refutation of these various modes of closure effected by the ideal of the organic state—as an embodiment of, in Cassin's words, "the unity of the human race regardless of frontiers, as opposed to theories like those of Hitler."[95]

Yet, the Nazi logic of sacralization is antithetical to the ethos of the Declaration in a subtler way as well, a way that only becomes apparent when we bear in mind the educational thrust of this document described above. We have seen that the Declaration's educational vision entails not merely a goal of transmitting information but of cultivating inward human progress—of enlisting individuals into committed, cosmopolitan moral communities. Though inherent human dignity unquestionably serves within the Declaration to embody a conception of the human prior to and independent of the machinations of particular communities, it was also intended by the Commission to serve as a focal point for the generation of social life. The *Volksgemeinschaft*, on the other hand, worked in dramatic opposition to such communalist logic, ultimately functioning to shut down the very human propensity for social life of the sort envisioned by the Commission.

Arendt again proves particularly relevant here, for she has famously portrayed totalitarianism not merely in terms of its unique political and legal characteristics but as a "moral" phenomenon in something like a Durkhemian sense of the term—that is, as a crisis of communal life and, ultimately, of "shared reality."[96] Totalitarianism as Arendt understands it is implicated in nothing less than the annihilation of "our ability to act in concert with others."[97] Given her conviction that life lived in concert with others is the fount of such human fundamentals as ethics, dignity, and meaning itself, it is thus hardly surprising that she invests the totalitarian movements of the twentieth century with a moral and existential gravity far beyond their already considerable political gravity.

Arendt's phenomenology of human social life is complex, and it grew in complexity as her scholarship unfolded. While she initially explored the moral ramifications of totalitarianism broadly in terms of the ability to act in concert with others, she came to insist in her later work upon a painstaking distinction, both historical and normative, between "political" and merely "social" modes of acting in concert with others. While she remained committed to the inextricable link between human flourishing and communal life—to the notion that "No human life, not even the life of the hermit in nature's wilderness, is possible without a world which directly or indirectly testifies to the presence of other human beings"—the realm of political life is given particular emphasis in her later works as the venue of uniquely human activity.[98] In contrast to the world of politics, the realm of mere social life as Arendt came to conceive of it is linked historically to the "private" realm of the household.[99] Because the private realm of the household remains permeated by the exigencies of biological necessity, it remains stubbornly tied to the logic of "animal life" and thus perpetually at a remove from the transcendent realm of politics as understood by ancients such as Aristotle.[100]

As Arendt traced the historical and theological shifts that had eroded the realm of the political as it was understood by the likes of Plato and Aristotle, she came to attribute some of modernity's most deep-seated ills to the ascendency of something like the very social realm that Durkheim locates at the heart of human meaning making.[101] Much like Durkheim's own understanding of social life, the social realm as Arendt came to understand it is ultimately "a normalizing realm" that aspires to channel the pluralism and unpredictability of human individuals into a semblance of homogeneity.[102]

Decidedly unlike Durkheim, however, Arendt understands this conformist dynamic of mere social existence to be a detriment to authentic human life—a dynamic that tends toward the exclusion of the very "spontaneous action [and] outstanding achievement" that elevates us above all other living organisms.[103] On one level, this makes Arendt an unlikely interlocutor in an exploration of the Declaration's particular social prescription. Yet, Arendt's analysis of the moral implications of totalitarianism—of the unique ways in which this system of governance served undermine the ability to act in concert with others—operates somewhat independently of her later analyses of the particular brand of human authenticity that stems from political life. Upon bracketing the distinction that Arendt eventually draws between the social and political realms of human life, we are left in her early explorations of totalitarianism with a valuable framework for making sense of the way in which the Nazi sacralization of the *Volksgemeinschaft* served to undermine— indeed, in many cases to extinguish—the most basic human capacity to act in concert with others. Moreover, while it is obvious enough how the sacralization of the *Volksgemeinschaft* would contribute to the extinction—or, at the very least, the dramatic deterioration—of this ability for those individuals singled out as threats and contaminants, Arendt's more striking observations concern the manner in which the logic of the *Volksgemeinschaft* leads to the erosion of the communal life of *all* inhabitants of the state, even those supposedly united under the auspices of the *Volksgemeinschaft* itself.

In *The Origins of Totalitarianism*, Arendt ties the erosion of the human capacity to act in concert with others to certain of the key logics by which Nazi ideologues secured the sacredness of the *Volksgemeinschaft*. While Nazi totalitarianism does not bear the sole burden for this development—indeed, throughout her career Arendt attributed the rise of totalitarianism and the decline of the authentic human comity of political life to an assortment of modern developments—the totalitarianism of the Reich marks an apex in this modern trajectory.[104] The racial and evolutionary scientism that served to naturalize the organic state and to legitimize the political measures taken to protect it from contamination bore the seeds of destruction for the collective life of the very community it claimed to bring together.

This self-destructive quality of the *Volksgemeinschaft* stems, according to Arendt, from the manner in which totalitarian ideologies tend to transform all laws into "laws of movement."[105] The idea of Nature, deployed in earlier times as a "stabilizing source of authority for the actions of mortal men," had become transformed within Nazi discourse into a process of ongoing struggle "which does not necessarily stop with the present species of human being."[106] This logic of perpetual movement had the effect of miring the politics of the *Volksgemeinschaft* in a nihilism that proved radically antithetical to the cultivation of social cohesiveness and stability. After all, observes Arendt,

> If it is the law of nature to eliminate everything that is harmful and unfit to live, it would mean the end of nature itself if new categories of the harmful and unfit-to-live could not be found. . . . In other words, the law of killing by which totalitarian movements seize and exercise power would remain a law of the movement even if they ever succeeded in making all of humanity subject to their rule.[107]

It is one of Arendt's enduring contributions to the phenomenology of totalitarianism to have elucidated the manner in which a stringent commitment to the preservation of the *Volksgemeinschaft* could go hand in hand with such a powerful communal nihilism—a nihilism that ultimately drove the very members of this community to "a kind of warfare which did not pay the slightest regard to the minimum requirements for the survival of the German nation."[108] In lieu of a stable, coherent moral prescription, the *Volksgemeinschaft* ultimately offered up nothing more than "stringent logicality as a guide to action"—a logicality that, while perhaps wholly in keeping with the impersonal unfolding of the evolutionary process of natural selection, worked in radical opposition to the cultivation and internalization of basic communal values.[109]

> The inhabitants of a totalitarian country are thrown into and caught in the process of nature or history for the sake of accelerating its movement; as such, they can only be executioners or victims of its inherent law. The process may decide that those who today eliminate races and individuals . . . are tomorrow those who must be sacrificed. What totalitarian rule needs to guide the behavior of its subjects is a preparation to fit each of them equally well for the role of executioner and the role of victim.[110]

In dramatic contrast to the educational project articulated by Roosevelt and other Commission members, the totalitarian brand of education serves not to instill moral convictions but, as Arendt puts it, "to destroy the capacity to form any."[111]

Such a system erodes the capacity for both political and personal corre-spondences—"correspondences" in the dual sense of both communication and connection building—and makes it nearly impossible for individuals to cultivate stable and meaningful communities. This erosion of communal life presents a formidable obstacle to political action and power, but this disem-powerment spans well beyond the "political sphere" that Arendt designates as the preeminent realm of collective human action.[112] Ultimately, claims Arendt, Nazi totalitarianism is unprecedented for the way in which it perme-ates the cognitive and psychological life of individuals as well as their capacity for political life—for the way in which it "destroys man's capacity for thought and deliberation just as certainly as his capacity for action."[113] The experi-ence of "loneliness"—which Arendt distinguishes from mere "isolation," and which she locates at the center of her phenomenology of totalitarianism—leads to the erosion not merely of human action but to the erosion of shared reality itself.[114] After all, "Even the experience of the materiality and sensu-ally given world depends upon my being in contact with other men, upon our *common* sense which regulates and controls all other senses and without which each of us would be enclosed in his own particularity of sense data which in themselves are unreliable and treacherous."[115]

The attenuation of this realm of basic human correspondence is, for Arendt, tantamount to the deterioration of objective knowledge and mean-ing making. It is hardly difficult to foresee the negative ethical implications of such an attenuation even if the history of the Reich had not served to make theses implications so brutally clear. The "living corpses" of the concentration camps represent the most radical product of such a system, but, as Arendt has so famously demonstrated, it is the ethical life of community members no less than those designated as outsiders that is ultimately at stake in the totalitarian state.[116] Indeed, Arendt's later assessment of Nazism famously deemphasized the "radical" evil of the camps and came to revolve around the more "banal" phenomenon of the moral stupefaction of those within the fold of the *Volksgemeinschaft* itself—those, such as Adolf Eichmann, whose crimes she understood to have resulted not from an excess of conviction but from "the abdication of judgment and the failure to imagine the world of the other as a fellow human being."[117] Such failures are not incidental to the par-ticular functioning of Nazism; they are, Arendt shows, intrinsic to a politics that endeavors to embody a natural lawfulness "without bothering with the behavior of men."[118]

Notwithstanding their differing appraisals of the social realm, Arendt is akin to Durkheim in her understanding of communal life as our most fundamental wellspring of human flourishing—not merely political flourishing, but moral and cognitive flourishing as well.[119] It is in light of such presumptions that Arendt laments at the end of *The Origins of Totalitarianism* that the rise of totalitarian systems of governance has not merely threatened the physical and mental wellbeing of certain populations, it has threatened "to ravage the world as we know it."[120] Admittedly, the framers of the Declaration merely skimmed the surface of this complex sociological vision; their treatment of Nazism and its horrors focused primarily upon the more straightforward phenomenon of physical mortality—of "the millions of men [who] had lost their lives" as a result of the nihilistic philosophies of the Reich.[121] Yet, running beneath their condemnation of the mortal toll of the wartime era is a robust prescription for social life in the era to follow—a presumption premised upon the notion that, to be effective in its protection of human life, the Declaration must do more than simply delineate basic human rights or outlaw their violation; rather, it must get "into the spirit of a people," as Roosevelt put it.[122] The Declaration must do more than merely proclaim the fact of inherent human dignity; it must function to give rise to a community bound together by a reverence for the irreducible worth of the human. By its very logic, such a reverence should produce a particular orientation toward others: a deep-seated conviction that, as Durkheim hopefully postulated long prior to the creation of the Declaration, a person "cannot take it as a goal for his conduct without being obliged to go beyond himself and turn toward others."[123]

The *Volksgemeinschaft* could hardly have been more antithetical to such a moral cosmopolitanism. Indeed, while the ideal of the organic state might certainly be understood to have functioned in the way of a sacred item—not merely in keeping with the situational definition described in Chapter 2, but in the eyes of the Commission as well—it can hardly be understood to have inspired authentically "religious" behavior in the sociofunctionalist understanding of the term. Notwithstanding the initial social resonance of the *Volksgemeinschaft*, this item ultimately proved incapable of generating, even for its own community members, the solidarity or the ethical orientation that theorists such as Durkheim have located at the heart of religious life. In clear contrast to this, and for all its sociological sparseness, the Commission's formulation of human rights unquestionably hinges upon the conviction that human flourishing is an eminently communal phenomenon—that the cultivation of individual dignity and the exercise of individual rights depend through and through upon the cultivation of a particular type of social life. As Lynn Hunt puts it in a somewhat different context,

> Human rights are not just a doctrine formulated in documents; they rest on a disposition toward other people, a set of convictions about what people are like and how they know rights and wrong in the secular world. Philosophical ideas, legal traditions, and revolutionary politics had to have this kind of inner emotional reference point for human rights to be truly "self-evident." And, as Diderot insisted, these feelings had to be felt by many people, not just the philosophers who wrote about them.[124]

The Declaration's invocation of the human family, and the attendant mandate that we act toward one another in the spirit of brotherhood, embodies precisely such an endeavor to translate the ideal of human dignity into a compelling social formation—to narrate human dignity not merely into an unquestioned reality but into an innate disposition toward all other human beings.

The Challenge of "Cosmopolitan Consciousness"

In Durkheim's earliest engagement with human rights, he depicts the religious logic of such rights as something that has effectively burst the bounds of conventional religiosity while still providing "all that is required to speak to its believers in a tone that is no less imperative than the religions it replaces."[125] His identification of the religious logic of human rights centered almost entirely upon the powerful social logic at work in the sacralization of the human person. When we conceive of humans as universally sacred—not sacred by virtue of particular qualities or criteria but sacred by virtue of the dignity we all possess through no powers of our own—a world emerges in which it becomes impossible *not* to feel moral obligation toward all others. For Durkheim, the coveted result of such a logic is an enshrinement within the modern world not of "egoism" but rather of "sympathy for all that is human, a wider pity for all sufferings, for all human miseries, a more ardent desire to combat and alleviate them, a greater thirst for justice."[126] True to his understanding of religion as a force that moves independently of mere pragmatism, the community engendered through the sacralization of human dignity would inevitably be motivated by more than "simply a hygienic discipline or a wise principle of economy."[127] Ultimately, such a community would be motivated by a deep-seated identification with—a genuine respect for—human dignity itself.

The history of the negotiation and broadcast of the Declaration reveals that the Commission harbored precisely such aspirations for human rights. Even as they almost uniformly emphasized the need for the development of concrete mechanisms of enforcement, the Declaration's framers repeatedly emphasized that the legal mechanisms of human rights must be undergirded by a "two-man-mindedness" that Chang translated roughly into "sympathy" or "consciousness of [one's] fellow men"—a sympathy that would operate independently of the legal mechanisms themselves.[128] As Malik would eventually put it in a 1951 article on the future of human rights, such enforcement measures must blossom from within an environment in which a human rights violation anywhere "sends a shudder throughout humanity everywhere"—a shudder that precedes and undergirds "the punishment of whoever has dared to commit sacrilege against the infinite worth and dignity of the human person."[129]

However, an educational project of the sort envisioned by framers such as Malik—a project aiming to transcend mere utilitarianism and incorporate itself into the "spirit" of societies everywhere—is, to put it mildly, a more difficult project than the Declaration's straightforward posit of the human family indicates. An unsurprising array of human dynamics stand in the way of a conversion of the sort demanded by the Declaration—dynamics ranging from the enduring hegemony of more localized mechanisms of human solidarity (nationalism and religion in particular), to the simple, well-documented correlation between proximity and human empathy. Such obstacles point to the way in which a moral cosmopolitanism of the sort envisioned by the Commission may very well operate *in opposition* to normal human social life. Such, indeed, is precisely Lefebvre's argument: for of all the allure of the logic of moral community brought together in its genuine respect for and identification with a sacred item, universal human rights, he claims, do not ultimately function according to such logic; in fact, they fly in the face of the logic by which moral communities typically function. "The real danger to human rights," he asserts, "is internal to a particular kind of morality and sociability."[130] The moral community that Durkheim understands to coalesce around a particular sacred item is, according to Lefebvre, qualitatively different from—and is actually antithetical to—the "universally inclusive" community demanded by the human rights of the Declaration.[131]

This conundrum is implicit, though easily overlooked, in Durkheim's own speculations on human rights. For all his talk of a novel "religion of humanity" currently in the process of being generated through the human rights discourse of his day, Durkheim unquestionably understood the religion of humanity to function according to the same social logic as any other religion—that is, in the service of a particular community. His predictions and prescriptions for the cultivation of a human rights community thus take as their template the dynamics of certain preexisting human communities. In particular, Durkheim hearkens to the nation-state, which he understands to be "the most highly developed" human group actually in existence, and therein merely a step away from "the society of mankind, at present unrealized and perhaps unrealizable, yet representing the limiting case, or the ideal limit toward which we must strive."[132]

The human family played a role within the negotiations of the Commission not unlike Durkheim's understanding of the nation-state: it was conceived as a means of bridging our more localized forms of social life with the expansive sociability demanded by inherent human dignity. Lefebvre, however, highlights the manner in which such logical leaps are the product of a potentially erroneous presumption of continuity between our preexisting forms of social life and the society of mankind. Hearkening to Bergson, he asserts that

> Certainly, obligation can be expanded to encompass more and more people. Bergson agrees with Durkheim that it is perfectly natural and possible for obligation to extend from a smaller group (a family, for example) to a larger group (a nation, for example). But with the next step, the two thinkers part company. For whereas between family and nation there is a quantitative difference of degree, between these two groups and the whole of humanity there is a qualitative difference of "kind." Expansion is not openness; and as [Vladimir] Jankélévitch says, "Who can fail to see that the human 'society' is not a society like the others?" It is no longer a question of smaller to bigger group, but instead of group to grouplessness.[133]

While neither Lefebvre nor Bergson deny the possibility that the discourse of human rights might transform and shape preexisting communities, their recognition of the dramatic distinction between the community called into existence by the Declaration and the community typically called into existence through our moral and religious narratives significantly complicates the neatness of Durkheim's own speculations concerning the moral community at the heart of human rights.

Ultimately, such reservations are by no means unique to Bergson; they mirror the concerns of a series of political theorists from across the ideological spectrum. The emphatic rejection of human rights ideals on the part of rightist theorists such as Carl Schmitt and Leo Strauss is heavily informed by a rejection of human rights' claim to be able to transport humanity out of the realm of the "political"—that is, out of the realm of discrete groups defined in part through their distinction from other groups.[134] Habermas has voiced a similar reservation from the opposite side of the ideological spectrum, lamenting that the universal community to which the Declaration aspires "lacks a basis of legitimacy on structural grounds."[135] In Habermas' understanding, the universal community of human rights is "distinguished from state-organized communities by the principle of complete inclusion—it may exclude nobody, because it cannot permit any social boundaries between inside and outside."[136] Yet, he asserts, "any political community that wants to understand itself as a democracy must at least distinguish between members and non-members."[137] Such distinctions, after all, are one of the driving forces of the "normative cohesion" that makes ethical-political behavior possible.[138] Insofar as the Declaration's notion of human family endeavors to sidestep these uncomfortable facts of political life—and there is little doubt that it does—it neglects and perhaps even occludes the key role of differentiation, of "closure," in sustaining human social life. Strauss charges as much in his admonition that such liberal political projects ultimately cast "a smokescreen over reality."[139]

It is hardly necessary to emphasize that the Declaration does not overtly endeavor to obscure such human realities—much less does it seek to inhibit an understanding of the combative world of Schmidt's "political." Yet, to claim that the Commission harbored no aspiration to soften the realities of social and political closure would also be inaccurate. The Declaration, as we have seen, aspires not merely to articulate a set of rights conducive to the preservation of human dignity and moral cosmopolitanism but to narrate such dignity and solidarity into existence, and against the backdrop of their dramatic negation, no less. As an item designed to assert, rather than argue or prove, the fact of our shared human dignity, the human family is thus both real and unreal; it hearkens to a distinction between humans and other animals that is "real" in the sense that it is broadly intuitive and even empirically provable, yet it derives from this factual distinction a solidarity that is aspirational to say the least. In so doing, it does not merely sidestep the palpable tension between the universalism of the Declaration and the parochialism of our actual real life relationships of mutual dependency, it claims to mediate this tension—to embrace our preexisting intermediate communities while simultaneously orienting them toward a global common responsibility appropriate to inherent human dignity.

Lefebvre's Bergsonian formulation of human rights revolves almost entirely around a suspicion of such a maneuver. While Lefebvre, unlike the political theorists above, refuses to foreclose upon the possibility of the "cosmopolitan consciousness" that Strauss and Habermas find so untenable, his refusal does not by any means take the form of an endorsement of the preexisting relationships of mutual dependency that permeate the logic and the text of the Declaration.[140] To the contrary, Lefebvre, through Bergson, understands universal human rights to have instituted a significant rupture with almost all existing patterns of human social life, much in the way that religious mysticism initiates a rupture with the comfortable concreteness of religious dogmatism.[141] Within this formulation, the insistence of someone like Durkheim—or Cassin, for that matter—that the community brought together through universal human rights can be conceived as simply a more expansive version of a preexisting community such as the nation-state or the family actually serves to veil the magnitude of the conversion demanded by the sacralization of all humans. The result, fears Lefebvre, is "an all too comfortable extension of everyday morality ... light enough to leave one's everyday orientation undisturbed yet deep enough to give a superior moral impression."[142]

Notwithstanding the Commission's early decision to commit to a nonbinding declaration, and notwithstanding the manner in which their invocation of human family unquestionably works to domesticate the uncomfortable logic of common responsibility—to render it, in Roosevelt's words, "readily understood by the ordinary man and woman"—the Declaration was by no means intended to engender a light morality of the sort critiqued by Lefebvre.[143] To the contrary, in invoking the human family, the Commission aspired to transform our understanding of our fellow humans—to set human dignity to the task not merely of highlighting our irreducible humanity but, equally, of converting us into members of a global moral community. Given Commission members' conviction that human flourishing is deeply dependent upon our participation in social life, it is hardly surprising to behold the manner in which the recognition and preservation of human dignity is portrayed by the Declaration's framers as an eminently social thing, dependent only secondarily upon laws and other coercive measures. If the Declaration's invocation of the human family does indeed contribute to a certain effacement of the magnitude of the moral reorientation demanded by inherent human dignity, this effacement can be understood at least in part as a feature of Commission members' conviction that the Declaration must complement and enhance, rather than contradict, the preexisting social matrices that they recognized to be so crucial to human flourishing.

Needless to say, such a complementary approach is also the only way to remain faithful to the Declaration's promise to have consolidated rather than supplanted the world's preexisting systems of value. The human family embodies the Commission's endeavor to strike a balance between the complex work of building upon our preexisting social foundations and simultaneously transforming those foundations. It embodies the Commission's aspiration to engender a moral orientation that places the local and the universal into concert, ultimately coalescing our various modes of communal life around a genuine respect for the sanctity of the human.

CHAPTER 4

The Legal Personality and
a New World Order

Notwithstanding the Commission's endeavor to facilitate the rise and spread of a moral community centered upon the sacredness of human dignity, the Declaration ultimately devotes itself to more than just sacralization and community building: it delineates "minimum conditions for a dignified life, a life worthy of a human being." Just as important, it designates a venue and an official vernacular for the codification, regulation, and enforcement of these minimum conditions. A number of months prior to its passage, Charles Malik characterized the Declaration as "the definitive explication of the pregnant phrase of the [UN Charter's] preamble, 'the dignity and worth of the human person.'"[1] Though the 1945 Charter proclaimed its commitment to the achievement of international cooperation in promoting and encouraging "respect for human rights and fundamental freedoms," nowhere, asserts Malik, did it "define precisely what these rights are."[2] The importance of such a definition cannot be overstated, for it represents the projection of human dignity and the moral cosmopolitanism appropriate to this dignity into the realm of orderly political practice. In so doing, it aspires to bridge the affective and the practical, and to furnish a concrete vision of the mechanisms through which the principles of human rights might become widely accessible and actionable.

This chapter highlights the manner in which this bridge between the conceptual and the actionable takes a decidedly legalistic form; that is, it takes shape in the Declaration as an endeavor to radically universalize the promise of the "rule of law" offered in the Preamble. The legalism of the Declaration, however, ultimately entails more than a straightforward delineation and codification of particular legal tenets. We have witnessed a number of ways in which the Declaration exceeds and complicates the logic of positive law, and the Commission's legal discourse is, ironically, no exception to this. This chapter approaches the Declaration's legal discourse as yet another manifestation of human rights' pervasive "extrajudicial" logic, highlighting the manner in which this document utilizes the language of law in an effort to translate the sacredness of human dignity into a system of order capable of standing above and regulating the life of the moral community brought together by this sacred item. Ultimately, the Declaration's legal language reaches beyond a straightforward logic of codification and enforcement, aspiring instead to lend systematicity, uniformity, and permanence to the Commission's more "effervescent" gestures of sacralization and community building.[3]

The notion of the rule of law was, of course, not a novel one in 1948; many, though certainly not all, people in the 1940s were able to take for granted some measure of access to the legal mechanisms of particular governments. Moreover, most people in the mid-twentieth century had not only the ability but also a strong incentive to look to their own governments rather than to the blossoming international community for their legal protections. Few people could better attest to the spuriousness of the legal protections offered by the evolving body of international institutions than could minorities and refugees in Europe, whose existence "outside the scope of any tangible law" had so recently rendered them grist for the mill of the nation-building projects of Germany and other states.[4]

Given the manner in which the Declaration's minimal conditions for a dignified life are ultimately enforceable only to the extent that they are first enshrined within, or at the very least endorsed by, the judicial systems of particular nations, this document's reference to the rule of law can easily appear to be little more than a formality. To understand the Declaration's invocation of the rule of law in this way, however, would be to neglect the ubiquity of legal language both within the body of this document and in the Commission's negotiations and speeches. After all, nearly one quarter of the Declaration's thirty articles trade specifically in the language of law. To dismiss the Declaration's invocation of the rule of law as a formality would also be to overlook the prominent role that law played for the Commission as an index of the Declaration's rupture with the previous epoch of barbarous acts. In fact, the rule of law was repeatedly offered up by the Commission as the preeminent practical antidote to the excesses of German totalitarianism. Finally, to dismiss the rule of law as a formality would be to ignore the way the Commission's particular legal vision proves to be intimately tied to human dignity, the sacred center of human rights. Far from a mere formality—and, far from a straightforward enumeration of rights—the legal language of the Declaration was calibrated to accomplish a very particular task: to externalize and codify inherent human dignity. In so doing, it functions as a crucial extension of the Declaration's broader mythopoeic logic.

Durkheim, whose scholarship on religion was informed in a variety of ways by an abiding interest in the sociology of law, once again offers a particularly fruitful resource for an exploration of this nexus of sacralization, solidarity, and law. Durkheim remained preoccupied throughout his career with the realm of law; indeed, he considered it one of the central foci of his sociological work.[5] Yet, for at least two reasons, his work is rarely used in any systematic way within legal sociology or within the study of law more broadly. This is the case in the first place because Durkheim himself was not systematic in his theorization of law and its function within society; rather, his insights remained scattered throughout his scholarship. A thorough understanding of his legal theory thus necessitates a certain creativity. This neglect of Durkheim's legal theory is due in the second place to the fact that his approach to law is, as Roger Cotterrell puts it, "unashamedly moralistic"—is basically inseparable from his theorizations of religion and morality.[6] This interpenetration has proven antithetical to prevailing trends in the sociology of law that have long presumed that the moral and religious logics of law can (and often should) be analytically separated from law's status as an enterprise of collective decision making within a particular political order.

Yet, Durkheim's approach remains very much in keeping with the orientation of many in the field of critical legal theory who have come to evince skepticism about this quest for analytical distinction, particularly the closer a legal system comes to its moments of founding and legitimation.[7] It is in such instances that law is most likely to reveal itself not as a rarefied or technical framework distinguishable from moral foundations and presumptions but as an expression of "the moral commitments of people living in relationships of community of many kinds, reflecting values that are real in the experience of those whose lives it regulates."[8] From this perspective, the very "moralism" that has rendered Durkheim's approach unattractive to many of his successors in sociology proves indispensable for approaching certain aspects of law. In particular, it proves indispensable to an understanding of those moments and gestures wherein political actors make the transition from "knowledge" to "legislation," or from what Jean-François Lyotard calls the "denotative utterances concerning what is true" to the "prescriptive utterances with pretensions to justice."[9] The creation of the Declaration, of course, endeavors to enact precisely such a transition. It is therefore worth taking some time to explore Cotterrell's reconstruction of Durkheim's diffuse sociology of law—to piece together Durkheim's legal theory and to consider the ways in which his moralistic understanding of law was strongly mirrored by members of the Commission on Human Rights.

The "Religion" of Regulation

Durkheim's earliest and most elaborate theorization of law unfolded in the context of his 1893 exploration of social solidarity. His endeavor in *The Division of Labor in Society* to generate a means of "measurement" of social solidarity led him to propose a trajectory of development from more primitive cultures exhibiting near seamless ("mechanical") solidarity to the more fragmented ("organic") solidarity predominant within modern societies.[10] He imagined the index of each type of solidarity to be its legal system: a strongly "repressive" or penal legalism is, he claimed, endemic to more primitive cultures and a "restitutive" or contractual system to more advanced cultures. This trajectory from the repressive to the restitutive has been roundly criticized by later theorists; not only does it fail to do justice to the sociolegal complexity of premodern societies, but it posits a simplistic and, in fact, a very selective vision of the real world functioning of law—a significant shortcoming for a book claiming to treat its subject matter "according to the method of the positive sciences."[11] Although in his later texts Durkheim moved beyond some of the most simplistic tenets of this framework, he never rearticulated his understanding of law with the same deliberateness as that of this first book.

While this fact has significantly compromised his usefulness as a resource for a broad understanding of the relationship between law and society, it has not foreclosed upon the relevance of his legal theory to the question of the interpenetration of religion and law. His early and his later scholarship is in fact united in its formulation of law as a mechanism whereby we render the social sentiments engendered through myth and ritual more tangible, permanent, and authoritative. In this manner, his understanding of law dovetailed almost inevitably with his theorization of religion. Whether he approached law as a means of charting social solidarity, as he tended to do in his early scholarship, or as a mechanism for the generation of a transhuman source of authority and value, as he tended to do later, Durkheim gradually came to propose an indissoluble link between law and the religious meaning making that brings individuals together into communities.[12]

Eventually, the effervescence of the community and the strictures of law became positioned within his theory of religion at opposite ends of a spectrum of increasing specificity and externality. Within such a formulation, law assumes the crucial role of bringing the mandates of the moral community, mandates that most often remain "diffuse," into the realm of external organization.[13] As Cotterrell synopsizes,

> Law has "specially authorized representatives" charged with the task
> of enforcement. Its rules "are instituted by definite organs and under
> a definite form and . . . the whole system which the law uses to realize
> its precepts is regulated and organised." . . . These criteria, Durkheim
> notes, do not distinguish legal rules from many religious precepts. In
> general, however, the manner of deciding responsibility and applying
> punishments is what distinguishes legal from moral rules. . . . In law,
> society judges, but in an organised way. Law thus requires *some* insti-
> tutional means for publicly declaring or affirming norms.[14]

When understood as the preeminent way by which the inclinations of the moral community become externalized, law comes to function not merely as a counterpart to Durkheim's theorization of religion but, in many ways, as its logical culmination.

Durkheim anticipated the work of postmoderns such as Derrida and Walter Benjamin in his endeavor to map out the often subtle connections between the logics of sacralization, community building, and law. His endeavors rested upon the presumption that there is a functional link between more overtly religious modes of legislation such as "ritual prescriptions" and more secular (even concertedly anti-metaphysical) modes such as legal positivism.[15] Legislation, whether it takes the form of religious prescriptions or secular prohibitions, is the primary means by which the solidarity of a given community becomes transposed from "a state of pure potentiality" to a state manifested "by sensible indices."[16] Put differently, law serves as "an external index which symbolizes" the less tangible moral orientations of a given community.[17] Durkheim thus ultimately invites an understanding of secular law as different "only in degree" from the regulatory systems of institutions conventionally understood as religious, for both types of regulatory system entail, as Cotterrell puts it, "'something that resists us, is beyond us, imposes itself on us and constrains us.'"[18] Both are "independent and dominating, 'resistant to the will,' so it is not just an internal state of mind, like a sentiment or habit" but rather a combination of "the idea of regularity with that of authority, authority being 'that influence which is imposed on us by any moral power that we acknowledge as superior.'"[19]

Within this broadly functionalist understanding, religion and law intertwine in their provision of "a source of meaning for individual lives, something individuals can relate to as greater than themselves, giving direction, confidence and a source of authority, a grand scheme to which the seemingly insignificant details of life can be related, an ultimate source of values and understandings."[20] This approach is markedly different from an approach merely seeking to highlight the "religious" ideas expressed in law. While it is certainly feasible to ask the question of how the ideas, practices, and texts of particular religious traditions inform the machinations of a particular legal system, Durkheim ended his career with an interest in a different connection between religion and law:

> law and religion have certain similarities *as social phenomena*. They are both foci of duty and commitment. They impose obligations on those subject to them, who accept their authority. And ultimately law, like religion, is not merely a matter of duty or obligation. The ultimate logic of Durkheim's position . . . is that, up to a point, law must also be, like religion, a focus of willing allegiance, something to be believed in and involved with.[21]

This approach to the connection between religion and law is markedly different from a "religious history" of law; it presumes that religion and law perform analogous or interrelated functions within society. This is a crucial insight that has been replicated and expanded many times over by theorists in the late twentieth and early twenty-first centuries.

Durkheim made some inconsistent efforts to distinguish the law-morality relationship in premodern and modern societies, but, as is so often the case with the functionalist approach, we ultimately discern little difference between the underlying logics of openly religious and avowedly secular legal systems. All such systems reveal themselves, according to Durkheim, to be in the essentially "religious" business of "impressing upon individuals a sense of the sacredness of something outside themselves, . . . of life lived not by the individual in isolation but in common with all other people, and by past and future generations."[22] Durkheim's conclusions along these lines have profound implications for our understanding of the relationship between religion and law: if religion is marked by the cultivation of "impersonal" forces designed to command our respect and orient our identities and behavior—to generate "a discipline willingly adhered to, believed in as a matter of commitment, internalized in the individual's way of thinking and acting"—then legislation itself can readily take on the mantle of a religious enterprise.[23] As Cotterrell puts it, "it seems that religious belief, in Durkheim's very specific sense, can be partly translated into a belief in regulation—including, no doubt, a belief in law—as necessary, welcome, natural, and obligatory."[24] As Cotterrell's final clause indicates, this religious logic hinges upon the pretension of a given legal system to command a nonutilitarian loyalty from its adherents—its claim to move beyond straightforward coercion and inspire a respect of the sort wielded by a sacred item. Given Durkheim's understanding of law as an extension of the sacred and a concretization of the moral community, this pretension toward genuine respect is hardly surprising; it is yet another facet of the religious logic that infuses all human institutions aspiring to imbue their claims and representations with affective power and "an aura of factuality."[25]

Most legal systems, of course, depend for their existence upon more than the genuine respect of their subjects; even the most reified legal tenets tend to operate through some combination of Durkheimian respect and Weberian monopoly on violence.[26] Durkheim, who takes as his point of analytical departure the affective charge of particular social representations—the radiation of energy that inspires individuals to see themselves as part of something larger than themselves—proved notoriously neglectful of such underlying questions of power and coercion. As unacceptable as this neglect has come to seem to later theorists, it is a natural product of his emphasis upon the phenomenon of genuine respect that arises from the sacred, unites the moral community, and undergirds the legal order that the community puts in place for itself. This approach is very much in keeping with Durkheim's broader understanding of religion and its social underpinnings, and it is therefore hardly surprising that his views on the logic of human legislation coalesced in the way that they did as his scholarship on religion blossomed later in his career. An approach to legislation that neglects the element of power/coercion, however, proves highly unsuited to the task of understanding most legal systems, as an impressive array of theorists have attested.[27]

Yet, Durkheim's approach offers a series of important insights into the particular logic of the rule of law embedded within the Declaration. Almost by its very nature, the Commission's vision of human rights' legal logic took a Durkheimian form. Given the reality that the Declaration would command no mechanisms of enforcement, and given its framers' claims that they were reflecting preexisting systems of value even as they worked to transform them, the Commission's formulation of the rule of law by necessity eschewed substantive engagement with matters of power and coercion. Instead, the Commission's depiction of the Declaration's legal logic consistently centered upon the sacredness of human dignity and upon the presumption that the rule of law would function as a natural mechanism for concretizing and codifying this inherent index of human worth.

In addition to its indebtedness to the sacredness of human dignity, the Commission's vision of the rule of law was, of course, also profoundly shaped by the juridico-political context of the preceding epoch of barbarous acts; it is in fact difficult to overstate the role that the "Nazification" of law played as a point of orientation for Commission members' own formulations of the legal orderliness appropriate to universal human rights. Ultimately, the negative exemplar of Nazi Germany permeates the legal language of the Declaration, as Morsink points out:

> The Universal Declaration includes seven articles that deal with legal rights. Article 6 gives everyone the right to a legal personality; Article 7 speaks of equality before the law; Article 8 asserts that everyone has fundamental constitutional rights; Article 9 rejects arbitrary arrest and detention; Article 10 calls for an independent judiciary; Article 11 enunciates the presumption of innocence in criminal cases; and Article 12 says that everyone has a right to certain areas of privacy. These seven articles cover nearly one quarter of a Declaration totaling thirty articles. Why so many? The delegates wanted to make sure that they stated separately the main legal rights that by 1948 had become part of the jurisprudential systems of all civilized nations. The Nazification of the German legal system during the Third Reich has gone so far and deep that only a clear statement of the separate issues involved could set the record straight.[28]

Morsink and many others have documented the complex breakdown of the German legal system under the leadership of the Nazi Party, and the likes of Arendt and Agamben have highlighted the ways in which the Nazification of German law was ultimately parasitic upon a much broader juridico-political crisis in Western Europe. The Commission's depiction of law under the Reich largely neglects this longer trajectory mapped by Arendt and Agamben, much in the way that it neglected the ways in which the very logic of human rights itself may be understood to have contributed to the sacralization of the *Volksgemeinschaft*. Not only were such matters hidden for the most part from the view of policymakers of the mid-twentieth century, but, even had these matters received the nuanced theoretical treatment that they would in the latter part of the twentieth century, they were tangential to the Commission's aim of grounding human rights within both the experience of the wartime era and the preexisting values of societies across the globe. In pursuit of these particular aims, the Declaration's framers engaged the legal crises of Nazi Germany not as indictments of broader elements within modern human rights law (à la Arendt), or of the western political tradition writ large (à la Agamben), but as concrete, incontrovertible evidence of the necessity of a reinvigoration— and a universalization—of the rule of law. This maneuver ultimately entails barely a hint of a systematic, self-critical reflection upon the field of international law itself; rather, it is underwritten by a thoroughly Durkheimian presumption of the indissoluble connection between legal orderliness and human flourishing.

The "Legal Personality": The Right to Have Rights

Commission members' heavy reliance on the foil of Nazi Germany propelled them toward a very particular vision of legal orderliness. Under the reign of the Reich, for example, the veneration of the *Volksgemeinschaft* had proven nearly synonymous with a willingness to suspend or amend German law in favor of the nearly absolute authority of the Führer.[29] In response, the Declaration's framers endeavored to articulate a vision of the rule of law that would specifically push back against the ability of a state to accomplish that hallmark of totalitarian governance: "the subordination of law and knowledge to politics."[30] The Reich, for example, had utilized denationalization as a key means of manipulating its populations and protecting its interests. In response, the Commission sought to formulate a legal orderliness that would prevent states from arbitrarily withdrawing the mantle of law from certain individuals and groups—a legal orderliness that would be capable of affording what Cassin describes as "access to justice" under all circumstances.[31] Finally, the history of the Final Solution had offered the most striking possible example of the manner in which the rights of stateless peoples exist in practice only to the extent that other states are willing to step up, often against their own national interests, and guarantee them. In response, the Commission endeavored to disrupt the state-centeredness of preexisting human rights mechanisms—to anchor the mechanisms of human rights law first and foremost within individuals and only secondarily within political bodies, and thus to rupture what Arendt famously identified as the practical equivalence of "the rights of man [and] the rights of peoples in the European nation-state system."[32] Though it is possible—and, within certain contexts, crucial—to raise the question of the Declaration's ultimate success in rectifying the various factors that gave rise to the legal violations of the wartime era, the history of the Commission's negotiations leaves no doubt that its members instinctively linked the success of the Declaration to its capacity to bring every human being irrevocably within the fold of a legal system in order to prevent anyone from ever again being "forced outside the pale of the law."[33] What is more, the Commission endeavored to accomplish this in a manner that would inspire universal compliance independently of any actual mechanisms of legal enforcement.

Precisely how did the Commission accomplish this goal of ensuring universal access to the rule of law? The Declaration's framers were most assuredly not "internationalists"; they did not seek merely to reinvigorate the state-centric orderliness of previous eras.[34] While they spoke on behalf of their governments, Commission members did not "negotiate on the basis of reciprocity, which is what nation-states do in most of their dealings with one another."[35] Rather, the Declaration's framers were driven together by what Morsink describes as

> a vision of cosmopolitan justice, which views all human beings as members of the same family of mankind, each of them born with inherent rights. . . . As cosmopolitans who had their minds set on individual human beings, they looked at the nation-states that dot our planet as no more (and no less) than the most important vehicles for the delivery of the enjoyment of people's—to use a redundancy— inherent birthrights.[36]

Even the persistent state-centric discourse of delegates from the Communist nations was not of a straightforwardly internationalist bent; rather, these delegates almost uniformly advocated for the cultivation of political systems that would eradicate "the contradiction between the government and the individual" and thus render the state fundamentally accountable to its citizens—would, in the words of Soviet delegate Andrei Vyshinsky, render the state an embodiment "of the collective individual."[37] Thus, in arguably all cases, the Commission's vision of the rule of law conceived of the preexisting constellation of nation-states as a means (and, in the eyes of most delegates, a perpetually untrustworthy means) to the goal of ensuring the protection of individual human beings. It is the human being—not the states, and not even the law itself—that stands at the heart of the Declaration's formulation of the rule of law.

How, then, does this principle of universal human empowerment become translated into a paradigm of legal orderliness? The answer lies in a term that was intrinsic to the negotiations of the Declaration from their very commencement: the "juridical personality." Ironically, this term does not actually appear in the English version of the Declaration: Article 6, which reads in French "Chacun a le droit à la reconnaissance en tous lieux de sa personalité juridique," states in English that "Everyone has the right to recognition everywhere as a person before the law." Notwithstanding the differences in terminology, the intention is identical, as Roosevelt makes clear in a 1949 account of the genesis of this term. Her account is worth quoting at length:

> I remember very well when Professor René Cassin in the early days of our discussion in the Human Rights Commission, suggested an article. It is not now in the words that he used in first suggesting it, though the idea is in that direction. I have often thought of it because it not only illustrated the difficulties of different legal systems, but it also illustrated the belief which many of the representatives in our Commission had, that certain things must never happen again because they had been one of the causes that brought on World War II. . . . His suggestion that we have an article that would read in French, "Personne ne droit être privé de sa personalité juridique," and I, without any legal knowledge, translated it into English as "No one shall be deprived of their juridical personality."
>
> Well, I didn't know what I had started. Behind my back, where lawyers sit from the departments in Washington, there was a storm. They all said, "There is no such expression as 'juridical personality' in English or American law." . . . Behind my back they kept arguing, saying what it means is "without due process of law," but how do you say it? Well, it took a long while to argue that out and finally one

day one of my Department of Justice youngish lawyers handed me a piece of paper and said, "You can accept the translation 'juridical personality,' it was once used in American law."

And when do you think it was used? It was used in the Dred Scott case when Justice Taney said "a slave has no juridical personality." So I accepted it.[38]

As the Commission deliberated on the Declaration's precise language, Roosevelt and others eventually came to conclude that, notwithstanding its legitimacy as a legal principle, the "legal personality" (as it was eventually transcribed into English) was an overly complicated term, inappropriate for a document aiming to speak to the broadest possible English-speaking audience.[39] The language of what would eventually become Article 6 was changed to its present iteration. The logic of this term, however, remains the same across both iterations: namely, the key to ensuring universal access to the rule of law is to ground the rule of law within each individual—to imbue each individual with a quality that serves as the foundation of his or her entitlement to legal protection under all circumstances, and thus to ensure that the individual, rather than the state, becomes the central focus of law. The legal personality is designed to accomplish precisely such a reorientation: to ensure, in the words of Cassin, that every individual "has a status in law" and is thus "able to be a bearer of rights, obligations, and responsibilities."[40] As Soviet delegate Koretsky put it in his own endeavor to define this term, "The legal personality means the ability to have rights."[41] This term embodies the Commission's overarching endeavor to translate inherent human dignity from a catalyst of diffuse social solidarity into an enduring system of organization—or, as Habermas puts it in a related context, to "cash out" human rights' moral promise in "legal currency."[42]

Human rights, Habermas observes, "exhibit a Janus face turned simultaneously to morality and to law."[43] In his own theorization of rights, Habermas draws a clear distinction between such logics, even as he acknowledges the existence of certain "bridges" between the relative abstractness of morality and the concreteness of law.[44] Though the Declaration's framers emphasized human rights' moral logic throughout their negotiations—"moral" very much in the Habermasian sense of something lacking concrete mechanisms of enforcement—they also regularly conflated the moral and the legal logics of human rights. After all, the Declaration's invocation of the rule of law certainly can't be understood as "legalistic" in any concrete sense of the term:

it lacks its own enforcement apparatus, and, as will become clear, it makes an ambiguous appeal to the apparatuses of preexisting legal systems. Ultimately, the rule of law was specifically conceived during the course of negotiations to offer a universalist, normative thrust reaching beyond the tenets and enforcement mechanisms of any particular legal regimes. Indeed, it was for this very reason that the Commission omitted the term "regime of law" from an early draft of the Preamble and opted instead for "rule of law"—a term that, according to UK delegate Ernest Davies, more cogently encompassed "the sources of law" and not merely the specific form it happens to assume within a given society.[45]

Inherent human dignity plays a key role in pushing the Declaration in this manner beyond a straightforward enumeration of legal rights and into the realm of the moral, as Habermas himself concedes:

> human dignity forms the "portal" through which the egalitarian and universalistic substance of morality is imported into law. The idea of human dignity is the conceptual hinge that connects the *morality* of equal respect for everyone with positive *law* and democratic lawmaking in such a way that their interplay could give rise to a political order founded upon human rights.[46]

The legal personality does not feature in Habermas's articulation of the mediating logic of human dignity. Yet, if dignity is the portal through which human rights values become imported into law, it is the legal personality that performs the actual "cashing out" of such values into legal practice, much in the way that, as we witnessed in the previous chapter, the human family performs the cashing out of human dignity into social life. Indeed, from this perspective, human dignity and the legal personality are essentially inseparable—mere loci on a broad, Durkheimian spectrum ranging from the relative ineffability of "genuine respect" to the concreteness of legal regulation.

Perhaps no theorist has more concisely articulated this connection between the ideals of human inviolability and access to the rule of law than has Arendt. Arendt, as we have seen, expressed profound pessimism about the human rights projects of the modern era. This wholesale critique of modern human rights is encapsulated by Arendt in the failure of human rights institutions to guarantee to all humans "the right to have rights"—the failure to guarantee, in other words, that we possess a claim upon the law simply by virtue of being human.[47] The rights declarations of the eighteenth century had let down those most in need of their protections precisely because they remained beholden to the enforcement mechanisms of nation-states. As Arendt famously lamented about the inalienable rights proclaimed in the French Declaration of the Rights of Man and of the Citizen,

> The Rights of Man . . . had been defined as "inalienable" because they were supposed to be independent of all governments; but it turned out that the moment human beings lacked their own government and had to fall back upon their minimum rights, no authority was left to protect them and no institution was willing to guarantee them.[48]

This failure to break human rights free of the legal apparatuses of nation-states had spelled disaster for millions of minorities and stateless peoples, and, although Arendt evinced enduring skepticism about the capacity of any secular human rights regime to remedy this, her reference to the right to have rights makes clear that, if there is any remedy to be discerned, such a remedy must involve an interlacing of human nature and human rights such that our access to law inheres in us as individuals qua individuals rather than as beneficiaries of a particular nation.

The right to have rights articulates precisely this aspiration, and it does so on multiple levels. On a straightforward political level, Arendt's right to have rights amounts to a call to imbue all individuals with a fundamental "right to belong to some kind of organized community."[49] The link between this political facet of the right to have rights and the Commission's human rights project is clear: the legal personality embodies the Commission's endeavor to ground the right to political belonging in every individual, independent of civil status—as Cassin puts it, to guarantee every individual everywhere "the right to have access to justice."[50] Ultimately, this would eliminate the prerogative of states to revoke citizens' access to the rule of law, and thus would begin to dismantle the intimate link between human rights and civil rights. This dismantling of the de facto power of nation-states was, as we have seen, dear to the hearts of many Commission members, and the notion of the legal personality ultimately proves as indispensable to this project as does the sacralization of human dignity.

In the course of making the case for the inclusion of the legal personality within the Declaration, Cassin described this term as "one of the most important texts of the Declaration, on a national as well as an international level."[51] In a manner similar to Arendt, Cassin understood stateless peoples to serve as a particularly important illustration of the need for such a principle within the framework of human rights. In the course of advocating on behalf of the idea of the legal personality, Cassin invoked the recent specter of "foreigners" who had been refused access to state legal systems—had been refused "the right to go before judges"—as the most concrete justification for the inclusion of a portion of text that would effectively enshrine the law within each individual.[52] The scenario of individuals facing the threat of "being deprived of their juridical personality by an arbitrary act of their government," as Canadian delegate H. H. Carter put it, rendered this somewhat abstract principle both current and concrete.[53]

Yet the right to have rights as Arendt conceives it also entails a more sweeping "ontological" dimension that is discernible in the logic of the Declaration as well.[54] Very much in keeping with her emphasis upon the importance of human communal life, Arendt ultimately conceives of the right to have rights not merely as a mandate to furnish all human beings with access to a court of justice, but to create an ethos in which all human beings have, in the words of Parekh, "the right to a place in the world where one can speak and act meaningfully."[55] To be placed beyond the pale of law is, from this perspective, not merely to be deprived of a particular set of rights or a particular place within a political community, it is to be expelled from "the human condition itself, which depends upon belonging to some human community."[56]

This ontological dimension of the right to have rights is frequently ignored within the discourse of human rights, and it was certainly not foregrounded by Commission members in their deliberations upon the legal tenets of the Declaration. Yet, even this ontological thrust lurks subtly within the Commission's emphasis on the social logic of human dignity: it lurks within Commission members' conviction that human dignity is actualized not through mere proclamation, rationalization, or coercion but through the cultivation of a genuine respect that, if successful, cannot help but to transform all individuals into ends in themselves rather than mere means for the furtherance of some political goal. This endeavor to elevate each individual to an end within a global community is ultimately very much in keeping with the ontological dimension of the right to have rights. It rests upon the conviction, intrinsic to the mythopoeic logic of this document, that the Declaration must accomplish more than the straightforward political task of outlining particular rights and erecting a particular governing body for their enforcement; it must also accomplish what Malik calls the "spiritual" task of enshrining the uniqueness of each individual in the face of modern conditions that threaten to efface this uniqueness.[57]

The particular conditions that threaten not just human rights but also human uniqueness are referenced only schematically by members of the Commission on Human Rights: Malik highlights the Industrial Revolution and the rise of nationalist ideologies as two significant causes of the modern descent into a "spirit of the masses."[58] Such an ethos, according to Malik, perpetually threatens to transform human beings into "atom[s] without distinction, without ontological differentiation of function."[59] His description looks markedly similar to Arendt's own description of human superfluousness.[60]

Ultimately, however, Commission members' concern for this "ontological" dimension of human rights manifests itself most specifically in the context of their condemnation of human slavery. Though Arendt, among others, has forcefully criticized the slavery analogy as a means of understanding the legal deprivations of the Holocaust,[61] framers such as Malik and Cassin (and Roosevelt, for that matter) raised the specter of slavery as a means of articulating the profound existential consequences of what Cassin referred to as "the negation of the legal personality."[62] The Nazification of Germany's legal system had, Cassin claimed, given rise to "a modern form of slavery" not merely by depriving certain people of their rights "to marry," "to be a creditor or to own property," or "to enter into contract," but, underlying these discrete deprivations, by reducing them to "property."[63] The right to legal personhood was eventually embraced by the Commission as a direct refutation of this logic, as a prophylaxis against the reduction of human beings to objects for use in the pursuit of nationalist or other projects. Whether or not the institution of slavery accurately captures the horrors of the Holocaust, the trope of slavery served during the course of the Commission's negotiation of the legal personality as the ultimate example of human disempowerment—the ultimate example of the denigration of human individuals to a means.

Commission members' repeated deployment of the trope of slavery in the context of discussions of the Declaration's legal prescriptions reveals the strength of the connection they perceived between access to law and basic human empowerment. The legal personality rests at the center of this logic, an embodiment of the intimate tie that framers such as Cassin discerned not merely between legal agency and human security, but between legal agency and all elemental acts of human self-assertion—acts including, but certainly not limited to, the ability to "enter into a contract," "to marry freely," and "to inherit or leave inheritances."[64] Though Cassin's enumeration of such basic modes of human empowerment might appear, like the trope of slavery itself, to understate the magnitude of the legal and existential deprivations of the

Holocaust as we now understand them, such enumerations worked in the service of his broader effort to draw a clear and compelling connection between legal agency and meaningful human existence. Ultimately, the practical and existential weight with which Cassin and others imbued "the right to a status in law" reaches beyond a simple endeavor to concretize particular legal measures; it bespeaks a logic deeply resonant with Durkheim's own "moralistic" understanding of law as a fundamental element of human flourishing—as a mechanism that secures and externalizes the various tenets that a community has converged upon to cultivate the wellbeing of its members.[65]

Humanity's Law

An appreciation of the logic of the legal personality is crucial for an understanding of the Declaration's unique legal vision, but it does not ultimately answer the question, raised above, of what sort of legal system the "right to have rights" demands in practice. The Declaration does not put in place any concrete political body for the implementation and enforcement of its rights; as with the social prescription explored in the previous chapter, the Declaration ultimately aspires to articulate a set of rights capable of enhancing rather than rupturing the world's preexisting legal systems. In this respect, the Declaration both does and does not prescribe a specific system for the translation of human rights' moral vision into law. It professes an openness to all political systems to the extent that such systems uphold the basic values enshrined in the Declaration—most centrally, the values of inviolable human dignity, common responsibility, and universal access to the rule of law. Thus, suitable political systems must obviously offer the specifically mentioned protections of, for example, equality before the law (Articles 7 and 8), independent judiciaries (Article 10), and presumption of innocence (Article 11). Each of these rights forms part of a legal constellation designed, often under painstaking negotiation, to secure impartial and equitable allocation of legal protection to all human beings.

These particular rights are also, of course, elementary characteristics of a liberal democratic political system, and here we are brought face to face with the fact that the Declaration does not deal in practice in just any "legal currency." As Habermas points out, the moral imperatives that are ultimately introduced into law through the portal of human dignity are fundamentally "egalitarian and universalistic"; they demand a political system committed to the principle that "human beings have certain natural ('inalienable') rights and that governments must accept a basic law, limiting [their] own powers, that secures them."[66] The framers were clear-eyed about the fact that the Nazi model was by no means the only example of a legal system incapable of making good on human rights' universalist mandate. As Soviet delegate Alexie Pavlov put it, "apart from attempts against whole groups, such as those against the Jews in Germany, account must be taken of the fact that civil legislation still contain[s] restrictive provisions regarding [the] juridical personality of individuals."[67] The Declaration's formulation of the rule of law is specifically designed to push against all such civil systems, and to give rise, in the words of Article 28, to "a social and international order in which the rights and the freedoms set forth in this Declaration can be fully realized."

Notwithstanding the universalist logic of the rule of law, there is thus little question that the constellation of goals that drove the Commission to enshrine this principle within the Declaration points toward something on the model of a liberal democratic political system.[68] Even given his general support for the principle of the rule of law, Koretsky admonished early in the drafting process that the Declaration's particular articulation of this legal ideal appeared be moving in the direction of transferring "certain principles of law accepted in the United Kingdom to other countries—not only principles but also the mechanisms of their implementation."[69] Such a maneuver, he warned, could appear "not quite applicable to other nations whose historical development was different."[70] On the whole, however, Koretsky's laments were overshadowed by the widespread presumption among Commission members that, while the legal personality certainly lends itself more readily toward particular political configurations over others, the term itself ultimately points beyond particular juridico-political prescriptions—that it embodies something closer to what Marcelo Neves describes as a normative expectation of "legal inclusion of each and every person in world society and hence of universal access to law as an (autonomous) social subsystem."[71]

Neves's articulation of the logic of human rights mirrors a point of broad consensus among Commission members: namely, that "Unlike citizenship in its broadest sense, which relates to general legal inclusion within the framework of a particular state order, human rights relate to legal inclusion on the level of a world society."[72] Inherent human dignity, the foundation for the notion that our value and our wellbeing transcend the interests of states and all other groups, can hardly demand less. The sacredness of human dignity must ultimately push all legal systems not merely toward the liberal democratic political values enumerated in the Declaration's specific articles, but toward a perpetual openness to modification—toward a legal "suprapositivity" that forces *all* domestic systems into conversation and comparison, with human well-being rather than national sovereignty serving as the ultimate lodestar of legitimacy.[73]

It is in this manner that the Declaration's legal prescription itself veers into the extrajudicial: even as it pays homage to law as an essential venue for human flourishing, it aspires to render the boundaries between domestic legal systems more porous, more open to "judicial dialogue and borrowing."[74] The legal personality rests at the center of this Janus-faced legal logic, simultaneously extolling the importance of our legal institutions while pushing us to reach beyond them—pushing all peoples toward an openness to alternative ways by which to make good on human rights' proclamation that, in Cassin's words, "there is not a single human being who could not possess both rights and obligations."[75] The Declaration, asserts Cassin in a related context, "contributes something new: the individual becomes a subject of international law in respect of his life and liberty, principles are affirmed, side by side with those already laid down by the majority of national laws, which no national or international authority had hitherto been able to proclaim, let alone enforce."[76]

Ultimately, then, the Declaration's enshrinement of the rule of law both does and does not promise to transform the preexisting international legal landscape. The Declaration prescribes no specific legal regime, though universal access to the rule of law clearly favors certain legal apparatuses over others. Notwithstanding this favoritism, there is little question that the Commission intended the Declaration's legal vision to be compatible with the widest possible array of domestic systems of governance—intended it, in the words of delegate Carlos Romulo, to "take into account all the different cultural patterns there are in the world, especially in respect to popular customs and legal systems."[77] In part, this compatibility is in keeping with the Commission's larger claim to have outlined rights and values that reflect those already in practice across the globe. However, it is also in keeping with Commission members' cognizance of the fact that, as Glendon puts it, "the nation-states would always have to provide the primary line of defense of human rights and that a 'universal' document would therefore have to leave room for an ample degree of pluralism in the understanding and implementation of many of its rights."[78] Cassin, certainly no advocate of unwarranted state sovereignty, pressed this particular point in his request to his fellow Commission members that they work to seize all opportunities "to prove that

the coexistence of States which have differing economic conceptions and differing regimes is possible and that it is not necessary for one conception to
triumph over another conception."[79]

It is in light of such concerns that the Declaration's vision of the rule of
law might well be understood to entail, on the one hand, something more
than a reinforcement of the preexisting nation-state system of international
governance and, on the other, something markedly less than a wholesale rein-
vention of this system. Ultimately, this formulation of the rule of law aspires
to "recalibrate" rather than to revolutionize, very much in keeping with what
Theodor Meron has described as the broader "humanization" of international
law in the nineteenth and twentieth centuries.[80] At stake in such a recalibration, asserts Ruti Teitel,

> is *the extended reach of legality*. This extension takes as a departure
> point classic conceptions of state sovereignty and state interests, and
> moves toward the incorporation of humanitarian concerns . . . as a
> crucial element in the justification of state action. Under the classic
> state-sovereignty-based approach, states were largely unconstrained
> in terms of what they did within their own borders. . . . And, exter-
> nally, apart from *jus cogens*, states were constrained only by norms
> to which they had consented, either by explicit agreement (as in the
> case of conventional law), or by state practice and *opinio juris* (as in
> the case of customary law).[81]

The infusion of a humanitarian logic into the classic "inter-State" model of
international law endeavors to "redefin[e] the struggle for justice in terms that
focus not on the preservation of state autonomy against the global legal order,
but on the effects of law on persons and peoples, and on our evolving understandings of human security."[82] Ideally, this extended logic of legality works
from within—and practically depends upon—the reigning international configuration of nation-states, yet it significantly alters both the scope and the
basis of law's legitimacy. It endeavors to shift the basis of both domestic and
international law to a "teleological" mode that takes as its starting point "the
concern for human dignity, which forms the basis of a list of fundamental
minimum standards of humanity."[83] In other words, this "humanitarian" legal
logic departs upon a presumption that the purpose of law is to ensure human
wellbeing and then endeavors to rally the discourses, institutions, and structures necessary for the provision of universal legal coverage.[84]

Teitel attributes the recalibration of law at the hands of the Declaration and other such human rights mechanisms primarily to a growth in awareness over the past century of legal "black holes": situations in which "insecurity cannot be countered by legal remedy."[85] This problem of legal black holes pre-dates the barbarous acts of the wartime era, of course, but we have witnessed the manner in which the specific legal black holes of this era served as the primary referent for the Declaration's own iteration of a more humanitarian mode of law.[86] The Nazification of law under the Reich served as an experien-tial anchor for Commission members' basic conviction that legal empower-ment is a key feature of the path to human well-being—not merely physical wellbeing but, as Arendt helps to show, a broader, existential well-being. This constellation of events and concerns comes together in the Declaration in the notion of the legal personality, which we have seen to be a term that, despite its scant precedence within the legal history of the west, embodies the legal core of this document and, ultimately, of human rights generally.

The Declaration's posit of the legal personality mirrors Arendt's own response to the legal black holes of the wartime era. Born out of her enduring suspicion of the capacity of our preexisting legal mechanisms to ensure the protection of all people, Arendt's notion of the right to have rights envisions a recalibration of law such that human beings become the guiding principle for the operation of law—at the emphatic expense of those monumental log-ics of "Nature," "*Volk*," and "History" that had proven so dramatically cata-strophic to both global peace and human flourishing.[87] Like Arendt's right to have rights, the legal personality endeavors to point beyond the preexisting landscape of nation-states and colonies, reaching for both a legal foundation and a legal praxis oriented toward the protection, everywhere and always, of individual human beings.

In a manner similar to Arendt's own prescription for human rights, the Declaration endeavors to enact a remedy to the problem of legal black holes by doing more than merely closing political and legal loops. Or, perhaps more accurately, it aspires to close loops in a way that ultimately depends upon a larger transformation of the "political consciousness" and even the moral sensibilities of people everywhere.[88] This endeavor toward the trans-formation of political consciousness takes place across various aspects of the Declaration, as we have seen, but it assumes its most concrete form in the Commission's endeavor to bind the rule of law to the individual such that it becomes inconceivable—or, more accurately, reprehensible, if not overtly sacrilegious—to place vulnerable people beyond the pale of law. The legal personality embodies this binding together of the human and the legal. Moreover, it demonstrates the manner in which Durkheim's spectrum from abstract to concrete—from the ineffability of social solidarity to the specificity of law—does not point merely in one direction: the legal order of a given community can be both a product and a generator of more diffuse moral sensibilities. As Cotterrell asserts, "Law is the most important means of planning the future, no less than regulating the present. It not only imposes duties— moral discipline—but can also facilitate social solidarity. Its task is somehow to frame and organise the complex social networks of attachment."[89]

The legal personality functions within the Declaration not merely to entrench human dignity within a realm of organized discourse and practice, but to transform our engagement with—indeed, our understanding of—certain central aspects of human life. To put it more concretely, the Declaration endeavors to establish the language of law as the preeminent vernacular for the articulation and navigation of matters of human justice.[90]

There is, moreover, ample evidence to indicate that the field of human rights law has indeed moved in this direction in the wake of the creation of the Declaration. As Sidonie Smith and Kay Schaffer point out, the rights language of the Declaration has, over the course of the twentieth and twenty-first centuries, become "the privileged mode of addressing human suffering."[91] This "juridicalization" of justice-seeking actors and activities is not merely the product but is also, ideally, the *producer* of a political consciousness that, overtly or not, understands human dignity to be sacred—understands human dignity to serve as both the uncontestable foundation and the uncontestable telos of law. Over time, the Declaration has served as a crucial point of focus in the gradual shift within international law from an orientation "almost entirely to relations among states, excluding, for the most part, matters concerning the relations between states and their own subjects," to an orientation that brings individuals to the fore as the primary subjects of international law—even if such foregrounding is merely conceptual, as it often is.[92]

Moreover, this humanization of the law has also engendered a shift within the practice of international law toward what might be called a "discursive" openness complementary to the juridical openness referenced above. In making good on the Declaration's enshrinement of the individual as the foundation of law, the field of human rights law has, over time, been forced to open itself to new sources and new expressions of human-generated information. The Declaration has served as the fount of a legal apparatus that, in the words of Schaffer and Smith,

signaled to the imagined international community as a whole, to the
nation-states within that imagined community, and to individuals
and communities within those nation-states, a collective moral
commitment to just societies in which all people live lives characterized by dignity, equality, bodily inviolability, and freedom. These
instruments of the United Nations position the victims of rights
violations as potential legal claimants in the international arena.[93]

The location of such individuals as claimants in the international arena
requires a commitment on the part of international institutions to "narrati-
bility"—a commitment to provide, as Slaughter puts it, "a public international
space that empowers all human beings to speak."[94] The blossoming of such a
commitment in the wake of the creation of the Declaration has served to push
human rights beyond both the bounds of the rarefied vernaculars of law and
beyond the authority of the political and legal elites who frequently control
such vernaculars. In short, the mandate to make good on the Declaration's
moral commitment to "all people" has arguably necessitated a shift in the
discourse of international law toward a more perceptible entanglement with
the "moral, aesthetic, and ethical aspects of culture."[95] A functionalist in the
spirit of Durkheim would, of course, assert that all legal systems ultimately
partake of such entanglements—that modern law's very claim to operate
independently of deep-seated moral and aesthetic sensibilities is itself a type
of fiction.[96] The Declaration—endeavoring as it does to afford humans, in
all their variety of "micronarratives and different language games," a central
position within the discourse and practice of law and, moreover, endeavoring
to do so without recourse to coercive measures—has merely served to bring
this constitutive extrajudicial logic of law into greater clarity.[97]

    None of this, however, is to deny that, even as the Declaration's concep-
tion of the legal personality potentially serves to push law farther into the
extrajudicial realms of moral, aesthetic, and ethical aspects of culture, this
item also epitomizes the Commission's deep-seated faith in the power of preexisting legal mechanisms to protect human dignity. There is good reason
for this enduring emphasis upon conventional legal mechanisms even in the
face of the Declaration's extrajudicial orientation: one of the key lessons of
the Holocaust to observers in the 1940s was that it was the Reich's depriva-
tion of access to the practical mechanisms of law that had served as its primary means for the disempowerment and even annihilation of large swaths
of Europe's population. The Commission's efforts to enshrine human dignity

at the heart of the burgeoning international legal landscape thus endeavors to strike a delicate balance between, on the one hand, members' general suspicion of state power and, on the other, their commitment to bolstering—indeed, universalizing—the real world legal protections offered by many preexisting political systems. The legal personality furnishes an enduring point of reference for the Commission's navigation of this terrain between the ideal of inherent human dignity and the reality of political life in the postwar era. The legal personality pointedly reaffirms the hegemony of domestic and international legal mechanisms even as it aspires to recalibrate humankind's understanding of the foundations and the telos of such mechanisms.

Ironically, this faith evinced by Commission members in the capacity of the universalization of the rule of law not merely to ensure the protection of human dignity but to aid in the transformation of humanity's political consciousness belies a lacuna within the framers' depiction of the rule of law—a blind spot that is reminiscent of their broader "Durkheimian" neglect of matters of power and coercion. After all, the juridicalization of justice to which the Declaration aspires can be both a positive and a negative development, as Foucault would remind us. The anchoring of the human dignity within the realm of law—precisely the purpose of the legal personality—does not merely serve as a means of granting justice seekers of all sorts access to the protections and remedies of law; it can just as readily serve as a means of *constraining* these same justice seekers into "objects of law and law-abiding citizens."[98] That the framers of the Declaration were ultimately inattentive to this subtle disciplinary logic of the legal personality—to the way in which, for instance, it might inspire the propagation of a human rights regime that "imposes a closure on the otherwise infinite possibilities of our justice-seeking practices"—is unsurprising given their presumption of the intimate connection between the sacralization of human dignity and the universalization of law.[99] Indeed, as this chapter has shown, the negotiations and speeches of the Commission largely rest upon a presumption that law is, to invoke Freud, essentially *heimlich*: "friendly" toward humans and naturally conducive to our wellbeing—that law functions, to paraphrase Durkheim, to "express, protect, and guarantee" the moral sentiments that elevate us above our individual limitations and bring us into solidarity with others.[100] The Commission's commitment to translating human dignity into public practice in the form of an innate "juridical essence," and their profound optimism about law's capacity to serve as a means of humanizing the uncharted international landscape of the postwar era, contribute to a striking blindness to the dangers of tying the Declaration's posit of inherent dignity so irrevocably to the matrix of law.[101]

Yet, notwithstanding the manner in which the notion of the legal personality runs the risk of "restrict[ing] the essence of man—of his freedom—to a legal entitlement," an exploration of the Declaration's Durkheimian orientation allows us to discern why the Commission could hardly have had it any other way.[102] In its effort to cash out inherent human dignity in the currency of law, and in the spirit of the Commission's broadly shared optimism that legal orderliness presents a crucial path to human well-being, the Declaration definitively binds together inherent human dignity and legal orderliness. Within the logic of the Declaration, the rule of law is singled out as the preeminent institutional expression and guarantor of human rights and the human dignity at their center. All that remains is for this legal principle to be universalized, which, of course, is precisely what the Declaration aspires to do over the course of its thirty articles.

While the prominence of the Declaration's legal language may appear to institute a decidedly contradictory interplay between, on the one hand, the regulatory logic of law and, on the other, the evocative, utopian posits of inherent dignity and the human family, Durkheim's moralistic approach to law allows us to perceive these different logics not as contradictions but as points on a continuum—a continuum between the relatively diffuse values and sentiments inspired by the sacred and the more organized regulations designed to externalize and protect items imbued with such a sacred status. "Law," Cotterrell synopsizes, "is a particular way in which the sanctioning of moral rules may be carried out," thus differing only in degree from the more evanescent moral proclivities of a given community.[103] Durkheim's approach to law provides an invaluable lens through which to make sense of the manner in which the Declaration's legal language aspires to do more than just enumerate "minimal conditions for a dignified life"—though it certainly does this. Ultimately, this legal language works in tandem with the ethos of the human family to transform inherent human dignity from a sacred item into a political reality.

Conclusion. Making and Unmaking Myth

Tony Evans distinguishes between three overlapping discourses at the heart of the modern human rights project: a "philosophical" discourse oriented toward the interrogation of human rights' foundations, a "legal" discourse oriented toward the juridical logic and external application of human rights laws, and a "political" discourse oriented toward a navigation of matters of power, hegemony, and interest.[1] The history of the negotiation and broadcast of the Declaration, of course, reveals the impossibility of neatly distinguishing these discourses; the Commission's efforts and concerns spanned indiscriminately across these various logics. However, in the years following the creation of the Declaration, asserts Evans, the "legal" discourse has assumed a dominant role in human rights meaning making.[2] The ascendency of the legal discourse in the wake of the Declaration is the product of a variety of factors, but one factor in particular bears mentioning here: by their very natures, the philosophical and political discourses of human rights push against each other, the political discourse calling attention to the very contingencies of power and history that serve to undermine the possibility of philosophical consensus on human rights, and the philosophical discourse appearing to mire human rights in a realm disconnected from political realities. The result over the long term has been a tendency among human rights proponents to shy away from both of these discourses—to treat the political "with suspicion" and the philosophical as pragmatically "settled" for the purposes of human rights advocacy (at least among "all rational nations").[3]

Intentionally or not, however, this neglect of human rights' philosophical and political dynamics has contributed to the rise of a relatively anemic body of human rights theory in the wake of the creation of the Declaration. Because the legal discourse tends to rivet human rights activism to questions of "compliance," to engender a substitution "of legal norms for human rights norms," and to vaunt legal discourse as "the sole source of truth-claims for the global human rights regime," the ascendency of this discourse has resulted in a lack of theoretical clarity on some of human rights' most fundamental philosophical and political characteristics, ultimately miring human rights scholarship in what Adamantia Pollis has called "a preparadigmatic state."[4] There is no shortage of scholars content to leave human rights' more philosophical and political dynamics alone, but Pollis is one among a growing body of human rights theorists who have asserted that that we must reckon with such dynamics before we can make good on more practical matters of compliance and truth. As Hajjar puts it in a similar vein, "While there could be no unifying 'theory of human rights' any more than there could be a 'theory of law,' there is a compelling need to develop and refine intellectual resources to understand and explain, to support and/or to criticize the transforming impact of international law on the global order."[5]

The intent of this book has been to propose that the sociofunctionalist formulation of myth provides a novel and promising means of engaging certain of the underlying philosophical and political dynamics of human rights and, in so doing, of enhancing our understanding of human rights' unique impact upon today's global order. The history of the framing and broadcast of the Declaration reveals that this document was intended to do more than enumerate fundamental rights, and to do more than lay the groundwork for a new international legal regime: it was intended to do the considerably more affective work of "building a set of expectations about how the new world order would operate."[6] As Roosevelt put it in 1948, the Declaration was intended to serve as "a compass" for the global community: "an instrument for determining the direction in which we are going" as we undertake "the difficult job of living together in international harmony while giving the other fellow his due."[7] This work of building expectations and facilitating communal life—work consisting not merely of the rejuvenation of international orderliness but also the generation and entrenchment of particular moral sensibilities—cannot be understood merely in terms of law and compliance; this work is fundamentally affective and, ultimately, extrajudicial. Such work draws upon and appeals to social, aesthetic, and religious logics. Contemporary scholarship on religion affords a series of invaluable insights into this complex territory.

Yet, to bring religious studies scholarship to bear on the Declaration is not to imply that the Declaration has betrayed the secular mandate that was clearly so important to its framers; rather, the religious logic of the Declaration must be understood as something more subtle, more elusive, than mere "idolatry"—more subtle than a simple case of, in Ignatieff's words, "humanism worshipping itself."[8] The sociofunctionalist approach allows us to locate the religious logic of this document not within the realm of metaphysics or transcendent meaning, but rather within the "ordinary" dynamics of the Commission's endeavor to generate a global moral community united in its ardent, multifaceted commitment to human dignity.

Interestingly, one of the insights afforded by scholarship on religion and myth involves the manner in which the contemporary ascendency of the "legal" discourse over the philosophical and the political discourses might be appreciated as evidence of the Declaration's success as a mythopoeic narrative. The juridicalization of human rights language, after all, poses advantages as well as potential disadvantages: it lends to human rights advocacy that brand of clarity that is the particular purview of law, and it offers something close to a universal language of justice seeking. In this respect, the ascendency of this legal discourse might well be understood as a fulfillment of one of the key aspirations of the Commission on Human Rights: namely, the aspiration to imbue the Declaration with a powerful logic by which inherent dignity could become concretized, codified, and put into practice around the globe—to ingrain the preeminence of the individual "within the public morality of world politics."[9] Approached from this perspective, we might pause to appreciate the possibility that today's neglect of human rights' philosophical and political vagaries serves as an index of human rights' *success* in having achieved the kind of sociopolitical entrenchment that makes it possible to downplay questions of foundations and power in the first place. Such sociopolitical entrenchment is, as we have seen, one of the preeminent aims of mythopoeic narratives.

This process whereby human rights have come to command a traction that by almost all accounts spans the globe has been neither straightforward nor inevitable. In his sweeping retelling of the history of the contemporary ascendency of human rights, Samuel Moyn puts the lie to the fairly prevalent notion that the Declaration was a direct progenitor of the global political consciousness that its framers worked so hard to inspire. Far from such a direct link, and following years of stagnation, today's human rights consciousness arose in the 1970s only after the rise and fall of various alternative postwar "universalistic schemes."[10] By this account, the palpable euphoria exhibited by delegates, Commission members, and press in the immediate aftermath of the adoption of the Declaration was less a harbinger of a significant moral and legal transformation than it was an ephemeral moment of "diplomatic consensus" among a cadre of elites claiming to speak for the world at large.[11] The myriad speeches, pamphlets, and other publications describing the Declaration's genesis and human rights' broad promise for human flourishing were, until their reappropriation by contemporary advocates and scholars, mere words shouted into the prevailing winds of the Cold War and the anti-colonial movements of the second half of the twentieth century.[12]

Such realities, crucial as they are, ironically bear only indirectly upon the question of the mythopoeic nature of the Declaration. The mythopoeic, as we have seen, refers to the logic of myth's production—the work of generating and propagating a particular narrative, potentially irrespective of the question of the reception of the narrative by its intended audience. The proclamations of prominent Commission members such as Roosevelt, Malik, Cassin, and Chang disclose their prolonged efforts to imbue the Declaration with the logic of innateness and inevitability that are hallmarks of myth, and in this respect there is little question that they were involved in a mythopoeic endeavor. This is the case even as they themselves declined to invoke the language of myth, and it might even be the case if they were ultimately unsuccessful in convincing their audience of the innateness and inevitability of the Declaration's basic tenets. The fact that these tenets *have* come over time—through the efforts of Commission members as well as a host of subsequent human rights advocates—to take on a cast of innateness and inevitability is problematic for the many reasons highlighted by Moyn, but it is worth considering the manner in which these very characteristics are also an indication of the Commission's *success* in, literally, creating a document of mythic proportions. If this transition from the mythopoeic to the mythic was ultimately accomplished at the hands of a much broader community of human rights advocates than those involved in the initial work of framing the Declaration, it does not change the nature of the Commission's own concerted efforts to make the contingencies of universal human rights appear eternal.

There is much evidence to support the idea that the Declaration has in fact achieved a mythic status in today's world, even if this status was not born immediately out of the efforts of the Commission on Human Rights. Its authority and its basic values have permeated domestic and international legal landscapes to the extent that almost no states remain in the world that are willing to contest the fundamental legitimacy of human rights.[13] Even as he acknowledges the "fits and starts" of the ascendency of human rights in the wake of the Declaration, Paul Gordon Lauren emphasizes that

> Never before in history has there been what is now widely described
> as a "universal culture of human rights" in which the rights of so
> many men, women, and children are given so much attention in

so many diverse places under the watchful eyes of the world and in which human rights is described as "the common language of humanity." Never before has the percentage of people living with freedom been higher. Never before in history have so many women been able to move into the public sphere as citizens, students, workers, and elected officials of have others far beyond their borders monitor the protection of their rights. Never before in history have human rights been such a part of the political, legal, and moral landscape, or played such an important role in world affairs.[14]

The contemporary ascendency of this human rights culture is emphatically not simply a product of the growth of human rights' (still relatively scarce) mechanisms of enforcement; it is in large measure a product of human rights' victory on what Moyn calls "the terrain of the imagination."[15] The Declaration has played an indispensable role in advocates' battles within this terrain, even if this role was not as direct and immediate as the framers themselves projected. In its claim to have channeled the horrors of World War II into a reaffirmation of human dignity, equality, and legal empowerment, the Declaration erects itself as the fulcrum of a global transition from barbarism to the rule of law. In its claim to "floa[t] above all local and regional contingencies," a claim made both necessary and possible by the Commission's resolution to create a nonbinding document, the Declaration vaunts itself as the embodiment of an unprecedented global consensus of values.[16] Moyn calls out his fellow historians for their role in furthering the current widespread perception—held both within and outside the academy—of human rights as "a cause both age-old and obvious."[17] He correctly identifies this phenomenon as "mythic," though he utilizes this term in the pejorative sense of an indictment of the role that theorists of human rights have played in stifling an awareness of human rights' contingency and in downplaying critical appraisals of their continued persuasiveness.[18] As this book has shown, however, the mythic qualities that render human rights so resistant to critical examination today are the very qualities that Commission members, faced with no prospects for coercing humans into an embrace of human rights, worked to engender in the course of their creation of the Declaration.

Moyn's critique highlights the manner in which an appreciation of the Declaration's mythopoeic logic ultimately cannot be separated from certain questions of methodology in the study of religion. Outside of the academic study of religion, the label of "myth" tends to imply that a narrative thus designated is false, deceptive, or, at the very least, outdated. That human rights advocates would seek to avoid implicating the Declaration with such a label is obvious. The sociofunctionalist approach, however, reorients us to the nature of myth. In doing so, this approach also has the potential to reorient us to the broader phenomenon of human rights' unique authority within the contemporary world. The sociofunctionalist framework of myth allows us to perceive the manner in which the Declaration, like all mythopoeic narratives, endeavors to "present" a series of tenets—to posit its authors' claims such that they broker minimal argument and no equivocation. In the face of the specific horrors of World War II and the broader uncertainties of the international legal landscape of the mid-twentieth century, the Declaration's creators endeavored to do much more than delineate particular rights: they endeavored to narrate into existence "a domain of social belief and procedures."[19] In keeping with the tautological quality that theorists of religion regularly attribute to myth, this domain to which the Commission aspired simultaneously derives from and gives rise to the sacredness of the human individual.

To appreciate the mythopoeic nature of the Declaration is not, however, to ignore the very real political work that went into the creation of this document. Far from pushing us to take the Commission at their decidedly effusive words that the Declaration is ultimately nothing more nor less than the consolidation of humankind's shared values, the sociofunctionalist approach to myth gestures emphatically toward the particular actors, agendas, and histories in the background of such narratives—toward the very actors, agendas, and histories that myths often so effectively hide. This approach, in other words, pushes us toward the work of *un*making the myth in human rights just as surely as it pushes us toward the work of appreciating this myth. As it pushes us toward an appreciation and even an embrace of the Declaration's location on the terrain of the imagination, this exploration of the Declaration's mythopoeic logic thus also remains in keeping with Moyn's own endeavor to reinstill the study of human rights with an attentiveness toward the political dynamics that tend to go missing in many of today's analyses of human rights.

This attentiveness to the manner in which today's human rights discourses are marked by an effacement of many of human rights' underlying political efforts and accidents represents an important step in human rights scholarship. Moyn's historical retelling is one example of this brand of more critical appraisal of contemporary human rights, but this critical questioning of human rights is not a novel enterprise; Arendt was undertaking a deconstruction of the narrative of human rights even as members of the Commission on Human Rights worked to broadcast their narrative of human dignity and global consensus in the immediate aftermath of the creation of the Declaration. Far from undermining the legitimacy of human rights, this brand of critical appraisal represents a crucial facet of what Derrida calls human rights "perfectibility."[20] Toward the end of his life, Derrida offered the important reminder that, while we have come to "need" human rights as a guarantor of justice and orderliness in the world, human rights themselves are also "in need":

> there is always a lack, a shortfall, a falling short, an insufficiency; human rights are never sufficient. Which alone suffices to remind us that they are not natural. They have a history—one that is recent, complex, and unfinished. From the French Revolution and the first Declaration right up through the declaration following World War II, human rights have been continually enriched, refined, clarified, and defined (women's rights, children's rights, the right to work, rights to education, human rights beyond "human rights and citizens' rights," and so on). To take this historicity and this perfectibility into account in an affirmative way we must never prohibit the most radical questioning possible of all the concepts at work here: the humanity of ma[n,] the very concept of rights or of law (*droit*), and even the concept of history.[21]

The sociofunctionalist conception of myth furnishes a valuable tool for an affirmative questioning of the sort prescribed by Moyn and Derrida. This framework of analysis allows for a serious consideration of the Commission's endeavors to efface human rights' contingency while nevertheless refusing to label these framers as naïve or hypocritical. It allows for a recognition of the Declaration's fabulous—fable-like—qualities while refusing to imagine that such qualities compromise the legitimacy or the truth of this document. It allows for an appreciation of the manner in which the Declaration was designed to, and continues to, operate in significant measure upon the terrain of the imagination—a terrain within which even the most glaring tautologies can be significant "if society is willing to accept them."[22]

Ultimately, to claim that the Declaration has made a transition from the mythopoeic to the mythic—that is, that it has attained some semblance of the uncontestable status with which its framers so clearly endeavored to imbue it—is by no means tantamount to a claim that human rights themselves are uncontestable. The debate over human rights' various strengths and weaknesses has blossomed in tandem with their increasing global hegemony, and in tandem with theorists' increasingly nuanced awareness of the many ways in which human rights can fail in their promise of universalism. The claim that the tenets and the rights laid out in the Declaration are west-centric— imperialistic in their pretension to represent a set of values shared by all peoples—is merely one of a range of critiques leveled in this spirit.

We witnessed in Chapter 3 that an understanding of the Declaration's logic of sacredness reveals flaws in the charge that this document essentially reiterates the Enlightenment era tenets of the French Declaration of the Rights of Man and the American Declaration of Independence. While the notion of human dignity unquestionably partakes of a history that stretches back into the philosophical and political orientations of the European Enlightenment, the Commission's setting apart of dignity as both an index of individual human worth and as an empty "concept" yet to be substantiated should give us pause in presuming a simple ideological connection between human dignity and the philosophy of the Enlightenment. Far from revealing a political or philosophical investment on the part of the framers in an Enlightenment notion of the unencumbered self, the sacralization of human dignity functioned in the service of untethering the human simultaneously from citizenship (a source of human oppression) and from the supernatural (a source of interminable disagreement). While an appreciation of the Declaration's mythopoeic logic can by no means settle the debate over human rights' "western" predilections, it furnishes the field of human rights theory with yet another useful vantage point from which to complicate oversimplified charges of cultural imperialism.

The framework of myth allows us to achieve some purchase on, if not a resolution of, a series of additional contestations over today's human rights values. One such contestation involves the question of the "aesthetics" of the human rights values enshrined within the Declaration.[23] The history of the negotiation and drafting of this document reveals Commission members' endeavors to capture the particular rights but also the broad moral orientations of human rights in an evocative, accessible narrative—a narrative that draws upon the barbarous acts of the wartime period and, more subtly, upon the enduring threat of state oppression in their effort to reaffirm our inherent dignity and prescribe particular means of preserving this dignity. The Declaration's narrative of human rights was designed to operate, as we have seen, on an affective rather than a straightforwardly rational or utilitarian register. There is an abundance of evidence to indicate that the Commission's efforts to pitch the Declaration to this register have contributed to human rights' success in having "permeated the pores of all regions across the world."[24]

However, this recognition of human rights' affective logic also begs the question of whether the Declaration's particular narrative has privileged certain imaginaries of human rights at the expense of others. Asad has famously highlighted the manner in which the Declaration's notion of inherent human dignity simultaneously rests upon and propagates an aesthetic of bodily "integrity."[25] This conflation of human dignity and bodily integrity is in many ways an unsurprising product of the Declaration's narrative; is a fairly natural outgrowth of a narrative that deploys the visceral, state-on-individual atrocities of World War II and the Holocaust as the primary anchor in experience for its formulation of the tenets and the rights of the Declaration. But, as Asad and a host of subsequent critics remind us, the human rights aesthetic of bodily integrity is undergirded by "a thick account of what being human is."[26] The "human" of human rights is, to quote Martha Nussbaum in a slightly different context, "A subject possessing bodily integrity, able freely to express himself or herself, and entitled to choose for herself or himself what to believe and how to behave."[27] While not precisely an "atomized" individual such as that posited by the likes of Yew and other cultural relativists, the "human" of the Declaration is unquestionably an individual pitched in a battle with states and other groups for the right to be left in peace to cultivate the social life most conducive to his or her existential and social flourishing.

Such an account of the human may or may not be desirable, but Asad's point is that it leads to very particular presumptions about how to foster human rights in the world. In the first place, it predisposes us to view only certain things as obstacles to the enjoyment of human rights (torture, for example), while remaining blind to phenomena that may inhibit human flourishing without specifically targeting the capacities outlined by Nussbaum. Asad identifies legal manipulations of the market as a prime example of an impediment to human flourishing that nevertheless sits uncomfortably within the Declaration's narrative of barbarism and rectification.[28] In the course of raising this critique, Asad highlights an additional implication of the particular "aesthetic" of the human enshrined within today's human rights discourse:

As a view of human nature it follows that where these capabilities are not being exercised due to their obstacles, their removal will allow humans either to exercise them spontaneously . . . or to freely choose not to do so. However, humans will have to be taught what *good* capabilities are and how to exercise them, and to be prevented from exercising vices that harm others. After all, humans are also capable of cruelty, greed, arrogance, treachery—indeed, there is scarcely anything they are *not* capable of.[29]

Who assumes the responsibility for teaching and reinforcing the exercise of good capabilities in the event that they don't arise spontaneously? Practically speaking, it is the state—a fact that pulls us immediately back into the problem, raised in Chapter 4, of the way in which the Declaration's narrative not only neglects but may actually occlude important matters of power. Asad is not alone in viewing human rights' hidden power dynamics as leading almost inevitably to a collapse of human rights norms into the "norms" of the nations that happen to be powerful enough to wield political authority within the international arena.[30]

Commission members, for their part, were quite clearly inattentive to this subtle collusion between the Declaration's particular aesthetic of human rights and the disciplinary matrices of powerful states. While certain Commission members unquestionably subscribed to the notion that a liberal democratic political system was the optimal system by which to make good on the Declaration's promise of universal access to the rule of law, and while they clearly embraced the possibility that individuals could be propelled into empathic behavior by a Durkheimian "radiation of mental energy" conveyed within particular social imaginaries, the subtle disciplinary logic that Asad discerns within the human rights narrative largely eluded them. An appreciation of human rights' mythopoeic logic does not resolve this matter, but it does highlight the manner in which the tenets and prescriptions of the Declaration are indeed embedded within a particular, affective narrative of human oppression and empowerment—a narrative that potentially "affirm[s] the universality of particular contents of human rights" while it "suppresses or *mis*-recognize[s] others."[31] As Asad has intimated, an attentiveness to such dynamics represents a crucial feature of a thorough understanding of human rights' strengths and weaknesses. The study of myth, attuned as it is to the dynamics of producing and propagating authoritative, affective narratives designed to efface their own contingency, offers a valuable supplement to Asad's and others' explorations of the aesthetics of human rights.

The possibility that the narrative at the heart of the Declaration encompasses only certain modes of human suffering and empowerment while neglecting others is, of course, a significant indictment of the universalism of this document. Such an indictment, however, can also be turned on its head, compelling us to ask whether the Declaration's narrative offers anything close to the substance capable of inspiring individuals to embrace its tenets, its moral orientation, and its strictures. In other words, given the fact that all individuals have preexisting, redolent systems of meaning to appeal to when navigating ethical, social, and political questions, is the Declaration capable of competing with—and, when necessary, superseding—preexisting values that potentially conflict with it?

Julie Owen has posed this question in the context of inquiring whether human rights can effectively function as a civil religion, and her prognosis is not optimistic.[32] She is far from the only commentator to have evinced skepticism about the capacity of human rights to command allegiance in the face of the more robust localized worldviews that the Declaration claims, ironically, to have consolidated within its narrative. This skepticism regarding what Carozza calls the "normative thinness" of human rights does not merely point to the uncertain fate of the Declaration when in direct competition with alternative narratives, it points to the larger question of whether this document can ultimately make good on its secular claim to mediate powerful, conflicting practices of the self that are so often derivative of differences in class, gender, and religion.[33]

The Commission's broader narrative of the universalism of the Declaration—intrinsic to the wording of this document but more overtly voiced in the course of framers' speeches and other broadcasts—does not merely ignore but actively obscures the fact that the Declaration's capacity to mediate differences depends upon its audience's willingness not merely to "plug in" their preexisting values to the narrative of universal human rights but to *prioritize* the principle of human rights itself. As Michael Freeman puts it, much human rights discourse ignores "the question as to whether the priority that human rights discourse gives to human rights over other values is itself a universally valid value."[34] This de facto commitment to the priority of human rights values has the potential to entail a considerably more jarring shift in sensibility than the "familiar" languages of human dignity and human family let on. As we witnessed in Chapter 3, the efforts the Commission made to imbue the Declaration's tenets with their always-already-given quality were the very efforts that were simultaneously designed to obscure the potential radicalism of the "conversion" demanded of its audience. Lefebvre engages this logic of conversion in terms of the ethical reorientation it demands, but human rights' logic of conversion also potentially entails a heavy dose of political coercion, as the likes of Piotr Hoffman and Saba Mahmood have pointed out.[35]

What is more, in the event that the Declaration's audience does prove willing to embrace the authoritativeness and self-evidence of this document's central tenets, these tenets in themselves contain no mechanisms for ensuring that they will not be infused with content that is antithetical to the broader spirit of the Declaration. Elsewhere, I have explored the manner in which key human rights tenets such as dignity and human family are amenable to decidedly "illiberal" iterations, and that the possibility of such alternative iterations should inform our understanding not only of these illiberal formulations themselves but also our understanding of human rights.[36] The focus of my inquiry, Sayyid Qutb, was an early, influential proponent of a militant form of Islamism who repeatedly deployed rhetorics of human dignity and brotherhood to justify the forceful spread of Islam throughout the Middle East and, by extension, throughout the world. Although Qutb did not level charges directly at the human rights community, his articulation of human dignity was formulated in direct contradiction to the universalist, "inherent" vision of dignity enshrined within the Declaration.

Human dignity as Qutb understood it is manifested in the capacity to make a "free moral choice"—the definitive capacity that distinguishes humans from other animals.[37] His militant brand of Islam was oriented in part toward the deployment of violence as a mechanism for the creation of contexts within which such a free moral choice could be made. Given Qutb's presumption that free moral choice will always lead to the choice to embrace Islam, the contexts Qutb envisioned were decidedly contrary to the spirit of the Declaration. To assert in the face of such an understanding of human dignity that, to be universal, dignity must be *inherent* is to ignore two interrelated features of Qutb's formulation. In the first place, the very idea of dignity's inherence is potentially an affront to a conception of dignity that rests upon choice rather than upon biology. In the second place, given the fact that the capacity for free moral choice as Qutb understood it is also universal, the Declaration's conception of dignity is arguably not the only universal vision of human dignity available to advocates wishing to make use of this term. The possibility of such opposing constructions of the Declaration's fundamental tenets is a development that the unequivocal narrative of this document, and the supporting narratives of Commission members, actively suppress.

These various points of ambiguity and contestation within today's human rights landscape lurk beneath the indubitable hegemony that the Declaration has come to command today. An appreciation of the mythopoeic logic of this document allows us to further Derrida's call for a questioning of human rights while simultaneously remaining attentive to the manner in which the Declaration was in a very real sense formulated to foreclose upon such questioning—the manner in which it was actively designed to speak with the "excessive self-assurance" that the likes of Derrida find so problematic.[38] Such self-assurance—essential to the Commission's task of bringing the broadest possible audience under the sway of the Declaration's fundamental tenets and, eventually, into alignment with the ambitious constellation of rights enumerated within its body—is a hallmark of a mythopoeic narrative. Yet this self-assurance unquestionably presents a conundrum for those seeking to imbue today's human rights discourse with an orientation toward critical self-reflexivity.

While the sociofunctionalist framework of myth cannot resolve this conundrum, it can attune us to the manner in which the global moral authority of human rights is tied, perhaps irrevocably, to a deliberate effort to sidestep the critical impulse that is such a defining characteristic of the late twentieth and early twenty-first centuries. As Stephen K. White puts it,

> One way in which late modernity is often characterized is as a time in which the fundamental notions of Western modernity have lost their self-certainty. In the emerging discourse of globalization, the idea of the nation state, for example, is rendered problematic in a number of ways. But there is at least one set of fundamentals that seems to be bucking this trend. Here I mean the idea of human rights, with something like an image of humanity hovering somehow behind, under, or beyond it. It is as if our ethical-political hopes and practices are increasingly attracted, by the implicitly gravitational force of our own language use, to this anchorage precisely as other fundaments lose their holding capacity.[39]

White does not attribute human rights' peculiar authority to the work of myth, but today's scholarship on religion invites precisely such a conclusion. The negotiations and subsequent activism of the Commission on Human

Rights disclose its members' efforts to secure the objective, indisputable status of human dignity and its attendant social and legal instantiations—to position it beyond questioning and thus to render it as durable, as real, as were "God," "nature," and "history" to the political projects of earlier centuries. Notwithstanding the skepticism of theorists such as Arendt, and notwithstanding the significant, enduring impediments and setbacks endemic to this project, there is broad consensus among theorists of human rights that the idea of human dignity has in fact taken on a sacred status—even if the precise definition of "sacredness" typically remains obscure. The framework of myth lends clarity to this definition, and to some of the central aspirations of the Declaration's creators, even as it encourages us to appreciate the obfuscations that have undergirded the transformation of human dignity into an anchor for our ethical-political hopes and practices.

Human rights are, in the words of Margaret Somers, "anything but natural."[40] At a seminal moment in the history of international relations, universal human rights were articulated by the creators of the Declaration to push deliberately against two venerable (and, arguably, much more intuitive) human tendencies: the tendency to tie the right to have rights to one's membership within a particular political community, and the tendency to hearken to the transcendent when grounding common political ideals and practices. This twofold endeavor gave rise to a document the likes of which had never before been seen: a declaration that predicates its tenets upon a secular, universal human reality that it brings into existence through no other means than by alleging to recognize this reality. Yet, for all the novelty of this maneuver, the Commission undertook its task by way of a time-honored logic whereby language is set to the task of unequivocally presenting a vision of the world and a set of attendant mandates appropriate to the maintenance of that world. As an exemplar of such logic, the Declaration is simultaneously constructed and objective—simultaneously a "pragmatic" device geared toward the production of certain results and, at the very same time, a proclamation of indisputable "truth."[41] While it is not uncommon for theorists to insist upon distinguishing these two dimensions of human rights, the framework of myth allows us to complicate any such distinction—to recognize the manner in which the Declaration is decidedly pragmatic in its endeavor to achieve a set of desired results within a particular context even as it simultaneously aspires to the status of objective truth. Indeed, as this book has demonstrated, the Declaration's practical goals could hardly have been met in any other way than through the construction and entrenchment of a powerful new human reality.

Like all myths, the Declaration was created to address the human needs of the day through the narration of a set of tenets specifically designed to forestall argument or protest. To see the myth in human rights is not to claim that the Declaration and its tenets are beyond dispute—or, conversely, that they are fraudulent. What we know today is that neither is the case. Rather, to see the myth in human rights is to recognize the unique way in which the first Commission on Human Rights executed the timeless human enterprise of endeavoring to transform a particular vision of human flourishing into an alluring, abiding mandate for belief and action.

APPENDIX. UNIVERSAL DECLARATION
OF HUMAN RIGHTS

PREAMBLE

Whereas recognition of the inherent dignity and of the equal and inalienable rights of all members of the human family is the foundation of freedom, justice and peace in the world,

Whereas disregard and contempt for human rights have resulted in barbarous acts which have outraged the conscience of mankind, and the advent of a world in which human beings shall enjoy freedom of speech and belief and freedom from fear and want has been proclaimed as the highest aspiration of the common people,

Whereas it is essential, if man is not to be compelled to have recourse, as a last resort, to rebellion against tyranny and oppression, that human rights should be protected by the rule of law,

Whereas it is essential to promote the development of friendly relations between nations,

Whereas the peoples of the United Nations have in the Charter reaffirmed their faith in fundamental human rights, in the dignity and worth of the human person and in the equal rights of men and women and have determined to promote social progress and better standards of life in larger freedom,

Whereas Member States have pledged themselves to achieve, in co-operation with the United Nations, the promotion of universal respect for and observance of human rights and fundamental freedoms,

Whereas a common understanding of these rights and freedoms is of the greatest importance for the full realization of this pledge,

Now, Therefore the General Assembly Proclaims this universal declaration of human rights as a common standard of achievement for all peoples and all nations, to the end that every individual and every organ of society, keeping this Declaration constantly in mind, shall strive by teaching and education to promote respect for these rights and freedoms and by progressive measures, national and international, to secure their universal and effective recognition and observance, both among the peoples of Member States themselves and among the peoples of territories under their jurisdiction.

ARTICLE 1
All human beings are born free and equal in dignity and rights. They are endowed with reason and conscience and should act towards one another in a spirit of brotherhood.

ARTICLE 2
Everyone is entitled to all the rights and freedoms set forth in this Declaration, without distinction of any kind, such as race, color, sex, language, religion, political or other opinion, national or social origin, property, birth or other status. Furthermore, no distinction shall be made on the basis of the political, jurisdictional or international status of the country or territory to which a person belongs, whether it be independent, trust, non-self-governing or under any other limitation of sovereignty.

ARTICLE 3
Everyone has the right to life, liberty and security of person.

ARTICLE 4
No one shall be held in slavery or servitude; slavery and the slave trade shall be prohibited in all their forms.

ARTICLE 5
No one shall be subjected to torture or to cruel, inhuman or degrading treatment or punishment.

ARTICLE 6
Everyone has the right to recognition everywhere as a person before the law.

ARTICLE 7
All are equal before the law and are entitled without any discrimination to equal protection of the law. All are entitled to equal protection against any discrimination in violation of this Declaration and against any incitement to such discrimination.

ARTICLE 8
Everyone has the right to an effective remedy by the competent national tribunals for acts violating the fundamental rights granted him by the constitution or by law.

ARTICLE 9
No one shall be subjected to arbitrary arrest, detention or exile.

ARTICLE 10

Everyone is entitled in full equality to a fair and public hearing by an independent and impartial tribunal, in the determination of his rights and obligations and of any criminal charge against him.

ARTICLE 11

(1) Everyone charged with a penal offence has the right to be presumed innocent until proved guilty according to law in a public trial at which he has had all the guarantees necessary for his defense.

(2) No one shall be held guilty of any penal offence on account of any act or omission which did not constitute a penal offence, under national or international law, at the time when it was committed. Nor shall a heavier penalty be imposed than the one that was applicable at the time the penal offence was committed.

ARTICLE 12

No one shall be subjected to arbitrary interference with his privacy, family, home or correspondence, nor to attacks upon his honor and reputation. Everyone has the right to the protection of the law against such interference or attacks.

ARTICLE 13

(1) Everyone has the right to freedom of movement and residence within the borders of each state.

(2) Everyone has the right to leave any country, including his own, and to return to his country.

ARTICLE 14

(1) Everyone has the right to seek and to enjoy in other countries asylum from persecution.

(2) This right may not be invoked in the case of prosecutions genuinely arising from non-political crimes or from acts contrary to the purposes and principles of the United Nations.

ARTICLE 15

(1) Everyone has the right to a nationality.

(2) No one shall be arbitrarily deprived of his nationality nor denied the right to change his nationality.

ARTICLE 16

(1) Men and women of full age, without any limitation due to race, nationality or religion, have the right to marry and to found a family. They are entitled to equal rights as to marriage, during marriage and at its dissolution.

(2) Marriage shall be entered into only with the free and full consent of the intending spouses.

(3) The family is the natural and fundamental group unit of society and is entitled to protection by society and the State.

ARTICLE 17
(1) Everyone has the right to own property alone as well as in association with others.
(2) No one shall be arbitrarily deprived of his property.

ARTICLE 18
Everyone has the right to freedom of thought, conscience and religion; this right includes freedom to change his religion or belief, and freedom, either alone or in community with others and in public or private, to manifest his religion or belief in teaching, practice, worship and observance.

ARTICLE 19
Everyone has the right to freedom of opinion and expression; this right includes freedom to hold opinions without interference and to seek, receive and impart information and ideas through any media and regardless of frontiers.

ARTICLE 20
(1) Everyone has the right to freedom of peaceful assembly and association.
(2) No one may be compelled to belong to an association.

ARTICLE 21
(1) Everyone has the right to take part in the government of his country, directly or through freely chosen representatives.
(2) Everyone has the right of equal access to public service in his country.
(3) The will of the people shall be the basis of the authority of government; this will shall be expressed in periodic and genuine elections which shall be by universal and equal suffrage and shall be held by secret vote or by equivalent free voting procedures.

ARTICLE 22
Everyone, as a member of society, has the right to social security and is entitled to realization, through national effort and international co-operation and in accordance with the organization and resources of each State, of the economic, social and cultural rights indispensable for his dignity and the free development of his personality.

ARTICLE 23
(1) Everyone has the right to work, to free choice of employment, to just and favorable conditions of work and to protection against unemployment.
(2) Everyone, without any discrimination, has the right to equal pay for equal work.

(3) Everyone who works has the right to just and favorable remuneration ensuring for himself and his family an existence worthy of human dignity, and supplemented, if necessary, by other means of social protection.

(4) Everyone has the right to form and to join trade unions for the protection of his interests.

ARTICLE 24

Everyone has the right to rest and leisure, including reasonable limitation of working hours and periodic holidays with pay.

ARTICLE 25

(1) Everyone has the right to a standard of living adequate for the health and well-being of himself and of his family, including food, clothing, housing and medical care and necessary social services, and the right to security in the event of unemployment, sickness, disability, widowhood, old age or other lack of livelihood in circumstances beyond his control.

(2) Motherhood and childhood are entitled to special care and assistance. All children, whether born in or out of wedlock, shall enjoy the same social protection.

ARTICLE 26

(1) Everyone has the right to education. Education shall be free, at least in the elementary and fundamental stages. Elementary education shall be compulsory. Technical and professional education shall be made generally available and higher education shall be equally accessible to all on the basis of merit.

(2) Education shall be directed to the full development of the human personality and to the strengthening of respect for human rights and fundamental freedoms. It shall promote understanding, tolerance and friendship among all nations, racial or religious groups, and shall further the activities of the United Nations for the maintenance of peace.

(3) Parents have a prior right to choose the kind of education that shall be given to their children.

ARTICLE 27

(1) Everyone has the right freely to participate in the cultural life of the community, to enjoy the arts and to share in scientific advancement and its benefits.

(2) Everyone has the right to the protection of the moral and material interests resulting from any scientific, literary or artistic production of which he is the author.

ARTICLE 28

Everyone is entitled to a social and international order in which the rights and freedoms set forth in this Declaration can be fully realized.

ARTICLE 29

(1) Everyone has duties to the community in which alone the free and full development of his personality is possible.

(2) In the exercise of his rights and freedoms, everyone shall be subject only to such limitations as are determined by law solely for the purpose of securing due recognition and respect for the rights and freedoms of others and of meeting the just requirements of morality, public order and the general welfare in a democratic society.

(3) These rights and freedoms may in no case be exercised contrary to the purposes and principles of the United Nations.

ARTICLE 30

Nothing in this Declaration may be interpreted as implying for any State, group or person any right to engage in any activity or to perform any act aimed at the destruction of any of the rights and freedoms set forth herein.

NOTES

Introduction

1. Bill Clinton, "A Message from the President," *The Universal Declaration of Human Rights at 50*, special issue, *Issues in Democracy* 3, 3 (October 1998): 6–7.

2. Ibid.

3. Although there were no dissenting votes for the adoption of the Declaration, there were eight abstentions (out of a total of fifty-six delegates). These abstentions consisted of South Africa, Saudi Arabia, and the Soviet-bloc countries of the USSR, the Ukrainian SSR, the Byelorussian SSR, the People's Federal Republic of Yugoslavia, the People's Republic of Poland, and Czechoslovakia.

4. Jack Donnelly, *Universal Human Rights in Theory and Practice* (Ithaca, N.Y.: Cornell University Press, 2003), 15–16.

5. Michael Ignatieff, *Human Rights as Politics and Idolatry*, ed. Amy Gutmann (Princeton, N.J.: Princeton University Press, 2001), 5.

6. Ibid., 7.

7. Joseph Slaughter, *Human Rights, Inc.: The World Novel, Narrative Form, and International Law* (New York: Fordham University Press, 2007), 25.

8. Ibid., 24–25.

9. Ibid., 29.

10. René Cassin, quoted in Commission on Human Rights Drafting Committee, First Session, Fifth Meeting, Summary Records (E/CN.4/AC.1/SR.5), 2; Vladimir Koretsky, quoted in Commission on Human Rights Drafting Committee, First Session, Sixth Meeting, Summary Records (E/CN.4/AC.1/SR.6), 4. Unless otherwise indicated, the UN documents cited in this book are from the years 1947 and 1948. The "E/CN.4/SR" designations refer to the numbered 1947 and 1948 sessions of the Human Rights Commission. When preceded by "AC.1," these designations refer to one of the Working Groups set up by the Commission. The "A/C.3" designations refer to the numbered meetings of the Third Session of the United Nations General Assembly, Third Committee, which took place over fall and winter 1948. The "A/PV" designations refer to the numbered meetings of the Plenary Meetings of the UN General Assembly, Third Session, that took place on 9 and 10 December, 1948. The final number in these UN document citations refer to the page number of the document being cited.

11. Mary Ann Glendon, A *World Made New: Eleanor Roosevelt and the Universal Declaration of Human Rights* (New York: Random House, 2002), 139.

12. Charles Malik, "The Drafting of the Universal Declaration of Human Rights," *UN Bulletin of Human Rights* 86, 1 (1986): 25.

13. Glendon, *A World Made New*, 86; Eleanor Roosevelt, *In Your Hands: A Guide for Community Action for the Tenth Anniversary of the Universal Declaration of Human Rights* (New York: Church Peace Union, 1958), *Milestone Documents*, accessed September 30, 2015, www.milestonedocuments.com.

14. See, for example, Ayten Gündogdu, "'Perplexities of the Rights of Man': Arendt on the Aporias of Human Rights," in *The Aporia of Rights: Explorations in Citizenship in the Era of Human Rights*, ed. Anna Yeatman and Peg Birmingham (New York: Bloomsbury, 2014); Slaughter, *Human Rights, Inc.*; Lynn Hunt, *Inventing Human Rights: A History* (New York: Norton, 2007); Alexandre Lefebvre, *Human Rights as a Way of Life: On Bergson's Political Philosophy* (Stanford, Calif.: Stanford University Press, 2013); Hans Joas, *The Sacredness of the Person: A New Genealogy of Human Rights* (Washington, D.C.: Georgetown University Press, 2013).

15. Pauline Tseng, "Beyond Myth and Reality in the Expedition to the Cosmopolitan Utopia: The Parable of Human Rights," *Non-State Actors and International Law* 2, 2 (2002): 147.

16. Ignatieff, *Human Rights as Politics and Idolatry*, xviii. Gutmann does not endorse this approach. Other prominent human rights pragmatists include John Rawls and Richard Rorty. Peg Birmingham deftly captures the logic of human rights pragmatism in *Hannah Arendt and Human Rights: The Predicament of Common Responsibility* (Bloomington: Indiana University Press, 2006), 2–3, and David Little does much the same in *Essays on Religion and Human Rights: Ground to Stand On* (Cambridge: Cambridge University Press, 2015), 25–30.

17. Ignatieff, *Human Rights as Politics and Idolatry*, 55.

18. Tseng, "Beyond Myth and Reality," 157. For a similar argument, see Rainer Forst, "The Justification of Human Rights and the Basic Right to Justification: A Reflexive Approach," *Ethics* 120, 4 (2010). See also Little, who asserts in *Essays on Religion and Human Rights* that many theorists of human rights "have not grasped or directly confronted the central purpose of human rights language or the basis on which the drafters of the UDHR believed that language to rest" (25).

19. Glendon, *A World Made New*, 239.

20. Donnelly, *Universal Human Rights in Theory and Practice*, 16.

21. Slaughter, *Human Rights, Inc.*, 25. See also Hunt, *Inventing Human Rights*.

22. Peter Fitzpatrick, *The Mythology of Modern Law* (New York: Routledge, 1992), 56. See also Jacques Derrida, "Force of Law: The 'Mystical Foundation of Authority,'" trans. Mary Quaintance, *Cardozo Law Review* 11 (1989–1990). Derrida famously wrestled with the contradiction between modern law's claim to embody the will of a given people and its ongoing implication with an "originary violence that must have established its authority and that could not itself have been authorized by any anterior legitimacy" (945). As

Fitzpatrick puts it, "law does not or cannot assume merely terrestrial dimensions. It continues to bear the characters of God. But it does this now in a mundane world" (55).

23. Simon Critchley, quoted in Beatrice Marovich, "Interview: Simon Critchley, Atheist Religious Thinker on Utopia and the Fiction of Faith," *Religion Dispatches* (August 20, 2012).

24. Derrida, "Declarations of Independence," *New Political Science* (1986): 10. All such documents, Derrida argues, are marked by an "obscurity, [an] undecidability between, let's say, a performative structure and a constative structure"—an obscurity that allows a people not only to "give birth to itself" but also to inspire subsequent generations of citizens to imagine themselves as fellow authorizers of a political vision that they were in no way actually present to authorize (10).

25. Ibid., 11.

26. Eric Michael Mazur and Kate McCarthy, eds., *God in the Details: American Religion in Popular Culture* (London: Routledge, 2011), 2.

27. Robert Bellah, *Beyond Belief: Essays on Religion in a Post-Traditional World* (Berkeley: University of California Press, 1991).

28. Bronisław Malinowski, quoted in Christopher Flood, *Political Myth* (New York: Routledge, 2002), 35. As Malinowski puts it, myths endeavor to establish "a sociological charter, or a retrospective moral pattern of behavior." Malinowski, *Myth in Primitive Psychology* (London: Souvenir Press, 1974), 89.

29. Donnelly, *Universal Human Rights in Theory and Practice*, 15.

30. Flood, for example asserts that "To state that a narrative is mythopoeic is merely to judge the properties of the discourse itself, without reference to how that discourse is received by an audience. But to be the expression of a *myth* the telling of a given narrative in any particular instance needs to be perceived as being adequately faithful to the most important facts *and* the correct interpretation of a story which a social group already accepts or subsequently comes to accept as true" (*Political Myth*, 43).

31. Clifford Geertz, *The Interpretation of Cultures: Selected Essays by Clifford Geertz* (New York: Basic, 1975), 90. Geertz is referring here not to the Declaration but to the broader logic of religion.

32. Durkheim, "Individualism and the Intellectuals," trans. Steven Lukes, *Political Studies* 17, 1 (1969): 25.

33. David Little, *For All Peoples and All Nations: The Ecumenical Church and Human Rights* (Washington, D.C.: Georgetown University Press, 2005), xi.

34. Recent treatments of this tendency to relegate "religion" to a discrete realm of human life abound, and will be discussed in the next chapter. Most often, such treatments highlight the role of the Protestant sensibilities of scholars of religion (whether or not such scholars are themselves adherents of Protestantism) in laying the groundwork for this widespread presumption that religion can be clearly delineated from other realms of human life.

35. Émile Durkheim, *Elementary Forms of Religious Life*, trans. Karen E. Fields (New York: Free Press, 1999), 429.

36. Geertz, *The Interpretation of Cultures: Selected Essays by Clifford Geertz*, 90.

37. Jonathan Z. Smith, *Imagining Religion: From Babylon to Jonestown* (Chicago: University of Chicago Press, 1988), xiii [italics omitted]. In this same text, Smith famously calls upon scholars of religion "to begin to interpret properly and appreciate *homo religiosus* as being, preeminently, *homo faber*" (89). See also Durkheim's admonishment that "Religious conceptions aim above all to express and explain not what is exceptional and abnormal but what is constant and regular. As a general rule, the gods are used far less to account for monstrosity, oddity, and anomaly than for the normal march of the universe. . . . [T]he most fundamental task of sacred beings has been to maintain the normal course of life by positive action" (Durkheim, *The Elementary Forms of Religious Life*, 26).

38. Commission on Human Rights Drafting Committee, First Session, Second Meeting, Summary Records (E/CN.4/AC.1/SR.2), 3.

39. Smith, *Imagining Religion.*, xi.

40. Ibid., xi–xii.

41. Johannes Morsink, *The Universal Declaration of Human Rights: Origins, Drafting, and Intent* (Philadelphia: University of Pennsylvania Press, 1999), 293.

42. Donnelly, *Universal Human Rights in Theory and Practice*, 15.

43. Theorists such as Jacques Derrida and Peter Fitzpatrick have asserted that the rule of law always partakes of precisely such a logic, but this will not be the focus of my argument.

44. Paul Gordon Lauren, *The Evolution of International Human Rights: Visions Seen* (Philadelphia: University of Pennsylvania Press, 2003), 239.

45. Samuel Moyn, *The Last Utopia Human Rights in History* (Cambridge, Mass.: Belknap Press of Harvard University Press, 2010), 9.

46. Ibid., 5.

47. Wendy Doniger, *The Implied Spider: Politics and Theology in Myth* (New York: Columbia University Press, 2011), 6. As Doniger puts it, "One way to define a myth is to conceptualize it on a continuum of all the narratives constructed of words . . .—all the various forms of narration of an experience" (6).

48. Ignatieff, *Human Rights as Politics and Idolatry*, 54.

49. William I. Hitchcock, "The Rise and Fall of Human Rights? Searching for a Narrative from the Cold War to the 9/11 Era," *Human Rights Quarterly* 34, 1 (February 2015): 87.

50. Glendon describes Roosevelt, Chang, and Malik as "the leadership of the Human Rights Commission throughout the entire period of the preparation of the document that became the Universal Declaration of Human Rights" (*A World Made New*, 33). Malik in particular commanded a role as spokesperson for the universal human rights propounded within the Declaration for a lengthy period of time following the Declaration's ratification. In addition to an academic career during which he lectured extensively on human rights theory and history, Malik took over the chairpersonship of the Commission on Human Rights upon Roosevelt's retirement, served as an ambassador to

the UN until 1955, and presided over the thirteenth session of the UN General Assembly in 1958.

51. Glenda Sluga, "René Cassin: Les droits de l'homme and the Universality of Human Rights, 1945–1966," in *Human Rights in the Twentieth Century*, ed. Stefan-Ludwig Hoffmann (Cambridge: Cambridge University Press, 2011), 124.

52. Many of the key framers of this document were unapologetic about couching their understanding of the Declaration's logic in overtly religious terms when speaking to specific religious communities. However, this willingness to deploy the language of religion in more sectarian settings was almost always counterbalanced with proclamations that the Declaration was ultimately compatible with any other religious idiom as well.

53. This notion of an "immanent" frame of reference refers in particular to the work of Charles Taylor. See, for example, Taylor, *A Secular Age* (Cambridge, Mass.: Belknap Press of Harvard University Press, 2007).

54. Slaughter, *Human Rights, Inc.*, 71. Jürgen Habermas describes much the same thing, though with a particular historical inflection: "In this entirely new category of rights, two elements are reunited that has first become separated in the course of the disintegration of Christian natural law, and has then developed in opposite directions. The result of this differentiation was on the one hand the internalized, rationally justified morality anchored in the individual conscience, which in Kant withdraws entirely into the transcendental domain; and on the other hand, the coercive, positive, enacted law that served absolutist rulers or the traditional assemblies of estates as an instrument for constructing the institutions of the modern state and a market society. The concept of human rights is a product of an improbable synthesis of these two elements." Habermas, "The Concept of Human Dignity and the Realistic Utopia of Human Rights," *Metaphilosophy* 41, 4 (July 2010): 470.

55. José Casanova, "The Secular, Secularizations, Secularisms," in *Rethinking Secularism*, ed. Craig Calhoun, Mark Juergensmeyer, and Jonathan VanAntwerpen (Oxford: Oxford University Press, 2011), 65.

Chapter 1. Sacred Myth, Political Myth

1. Glendon, *A World Made New*, 240–41.

2. Roosevelt, quoted in Glendon, 239.

3. Kees Bolle, "Myth: An Overview, *Encyclopedia of Religion*, ed. Lindsay Jones, 2nd ed., vol. 9 (Detroit: Macmillan Reference, 2005), 6359: "the words of myth have an extraordinary authority and are in that perceivable manner distinct from common speech. The language of myth does not induce discussion; it does not argue, but presents."

4. Roland Barthes, *Mythologies*, trans. Annette Lavers (New York: Hill and Wang, 1972), 142.

5. See, for example, Sigmund Freud, *The Future of an Illusion*, trans. and ed. James Strachey (New York: Norton, 1961).

6. See, for example, E. B. Tylor, *Primitive Culture: Researches into the Development of Mythology, Philosophy, Religion, Art, and Custom* (London: Bradbury, Evans, 1871).

7. See, for example, Rudolph Otto, *The Idea of the Holy*, trans. John W. Harvey (New York: Oxford University Press, 1958).

8. Laurie L. Patton and Wendy Doniger, "Introduction," in *Myth and Method*, ed. Patton and Doniger (Charlottesville: University Press of Virginia, 1996), 13.

9. Ibid., 4.

10. Doniger, *The Implied Spider*, xii, 2.

11. Smith, *Imagining Religion: From Babylon to Jamestown*, 89.

12. Mircea Eliade is a vocal accuser along these lines; his theorizations of religion pushed strongly against the sociofunctionalist reduction of religion to everyday social and political matters. For a phenomenologist of religion such as Eliade understood himself to be, the important thing "is to bring out the specific characteristics of the religious experience, rather than to show its numerous variations and the differences caused by history." Mircea Eliade, *The Sacred and the Profane: The Nature of Religion* (London: Harcourt, 1957), 16.

13. Talal Asad, *Genealogies of Religion: Disciplines and Reasons of Power in Christianity and Islam* (Baltimore: Johns Hopkins University Press, 1993), 14. See also Bruce Lincoln, *Holy Terrors: Thinking About Religion After September 11* (Chicago: University of Chicago Press, 2006); Brent Nongbri, *Before Religion: A History of a Modern Concept* (New Haven, Conn.: Yale University Press, 2013); and Tomoko Masuzawa, *The Invention of World Religions: Or, How European Universalism Was Preserved in the Language of Pluralism* (Chicago: University of Chicago Press, 2005).

14. There are important exceptions to the ahistoricism of religious studies scholarship—even within scholarship prior to the second half of the twentieth century. When faced with the striking variation of religious belief and practice throughout the world, theorists ranging from Tylor to Freud have proposed an evolutionary model for framing such differences. At its heart, such evolutionism owes a debt to the analyses of modernity's very first scholars of religion: Christian missionaries endeavoring to document and make sense of their encounters with the "primitive" civilizations of Africa, Asia, and the Americas. In the evolutionist approach, religions are imagined to develop from simpler to more complex systems. Not surprisingly given the ancestry of this approach, and given the Eurocentrism of the great majority of these pre-twentieth-century scholars of religion, the religion most often posited at the pinnacle of this evolutionary process is Christianity. Such evolutionism certainly contains an element of historicism, but it is a historicism with an almost Hegelian inevitability to it; nonmonotheistic religions are understood to be either on a path to monotheism or mired in a state of cultural stagnation, and the evolution of a particular religion is a process that can be understood without a foray into the political dynamics that so profoundly shape other social institutions. Needless to say, contemporary theorists of religion have endeavored to stake out a different approach from this evolutionary model.

15. Lincoln, *Holy Terrors*, 2.

16. See, for example, Asad, *Genealogies of Religion*; Lincoln, *Holy Terrors*; David Chidester, *Savage Systems: Colonialism and Comparative Religion in Southern Africa* (Charlottesville: University of Virginia Press, 1996).

17. Smith, *Imagining Religion*, xi.

18. Nongbri, *Before Religion*, 2.

19. Asad, *Genealogies of Religion*; Lincoln, *Holy Terrors*.

20. Diana Eck, *Darsan: Seeing the Divine Imagine in India* (New York: Columbia University Press, 1998); Robert Orsi, *The Madonna of 115th Street: Faith and Community in Italian Harlem, 1880–1950* (New Haven, Conn.: Yale University Press, 2010). Winnifred Fallers Sullivan offers a somewhat different exploration of this phenomenon as it relates to Christianity in *The Impossibility of Religious Freedom* (Princeton, N.J.: Princeton University Press, 2007).

21. Casanova, "The Secular, Secularizations, and Secularisms," 61.

22. To name just a few examples: Taylor, *A Secular Age*; Brad S. Gregory, *The Unintended Reformation: How a Religious Revolution Secularized* Society (Cambridge, Mass.: Belknap Press of Harvard University Press, 2012); Talal Asad, *Formations of the Secular* (Stanford, Calif.: Stanford University Press, 2003); Casanova, "The Secular, Secularizations, Secularisms."

23. Otto, *The Idea of the Holy*, 26.

24. Bruce Lincoln, *Theorizing Myth: Narrative, Ideology, and Scholarship* (Chicago: University of Chicago Press, 1999), 147 [italics omitted].

25. Smith raises the issue of the "anthropo-logic" of mythmaking in his engagement with Géza Róheim's analysis of a myth of the Tjilpa of Australia: "It is anthropology, not cosmology, that is to the fore. It is the ancestral/human alteration of and objectification of the landscape that has transformed the undifferentiated primeval space during the Dream-time into a multitude of historical places in which the ancestors, though changed, remain accessible." Jonathan Z. Smith, *To Take Place: Toward and Theory of Ritual* (Chicago: University of Chicago Press, 1992), 11.

26. Lincoln pursues what he describes as an undeveloped line of thought in an important work by Durkheim and Marcel Mauss: "These ruminations have led me back to one extraordinary sentence in Durkheim and Mauss, which I take to have been particularly influential on both [Georges] Dumézil and Lévi-Strauss. This appears toward the end of their essay, *Primitive Classification*, where they introduced, but failed to develop, the idea that myth may be understood as taxonomy in narrative form. . . . While I would hardly insist that this formulation accounts for all myths, let along all aspects of myth, I find it terribly suggestive, and I suspect that pursuing its implications led to all that is best in Dumézil and Lévi-Strauss alike. What is more, I think it can lead us further still. Like all Durkheimian formulations, it is relatively unattuned to issues of politics and history. To give it a sharper critical edge, I would introduce an orientation more associated with cultural theorists from Antonio Gramsci to Roland Barthes, to Pierre Bourdieu. . . . Pursuing these lines of thought, I am thus inclined to argue that when a taxonomy is encoded in mythic form, the narrative packages a specific, contingent

system of discrimination in a particularly attractive and memorable form" (*Theorizing Myth*, 146–47).

27. Lincoln, *Discourse and the Construction of Society: Comparative Studies of Myth, Ritual, and Classification* (New York: Oxford University Press, 1989), 24.

28. Doniger, *The Implied Spider*, 2.

29. Flood, *Political Myth*, 38–39.

30. Ibid., 140. Plato, who repeatedly equated myth with fiction and antirationalism, nevertheless acknowledges this quality of what Philippe Lacoue-Labarthe, Jean-Luc Nancy, and Brian Holmes call "exemplarity" in Labarthe and Holmes, "The Nazi Myth," *Critical Inquiry* 16, 2 (1990): 297: "Myth is a fiction in the strong, active sense of 'fashioning,' or, as Plato says, of 'plastic art': it is, therefore, a *fictioning*, whose role is to propose, if not to *impose*, models of types, . . . types in imitation of which an individual, or a city, or an entire people, can grasp themselves or identify themselves."

31. Two seminal critical engagements with the secularization thesis include Peter Berger, "The Desecularization of the World: A Global Overview," in *The Desecularization of the World: Resurgent Religion and World Politics*, ed. Peter Berger (Ann Arbor, Mich.: Eerdmans., 1999) and José Casanova, *Public Religions in the Modern World* (Chicago: University of Chicago Press, 1994).

32. Ernst Cassirer, *The Myth of the State* (New Haven, Conn.: Yale University Press, 1974), 3. See also Max Horkheimer and Theodor Adorno's depiction of myth as a "recidivist element" in western culture in *Dialectic of Enlightenment*, trans. John Cumming (New York: Continuum, 1999), xiii.

33. Kim Dovey, *Framing Places: Mediating Power in Built Form* (London: Routledge, 1999), 30. Flood is unhesitating in his embrace of this logic: "to the extent that [a narrative] signals its teller's political values and is thus a vehicle for their potential transmission, it is marked by ideology and is therefore mythopoeic" (Flood, *Political Myth*, 43).

34. Lincoln, *Discourse and the Construction of Society*, 24.

35. Ibid., 25: "Myth is not just a coding device in which important information is conveyed, on the basis of which actors *can then* construct society. It is also a discursive act through which actors evoke the sentiment out of which a society is actively constructed."

36. Ibid., 24. Here, Lincoln hearkens directly to Geertz, *The Interpretation of Cultures*.

37. Flood ultimately insists upon what amounts to a substantive distinction between political and sacred myth (*Political Myth*, 35).

38. I have discussed this aspect of Rawls' political philosophy in an earlier work (as have many others): "John Rawls posed a question that has come to emblemize the field of contemporary liberal political philosophy: 'how is it possible that there can be a stable and just society whose free and equal citizens are deeply divided by conflicting and even incommensurable religious, philosophical, and moral doctrines?' For Rawls, and for many legal professionals, the answer to this question lies in a political system that insists on the public deliberation of core political values in a *lingua franca* 'that others, as free and equal citizen[s,] might also reasonably be expected reasonably to endorse.'

Rawls emphasized that a political system of the sort he had in mind might take a variety of forms, but he harbored little doubt that religions—comprehensive doctrines *par excellence*—will almost inevitably fail to meet the criteria of a *lingua franca* for a pluralistic society committed to freedom and equality for all of its citizens." Reinbold, "Sacred Institutions and Secular Law: The Faltering Voice of Religion in the Courtroom Debate over Same-Sex Marriage," *Journal of Church and State* 56, 2 (2014): 264.

39. Chiara Bottici and Benoît Challand, "Rethinking Political Myth: The Clash of Civilizations as a Self-Fulfilling Prophecy," *European Journal of Social Theory* 9, 3 (2006): 317.

40. Hans Blumenberg, *The Legitimacy of the Modern Age*, trans. Robert M. Wallace (Cambridge, Mass.: MIT Press, 1983), 78.

41. Ibid.

42. Examples of such "post-traditional" mythmaking abound. See, for example, Flood, *Political Myth*; Bottici and Challand, "Rethinking Political Myth"; Catherine Albanese, *Sons of the Fathers: The Civil Religion of the American Revolution* (Philadelphia: Temple University Press, 1977); Ajume Wingo, *Veil Politics in Liberal Democratic States* (Cambridge: Cambridge University Press, 2003); Leslie Dorrough Smith, *Righteous Rhetoric: Sex, Speech, and the Politics of Concerned Women of America* (Oxford: Oxford University Press, 2014).

43. Smith, *Imagining Religion*, xiii.

44. Blumenberg, *Work on Myth*, trans., Robert M. Wallace (Cambridge, Mass.: MIT Press, 1985), 43, 113.

45. Smith, *Imagining Religion*, 101.

46. Rudolf Bultmann, quoted in Robert A. Segal, "Does Myth Have a Future?" in Patton and Doniger, *Myth and Method*, 90.

47. Ibid.

48. Smith, *Imagining Religion*, 101.

49. See, for example, Durkheim, *The Elementary Forms of Religious Life*, 432.

50. Doniger, *The Implied Spider*, 3.

51. Ibid.

52. Taylor, *A Secular Age*, 3.

53. Gordon Lynch, *The Sacred in the Modern World* (Oxford: Oxford University Press, 2012), 13.

54. Stephen K. White, *Sustaining Affirmation: The Strengths of Weak Ontology in Political Theory* (Princeton, N.J.: Princeton University Press, 2000), 9.

55. Patton and Doniger, *Myth and Method*, 4.

56. Ibid.

57. White, *Sustaining Affirmation*, 9.

58. This phrase was famously coined by Jeremy Bentham in "Anarchical Fallacies; Being An Examination of The Declaration of Rights Issued During the French Revolution By Jeremy Bentham", in *The Works of Jeremy Bentham*, vol. 2, ed. John Bowring (Edinburgh: Simpkin, Marshall, 1843), 501.

59. Herman van Roijen, delegate to the Netherlands, quoted in General Assembly, Third Session, Hundred and Eightieth Plenary Meeting, Report of the Third Committee, December 9, 1948 (A/PV.180), 873.

60. Ibid., 853.

61. Commission on Human Rights Drafting Committee, First Session, Fifth Meeting, Summary Records (E/CN.4/AC.1/SR.5), 6.

62. Ibid.

Chapter 2. The Sacred Center of Human Rights

1. See, for example, Joas, *The Sacredness of the Person*, 140–72; Nicholas Wolterstorff, *Justice: Rights and Wrongs* (Princeton, N.J.: Princeton University Press, 2010); or for a more nuanced and critical version of this, Asad, *Formations of the Secular*, 127–58.

2. See, for example, Joas, *The Sacredness of the Person*, 97–139; Hunt, *Inventing Human Rights*, Slaughter, *Human Rights, Inc.*; Richard Rorty, "Human Rights, Rationality, and Sentimentality," in *Truth and Progress: Philosophical Papers* (Cambridge: Cambridge University Press, 1998).

3. The fact that the Preamble was ultimately the final portion of the Declaration composed does not alter its importance, as the painstaking negotiations over its language attest.

4. Charles Malik, "What Are Human Rights?" *The Rotarian* (August 1948): 9.

5. Derrida, "Declarations of Independence," 10; Slaughter, *Human Rights, Inc.*, 63–64.

6. Strong foundational arguments, Donnelly explains, "operate within (social, political, moral, religious) communities that are defined in part by their acceptance of, or at least openness to, particular foundational arguments. For example, all the major parties in the English Civil War took for granted that God was a central source of rights and that the Bible provided authoritative evidence for resolving political disputes. Their disagreements, violent as they ultimately became, were 'internal' disputes over who spoke for Him, when, and how, and what He desired" (Donnelly, *Universal Human Rights in Theory and Practice*, 18).

7. Slaughter, *Human Rights, Inc.*, 63–64.

8. Commission on Human Rights, Third Session, Seventy-Fifth Meeting, Summary Records (E/CN.4/SR. 75), 4–5.

9. Michael Perry, *The Idea of Human Rights: Four Inquiries* (New York: Oxford University Press, 1998), 28. Perry offers what is perhaps the most salient version of this argument, which he articulates primarily in the negative—that is, in opposition to the claim that there is a convincing secular argument to be made for the sacredness of human dignity: "it is not obvious that either a secular cosmology or cosmological agnosticism can yield the requisite conviction about how things really are. How do we get from 'the universe is (or might be) nothing but a cosmic process bereft of ultimate meaning' to 'every human being is nonetheless sacred (in the strong or objective sense)'?" (28).

10. Ibid., 15.

11. Asad, *Formations of the Secular*, 36.

12. Ibid., 31.

13. Ibid., 33.

14. Durkheim, *The Elementary Forms of Religious Life*, 44. It bears mentioning that Asad himself identified Durkheim as part of this problem that he is addressing in the above quote (Asad, *Formations of the Secular*, 30–33). While there is no question that Durkheim ventures at certain points into a more "substantial" formulation of the sacred, the key point that I am highlighting here, in conjunction with Chidester and Linenthal, is that a particular substance is not essential to Durkheim's formulation of the sacred.

15. David Chidester and Edward T. Linenthal, Introduction, in *American Sacred Space*, ed. Chidester and Linenthal (Bloomington: Indiana University Press, 2001), 5–6. For a related discussion from Jonathan Z. Smith, see Smith, *To Take Place*, 106–8.

16. Chidester and Linenthal, 6.

17. Ibid., 17.

18. Ibid. In reality, the distinction between substantial and situational theories of the sacred is often difficult to maintain. Chidester and Linenthal admit as much in their avowal that "the politics of construction and contestation has always been a subtext" even in the more substantial formulations of theorists such as Otto, Eliade, and van der Leeuw (Chidester and Linenthal, 6). Eliade's phenomenological (and decidedly apolitical) definition of the sacred as a manifestation of "reality," for example, is balanced to some extent by his attentiveness toward the ongoing within all religious traditions of devaluation and revaluation. Eliade, *Patterns in Comparative Religion*, trans. Rosemary Sheed (London: Sheed and Ward, 1958). To make things even more complicated, Durkheim and Lévi-Strauss's location within the "situational" school of thought has been contested by others. Smith, for example, locates Durkheim at the forefront of the "substantial" school of thought (Smith, *Imagining Religion*, 105–6). Agamben, for his part, accuses Lévi-Strauss of formulating a definition of the sacred that papers over human agency and sociopolitical context in favor of "by a scientific mythologeme that not only explains nothing but is itself in need of explanation." Giorgio Agamben, *Homo Sacer: Sovereign Power and Bare Life*, trans., David Heller-Roazen (Stanford, Calif.: Stanford University Press, 1998), 80.

19. Berger, quoted in Morgan Marietta, *The Politics of Sacred Rhetoric: Absolutist Appeals and Political Persuasion* (Waco, Tex.: Baylor University Press, 2012), 11.

20. See Agamben, *Homo Sacer*, 80.

21. See, for example, Marietta, *The Politics of Sacred Rhetoric*; Lynch, *The Sacred in the Modern World*; Joas, *The Sacredness of the Person*. Indeed, Lynch calls the phenomenon of sacralization in the modern world "the crucial intellectual project of our time" (Lynch, *The Sacred in the Modern World*, 3).

22. Peter Berger and Thomas Luckmann, quoted in Marietta, *The Politics of Sacred Rhetoric*, 12.

23. Durkheim, "Individualism and the Intellectuals," trans. Steven Lukes, *Political Studies* 71, 1 (1969): 21.

24. This essay was written in the context of the Dreyfus Affair and is, as Steven Lukes states, an "expression of the views and attitudes of the *Dreyfusard* 'intellectuals.'" Lukes, introduction to "Individualism and the Intellectuals," *Political Studies* 17, 1 (1969): 15. Jane F. Collier offers a broader contextualization of Durkheim's vision of human rights: "Growing up in the aftermath of the failed social revolutions of 1848, as a time that historian Eric Hobsbawm has characterized as the 'Age of Capital,' Durkheim wanted to find a moral discourse that avoided laissez-faire capitalism's apparent celebration of amoral self-interest without reinscribing the religious moralities of the past or succumbing to Communist class warfare." Collier, "Durkheim Revisited: Human Rights as the Moral Discourse for the Postcolonial, Post-Cold War World," in *Human Rights: Concepts, Contests, and Contingencies*, ed. Austin Sarat and Thomas R. Kearns (Ann Arbor: University of Michigan Press, 2001), 63.

25. Asad, *Formations of the Secular*, 31.

26. Marietta, *The Politics of Sacred Rhetoric*, 15 [italics omitted].

27. Ibid.

28. Eliade remains a paragon of this dualistic approach to the sacred. *The Sacred and the Profane: The Nature of Religion* (London: Harcourt, 1957), 10. Durkheim has also subscribed to a (somewhat less substantive) dualism of sacred and profane: all religious, he asserted, "presuppose a classification of the real or ideal things that men conceive of into two classes—two opposite genera—that are widely designated by two distinct terms, which the words *profane* and *sacred* translate fairly well. The division of the world into two domains, one containing all that is sacred and the other all that is profane—such is the distinctive trait of religious thought" (*The Elementary Forms of Religious Life*, 34).

29. This emphasis upon the situational quality of the sacred allows us to sidestep the theoretical gymnastics of theorists (Durkheim among them, in his more speculative moments) who have attempted to describe the sacred as locked in an "ambivalent" relationship with the profane (Agamben, *Homo Sacer*, 71–80).

30. Dignity is invoked in this unequivocal way twice within the Preamble and then subsequently in Articles 1, 22, and 23.

31. Werner Hamacher, "The Right Not to Use Rights: Human Rights and the Structure of Judgments," *Political Theologies: Public Religions in a Post-Secular World*, ed. Hent de Vries and Lawrence E. Sullivan (New York: Fordham University Press, 2006), 671.

32. Michael Taussig, *Defacement: Public Secrecy and the Labor of the Negative* (Stanford, Calif.: Stanford University Press, 1999), 141. Acts of profanation and defacement, Taussig claims, do not merely spoil but also "animate the thing defaced" (3). See also Georges Bataille, *The Accursed Share: An Essay in General Economy*, trans., Robert Hurley (New York: Zone, 1988); Mary Douglas, *Purity and Danger: An Analysis of Concepts of Pollution and Taboo* (London: Routledge, 1966).

33. In "World War II and the Universal Declaration," Johannes Morsink claims that this "anchor in experience" serves as the central foundation for the Declaration. While I do not dispute Morsink's argument concerning the importance of the wartime

era—indeed, it will be central to my own discussion in this chapter—his argument does ignore the important role played by inherent human dignity within the deliberation and the logic of the Declaration. In a more recent work, Morsink has devoted much more analysis to this item, though at no point does he engage it through the lens of myth and sacralization. Morsink, *Inherent Human Rights: Philosophical Roots of the Universal Declaration* (Philadelphia: University of Pennsylvania Press, 2009).

34. Hamacher, "The Right Not to Use Rights," 671–72. Here, Hamacher quotes the French Declaration of the Rights of Man and of the Citizen, which he references as an analogue for all other modern human rights declarations, including the Universal Declaration of Human Rights.

35. The manner in which the wartime period is simultaneously foregrounded and sidelined within the Declaration has led me to argue elsewhere that the "barbarous acts" of the wartime period serve within this document as a type of cosmogony: a deployment of a particular chronology for the purpose of staking out "a retrospective moral pattern of behavior." Malinowski, *Myth in Primitive Psychology*, 89; Reinbold, "Political Myth and the Sacred Center of Human Rights: The Universal Declaration and 'Inherent Human Dignity,'" *Human Rights Review* 12, 2 (2011): 150–53. Cosmogonies are marked by the manner in which they use a momentous epoch in an (empirical or fictitious) history as a means of exemplifying desirable patterns of belief and action—as a vehicle for relating "basic notions of the origins of the reality in which [we live] to the patterns of action that [we] consider to be dependable and worthy of choice." Robin Lovin and Frank E. Reynolds, Introduction, in *Cosmogony and Ethical Order: New Essays in Comparative Ethics*, ed., Lovin and Reynolds (Chicago: University of Chicago Press, 1985), 8. While the barbarous acts of the wartime era, and the broader threat of violence toward which these acts signal, can certainly be understood to function in such a way within the Declaration, this approach runs the risk of entrenching the Commission's invocation of inherent human dignity within a utilitarian logic that is very clearly anathema to the spirit of this document.

36. Hannah Arendt, *The Origins of Totalitarianism* (Cleveland: World, 1958), 278.

37. Adolf Hitler, quoted in Morsink, "World War II and the Universal Declaration," *Human Rights Quarterly* 15, 2 (1993): 361.

38. Arendt, *The Origins of Totalitarianism*, 267.

39. Michel Foucault, "The Political Technologies of Individuals," in *Technologies of the Self: A Seminar with Michel Foucault*, ed. Luther H. Martin, Huck Gutman, and Patrick H. Hutton (Amherst: University of Massachusetts Press, 1998), 147.

40. Zygmunt Bauman, *Modernity and the Holocaust* (Ithaca, N.Y.: Cornell University Press, 1989), 91.

41. Arendt, *The Origins of Totalitarianism*, 293.

42. Agamben, *Homo Sacer*, 126.

43. Heinrich Himmler, quoted in Robert Jay Lifton, *The Nazi Doctors: Medical Killing and the Psychology of Genocide* (New York: Basic, 1986), 153.

44. Serena Parekh, *Hannah Arendt and the Challenge of Modernity: A Phenomenology of Human Rights* (New York: Routledge, 2008), 15.

45. As Parekh puts it, "Europe's inability to prevent the persecution of individuals who were not its members was essential to the success of totalitarianism. In other words, the connection between rightlessness and totalitarian annihilation is not accidental; but rather, rightlessness is the necessary precondition for totalitarian persecution" (13).

46. Agamben, *Homo Sacer*, 114.

47. Ibid., 82.

48. Ibid. "[T]he production of bare life," Agamben claims, "is the originary activity of sovereignty."

49. "Sacredness is a line of flight still present in contemporary politics, a line that is as such moving into zones increasingly vast and dark, to the point of ultimately coinciding with the biological life itself of citizens. If today there is no longer any one clear figure of the sacred man, it is perhaps because we are all virtually *hominess sacri*" (ibid., 114–15).

50. Ernst Cassirer famously explored this topic in *The Myth of the State*, though, as we witnessed in the previous chapter, his analysis rests to some extent on the problematic presumption that myth is opposed to rationalism. For a discussion of the mythopoeic logic of Nazism that does justice to the sociofunctionalist formulation of myth, see Lacoue-Labarthe, Nancy, and Holmes, "The Nazi Myth": "we wish, in the case of Nazism, to mark our suspicion and skepticism of the hasty, crude, and usually blind accusation of *irrationality*. There is, on the contrary, a *logic of fascism*. This also means that *a certain logic is fascist*, and that this logic is not wholly foreign to the general logic of rationality.... We do not say that only to underline the degree to which the standard opposition—accepted both *within* and *with respect to* Nazi ideology—of *muthos* and *logos*, while seemingly elementary, is in fact very complex; nor only to recall that, like all totalitarianisms, Nazism claimed to be based on a science.... We say it above all because it must not be forgotten that one of the essential ingredients in fascism is *emotion*, collective, mass emotion . . . and neither must it be forgotten that this emotion always joins itself to *concepts*" ("The Nazi Myth," 294).

51. Arendt, *The Origins of Totalitarianism*, 461. Arendt perceives such a tendency in all ideologies: "Ideologies are known for their scientific character: they combine the scientific approach with results of philosophical relevance and pretend to be scientific philosophy" (468). Though Arendt neither proposes nor builds upon a theory of myth in her exploration of totalitarianism, her analysis of the ideological aspects of the *Volksgemeinschaft* strongly resonates with the formulation of myth that I have articulated here (361–64).

52. This biological/racial element is, of course, more complicated than this; race itself ultimately proved malleable in the hands of Nazi policymakers (Agamben, *Homo Sacer*, 172).

53. As Agamben puts it, "Until this time, the questions 'What is French? What is German?' had constituted not a political problem but only one theme among others discusses in philosophical anthropologies. Caught in a constant work of redefinition, these questions not begin to become essentially political, to the point that, with National

Socialism, the answer to the question 'Who and what is German?' (and also, therefore, 'Who and what is not German?') coincides immediately with the highest political task. Fascism and Nazism are, above all, redefinitions of the relations between man and citizen, and become fully intelligible only when situated—no matter how paradoxical it may seem—in the biopolitical context inaugurated by national sovereignty and declarations of rights" (130).

54. Arendt, 293. As Agamben puts it, "Declarations of rights represent the originary figure of the inscription of natural life in the juridico-political order of the nation-state. The same bare life that in the ancien régime was politically neutral and belonged to God as creaturely life and in the classical world was (at least apparently) clearly distinguished as *zoe* from political life (*bios*) now fully enters the structure of the state and even becomes the earthly foundation of the state's legitimacy and sovereignty" (*Homo Sacer*, 127).

55. Parekh, *Hannah Arendt and the Challenge of Modernity*, 26. See also Birmingham, *Hannah Arendt and Human Rights*, 4–12.

56. Agamben designates the predominant blind spot of today's human rights organizations to be the failure of many such organizations to sufficiently appreciate the coimplication of humanitarianism, based upon the "sacred and inviolable rights of man," and politics (or, more specifically, political sovereignty)—a failure that engenders "a secret solidarity with the very powers [such organizations] ought to fight" (Agamben, *Homo Sacer*, 133–34). For, says Agamben, "A humanitarianism separated from politics cannot fail to reproduce the isolation of sacred life at the basis of sovereignty, and the [concentration] camp—which is to say, the pure space of exception—is the biopolitical paradigm it can't master" (134).

57. Over the course of his scholarship on the Declaration, Morsink has traced the framers' indebtedness to the particularities of the Third Reich for the formulation of the Declaration's rights. See Morsink, "World War II and the Universal Declaration" *Human Rights Quarterly* 15, 2 (1993): 357–405 and *The Universal Declaration of Human Rights*, 36–91.

58. Glendon, *A World Made New*, 9–10. See also Morsink, "World War II and the Universal Declaration," and Lauren, *The Evolution of International Human Rights*, 216.

59. Agamben, *Homo Sacer*, 142.

60. Morsink, *The Universal Declaration of Human Rights*, 290. See also Paul W. Kahn's discussion of "depoliticized individuals" in Kahn, "American Hegemony and International Law: Speaking Law to Power: Popular Sovereignty, Human Rights, and the New International Order," *Chicago Journal of International Law* (Spring 2000): 1–18.

61. Roosevelt, quoted in Glendon, *A World Made New*, 146.

62. Charles Malik, "The UN and Essential Human Rights," in *The Challenge of Human Rights: Charles Malik and the Universal Declaration*, ed. Habib C. Malik (Oxford: Charles Malik Foundation Center for Lebanese Studies, 2000), 105 [italics in original].

63. Malik, "An International Bill of Rights," in *The Challenge of Human Rights: Charles Malik and the Universal Declaration*, 58. The very idea of "the rights of man,"

Malik asserted in the course of negotiations, "means that man in his own essence has certain rights; that, therefore what we [the Commission] are going to elaborate must answer to the nature and essence of man."

64. Byelorussian delegate Leonid Kaminsky, quoted in General Assembly, Third Session, Hundred and Eighty-Second Plenary Meeting, Report of the Third Committee, December 10, 1948 (A/PV.182), 896.

65. Ibid., 896–97.

66. As Koretsky put it in an early session of the Drafting Committee, "The basic characteristics of the drafts that have been presented to the Committee was their tendency to liberate man not from persecution but from his own government, from his own people. . . . This meant putting him in opposition to his own government and to his own people." Commission on Human Rights Drafting Committee, First Session, Fifth Meeting, Summary Records (E/CN.4/AC.1/RS.5), 6.

67. Union of Soviet Socialist Republics: Draft Preamble to the International Declaration on Human Rights, Commission on Human Rights, Third Session, June 15, 1948 (E/CN.4/139). The Soviet draft preamble begins, "In accordance with the principle of respect for human rights and fundamental freedoms for all without distinction of race, sex, language, and religion, and for the dignity and worth of the human person, proclaimed by the Charter of the United Nations," and then sets itself with "the aim of guaranteeing the observation of all the said rights and freedoms, and of promoting the common progress and the improvement of the living conditions of the people and the development of friendly relations among the nations."

68. Preamble, proposed by the Committee on the Preamble, Third Session, June 15, 1948 (E/CN.4/138).

69. For a fuller discussion of the dynamics of this longstanding disagreement, see Morsink, *The Universal Declaration of Human Rights*, 21–24.

70. Commission on Human Rights Drafting Committee, First Session, Second Meeting, Summary Records (E/CN.4/AC.1/SR.2), 4.

71. Commission on Human Rights, Third Session, Forty-Eighth Meeting, Summary Records (E/CN.4/RS.48), 9.

72. See also Joas, *The Sacredness of the Person*, 69–96.

73. Glendon, *A World Made New*, 176.

74. Malik, "The UN and Essential Human Rights," 109–10.

75. As Morsink puts it, Communist delegates such as Koretsky "wanted to condemn [Hitler] even more than most of their colleagues. In one of the first meetings of the Drafting Committee, [Koretsky] pointed out 'that the United Nations must first fight the remnants of fascism. Having beaten fascism it must formulate a Bill of Rights which would prevent the rebirth of fascist systems and fascist ideology' (SR.5/p. 7). The deep animosity that exists between Marxist egalitarianism and Nazi racism led the USSR delegation to propose amendments to what became Articles 19 and 20 stating that fascists and Nazis did not have human rights to freedom [of] expression and association. When those amendments were rejected the Communists, rather than abstaining, which

was their custom, voted against these articles" (Morsink, *The Universal Declaration of Human Rights*, 23).

76. Cassin, quoted in Glendon, *A World Made New*, 176.

77. This broader argument is a mainstay of human rights pragmatists. See, for example, Ignatieff's assertion that "people from different cultures may continue to disagree about what is good, but nevertheless agree about what is inarguably, insufferably wrong" (Ignatieff, *Human Rights as Politics and Idolatry*, 56).

78. Malik, "The UN and Essential Human Rights," 109–10.

79. Roosevelt, quoted in Glendon, *A World Made New*, 146.

80. Morsink, *The Universal Declaration of Human Rights*, 320.

81. Ibid., 319 [italics added].

82. General Assembly, Third Session, Hundred and Eighty-First Plenary Meeting, Report of the Third Committee, December 10, 1948 (A/PV.181), 887.

83. Ibid.

84. Ibid.; Slaughter, *Human Rights, Inc.*, 26.

85. Christopher McCrudden enumerates three conventional modes of justifying the uniqueness of the human being, none of which capture the logic of the Declaration. McCrudden, "Human Dignity and Judicial Interpretation of Human Rights," *European Journal of International Law* 19, 4 (2008): 658.

86. Slaughter, *Human Rights, Inc.*, 26.

87. Malik, "Spiritual Implications of the Universal Declaration," in *The Challenge of Human Rights*, 134.

88. Morsink, *The Universal Declaration of Human Rights*, 281.

89. Ibid., 284. See also Little, *Essays on Religion and Human Rights: Ground to Stand On*, 35.

90. Ibid., 283. Morsink explains that, "While it is true that the natural rights philosophies of the eighteenth century presumed to have found a sound basis for a morality that was universal and at the same time secular, the secularism involved was often of a rather mixed kind where Nature and Reason—the two secular components of the triad—were still kept in close proximity to the God from which they flowed. Thinkers like Paine, Locke, Rousseau, and Jefferson regularly and interchangeably appeal to God, Nature, and Reason as the source of value. Since these thinkers did not keep the members of this triad separated, one gets the impression that for them value trickles down from the Creator-God to His Nature and Reason, which is why—contrary to our own linguistic habits—these two secular members of the triad are often capitalized in the writings of this era" (282). See also Glendon, *A World Made New*, 147; Malik, "The Drafting of the Universal Declaration of Human Rights," 20; Jack Mahoney, *The Challenge of Human Rights: Origin, Development, and Significance* (Oxford: Blackwell, 2007), 124.

91. Morsink, *The Universal Declaration of Human Rights*, 283.

92. Roosevelt, "Making Human Rights Come Alive," in *What I Hope to Leave Behind: The Essential Essays of Eleanor Roosevelt*, ed. Allida M. Black (New York: Carlson, 1995), 561.

93. McCrudden, "Human Dignity and Judicial Interpretation of Human Rights," 679–80. See also Paolo G. Carozza, "Human Dignity and Judicial Interpretation of Human Rights: A Reply," *European Journal of International Law* 19, 5 (2008): 937.

94. Asad, *Formations of the Secular*, 5.

95. Carozza, "Human Dignity and Judicial Interpretation of Human Rights: A Reply," 934.

96. Jacques Maritain, introduction to *Human Rights: Comments and Interpretations* (New York: Allan Wingate, 1949), 16.

97. Malik, "The Drafting of the Universal Declaration of Human Rights," 24.

98. Ibid. See also Malik's assertion that "previous great statements were responsive each to a particular culture or outlook or nation or revolutionary movement. The new declaration, however, is absolutely the first pronouncement in history on this topic on a universal scale. In other words, it is a kind of synthesis of all these previous insights, one to which not only western Europe and the United States contributed their wisdom, but also the Slavic world, China, India, the Near East and the Latin American world. The universal character of the declaration, in the double sense of being universal in origin and universal in intent of application, is one of its most important features" ("The Twin Scourges: Materialism, Human Self-Sufficiency," in *The Challenge of Human Rights*, 207).

99. Mahoney, *The Challenge of Human Rights*, 51.

100. René Cassin, *La pensée et l'action*, ed. François-Joachim Beer (Paris: F. Laclou, 1972), 116 [author's translation]. In the original French, Cassin states that "Il importe enfin de marquer que la laïcité de la Déclaration est en relation direct avec son universalité. Nombre de délégations dont la Constitution nationale et les institutions ont un caractère religieux ont renoncé à obtenir dans la Déclaration tout mention de la Divinité ou de l'origine divine de l'homme. . . . Cet œcuménisme de la Déclaration, à laquelle les Églises et Confessions ont donné leur adhésion solennel, sans abdiquer aucunement leurs dogmes et principes, a incontestablement exercé par la suite une très grande influence."

Chapter 3. The Sacred and the Social

1. Fareed Zakaria, "Culture Is Destiny: A Conversation with Lee Kwan," *Foreign Affairs* 73, 2 (1994): 113. See also Asad's discussion of the "self-owning human," in *Formations of the Secular*, 148–55. For a more developed example of the cultural relativist critique geared specifically toward universal human rights, see Makau Mutua, "Savages, Victims and Saviors: The Metaphor of Human Rights," *Harvard International Law Journal* 42 (2001): 201–45 and Mark Goodale, "Encountering Relativism: The Philosophy, Power, and Politics of a Dilemma," in *Surrendering to Utopia: An Anthropology of Human Rights* (Stanford, Calif.: Stanford University Press, 2009), 40–64.

2. Zakaria, ""Culture Is Destiny," 111.

3. Ibid.

4. Ibid., 112.

5. American Anthropological Association Executive Board, "Statement on Human Rights," *American Anthropologist* 49, 4 (1947): 539.

6. White, *Sustaining Affirmation*, 22.

7. Taylor, *A Secular Age*, 15.

8. Ibid., 15–20. See also Mark Lilla, *The Stillborn God: Religion, Politics, and the Modern West* (New York: Vintage, 2007).

9. Marcel Gauchet, *The Disenchantment of the World: A Political History of Religion* (Princeton, N.J.: Princeton University Press, 1997), 159. See also Emilio Gentile's description of the "sacralization of politics," *Politics as Religion*, trans. George Staunton (Princeton, N.J.: Princeton University Press, 2006), xvi.

10. John Rawls, *A Theory of Justice* (Cambridge, Mass.: Belknap Press of Harvard University Press, 1971), 11.

11. Gregory, *The Unintended Reformation*.

12. Ibid., 116.

13. Ibid.

14. Moyn, *The Last Utopia*, 20.

15. Ibid., 25.

16. Asad, *Formations of the Secular*, 137.

17. Donnelly, *Universal Human Rights in Theory and Practice*, 27.

18. As Ignatieff puts it, the human rights instruments created after 1945 were "a war-weary generation's reflection on European nihilism and its consequences. Human rights was a response to Dr. Pannwitz, to the discovery of the abomination that could occur when the Westphalian state was accorded unlimited sovereignty, when citizens of that state lacked normative grounds to disobey legal but immoral orders" (Ignatieff, *Human Rights as Politics and Idolatry*, 4).

19. Michael Hardt and Antonio Negri, *Empire* (Cambridge, Mass.: Harvard University Press, 2000), 5; Cassin, *La pensée et l'action*, 116 [author's translation].

20. Carozza, "Human Dignity and Judicial Interpretation of Human Rights: A Reply," 932.

21. Glendon, *A World Made New*, xviii.

22. Roosevelt, quoted in ibid., xix.

23. McCrudden, "Human Dignity and Judicial Interpretation of Human Rights," 675.

24. Durkheim, *The Elementary Forms of Religious Life*, 44.

25. Ibid., 34.

26. Ibid., 41.

27. Ibid.

28. Ibid., 419.

29. Ibid., 227.

30. Henri Bergson, quoted in Lefebvre, *Human Rights as a Way of Life*, 115.

31. Melanie White, "Habit as a Force of Life in Durkheim and Bergson," *Body and Society* 19, 2–3 (2013): 244.

32. Durkheim, *The Elementary Forms of Religious Life*, 44.

33. Ibid., 305. As Joas puts it, "It is a sociological truism that 'a society cannot hold together unless there exists among its members a certain intellectual and moral

community," but simply calling for such community does little to help develop it" (*The Sacredness of the Person*, 53).

34. Ibid., 209.

35. Ibid.

36. Ibid. [italics added].

37. Ibid.

38. Ibid. 210.

39. Durkheim also places a heavy emphasis upon the work of "practices" such as rituals and ceremonies in the cultivation of the moral community (ibid., 44).

40. Glendon, *A World Made New*, 227.

41. Ibid.

42. Hansa Mehta, quoted in *United Nations Yearbook of Human Rights for 1948* (New York: UN, 1950).

43. Commission on Human Rights Drafting Committee, First Session, Fifth Meeting (E/CN.4/AC.1/SR.5), 7.

44. Draft International Declaration of Rights submitted by Working Group of Drafting Committee (Preamble and Articles 1–6) (E/CN.4/AC.1/W.1).

45. Morsink, *The Universal Declaration of Human Rights*, 326–27.

46. Glendon, *A World Made New*, 228.

47. Charles Malik, "Talk on Human Rights," Speech given to the Committee on International, Political and Social Problems of the U.S. Chamber of Commerce (1949), 1–2 [italics added]. Though Malik is arguably giving only one possible reading of this clause of Article 29, his reading seems to be borne out by the second clause of this article, which states that "In the exercise of his rights and freedoms, everyone shall be subject only to such limitations as are determined by law solely for the purpose of securing due recognition and respect for the rights and freedoms of others and of meeting the just requirements of morality, public order and the general welfare in a democratic society."

48. Morsink, *Inherent Human Rights*, 148.

49. Ibid. See also Seyla Benhabib, *Dignity in Adversity: Human Rights in Troubled Times* (Malden, Mass.: Polity, 2011), 124–26.

50. Ibid., 151.

51. Lefebvre, *Human Rights as a Way of Life*, 68.

52. Ibid., 68 [italics added].

53. Ibid.

54. In advocating for a bolstering of what he calls "intermediate sources of freedom" such as family and religious groups, Malik endeavors to strike precisely such a balance between support for our preexisting modes of social life and support for inherent human dignity (Malik, "What Are Human Rights?" 10). He laments a world in which "The family is subject to terrible strain, the church is on the defensive, modern man has no friends, truth has become a matter of pragmatic convenience," and holds up the Declaration as a vehicle for the creation of "conditions which will allow man to develop

ultimate loyalties with respect to these intermediate sources of freedom, over and above his loyalty to the State."

55. Roosevelt, "Making Human Rights Come Alive," 563: "We had a very good illustration of our difficulties from a different point of view between the U.S.S.R. and ourselves. Their chief amendments were two: one was to come at the end of many articles and say 'these rights,' whatever they may be, 'are guaranteed by the state.' That was a kind of national implementation which many of us thought very unwise and so it was not accepted, but it gave the U.S.S.R. a reason for abstaining in the end because they said there was no way for the things that were written here to be guaranteed, which is completely true. There is no way. It is an educational Declaration and the only way we can guarantee that these rights will be observed is by doing a good job educationally."

56. Commission on Human Rights, Third Session, Fifth Meeting, Summary Reports (E/CN.4/SR.50), 7.

57. Ibid.

58. Roosevelt, in *Our Rights as Human Beings: A Discussion Guide on the Universal Declaration of Human Rights* (Lake Success, N.Y.: UN Department of Public Information, 1949), 16: "It must be kept in mind that many differing legal systems, social philosophies, cultural traditions, and economic concepts must be reconciled before the covenants can be finally defined, codified and organized into documents of international responsibility having binding legal effect. Public opinion . . . will determine whether these rights and freedoms as outlined in the two draft covenants and proclaimed in the Declaration are to become a reality."

59. White, *Sustaining Affirmation*, 11, 10.

60. Durkheim, *The Elementary Forms of Religious Life*, 210.

61. Durkheim, *Les formes élémentaires de la vie religieuse* (Paris: Presses Universitaires de France, 1960), 296–98.

62. Durkheim, *The Elementary Forms of Religious Life*, 210, translator's note.

63. Richard Pritchard, quoted in Morsink, *Inherent Human Rights*, 109.

64. Ibid., 110.

65. Commission on Human Rights, Third Session, Fifty-First Meeting, Summary Records (E/CN.4/SR.51), 6 [italics added].

66. Ibid.

67. Ibid.

68. Durkheim, *Moral Education* (Mineola, N.Y.: Dover, 2002), 11.

69. Commission on Human Rights Drafting Committee, First Session, Eighth Meeting, Summary Records (E/CN.4/AC.1/SR.8), 2.

70. Ibid.

71. Ibid., 2–3.

72. Roosevelt, "The Promise of Human Rights," in *What I Hope to Leave Behind: The Essential Essays of Eleanor Roosevelt*, ed. Allida M. Black (New York: Carlson, 1995), 558.

73. Roosevelt, quoted in Glendon, 239.

74. Chang, quoted in ibid.

75. Cassin, quoted in ibid., 239.

76. White, "Habit as a Force of Life in Durkheim and Bergson," 244.

77. Ibid.

78. Ibid.

79. Lefebvre, *Human Rights as a Way of Life*, 74–81.

80. Ibid., 76.

81. Roosevelt pointedly placed the onus of national conversion on the individual and intermediary group. Such entities were in her mind the primary encouragers of "local and national governments to act in the spirit of the Declaration" (*Our Rights as Human Beings*, 16).

82. Lefebvre, *Human Rights as a Way of Life*, 78–79: "A key feature of both the Declaration of the Rights of Man and the Declaration is their addressee. The first speaks to 'all members of the social body,' and the second targets 'every individual' as its recipient. It would appear, therefore, that contrary to the widespread impression that nation-states are the primary addressee of human rights documents, these declarations explicitly name another subject."

83. Commission on Human Rights, Third Session, Fiftieth Meeting, Summary Records (E/CN.4/SR.50), 10.

84. Morsink, *Inherent Human Rights*, 188.

85. Ibid., 41.

86. Ibid., 39.

87. Arendt, quoted in Birmingham, *Hannah Arendt and Human Rights*, 4.

88. Ibid.

89. See, for example, Samantha Power, *A Problem from Hell: America and the Age of Genocide* (New York: Basic, 2002).

90. In his exploration of "the metaphysics of inherence," Morsink describes the approaches of a number of such theorists (Morsink, *Inherent Human Rights*, 40–54). Moments before the final adoption of the Declaration, in fact, the Commission also adopted an Egyptian motion acknowledging the need for future elaboration on the matter of duties (41).

91. Ibid., 44.

92. Ibid., 41. "A legal right is created and maintained by actual, historical (legal) practices and systems that govern the behavior of the relevant group of people. Such social and historical practices and actual systems of positive law are the breathing space of legal rights and duties that are inextricably linked to by the rules of the system that created them. Thus, a legal right is defined in terms of the system of institutionalized rules of which it forms a part. If a human right were to be real in the only way a legal right can be said to be real, it would from day one need to be embedded in, and so be dependent on, a minimum of such institutionalized practices. In that case, the right would not be inalienable and not be inherent in the newborn human being" (48).

93. Hent de Vries, "Introduction: Before, Around, and Beyond the Theologico-Political," in de Vries and Sullivan, *Political Theologies*.

94. Lefebvre, *Human Rights as a Way of Life*, 25–26.

95. Cassin, quoted in Morsink, "World War II and the Universal Declaration," 362–63. Cassin is referring here to the "spirit of brotherhood" invoked in Article 1.

96. Parekh, *Hannah Arendt and the Challenge of Modernity*, 6.

97. Ibid., 29.

98. Hannah Arendt, *The Human Condition* (Chicago: University of Chicago Press, 1958), 22.

99. Ibid., 24.

100. Ibid., 38, 24. "The natural, merely social companionship of the human species was considered [by the ancient Greeks] to be a limitation imposed on us by the needs of biological life, which are the same for the human animal as for other forms of animal life" (24). Within the political realm, however, men could be enrolled in a fellowship that "transcended the mere togetherness imposed on all—slaves, barbarians, and Greeks alike—through the urgencies of life. The 'good life,' as Aristotle called the life of the citizen, therefore was not merely better, more carefree or nobler than ordinary life, but of an altogether different quality. It was 'good' to the extent that by having mastered the necessities of sheer life, by being freed from labor and work, and by overcoming the innate urge of all living creatures for their own survival, it was no longer bound to the biological life process" (36–37).

101. Ibid., 24.

102. Elke Schwarz, "@hannah_arendt: An Arendtian Critique of Online Social Networks," *Millennium: Journal of International Studies* 43, 1 (2014): 170.

103. Arendt, *The Human Condition*, 40: "society expects from each of its members a certain kind of behavior, imposing innumerable and various rules, all of which tend to 'normalize' its members, to make them behave, to exclude spontaneous action or outstanding achievement."

104. Ibid., 36.

105. Arendt, *The Origins of Totalitarianism*, 463.

106. Ibid.

107. Ibid., 464.

108. Ibid., 472.

109. Ibid., 470.

110. Ibid., 468.

111. Ibid.

112. Ibid., 474.

113. Ibid., 474–77.

114. Ibid., 475–76.

115. Ibid., 475–77.

116. Ibid., 451.

117. Patrick Hayden, "The Relevance of Hannah Arendt's Reflections on Evil: Globalization and Rightlessness," *Human Rights Review* 11 (2010): 455. See also Hannah Arendt, *Eichmann in Jerusalem: A Report on the Banality of Evil* (New York: Penguin, 1964).

118. Arendt, *The Origins of Totalitarianism*, 462.

119. Durkheim pointedly links the capacity for "objective" thought to our embeddedness within social life (*The Elementary Forms of Religious Life*, 433–40).

120. Arendt, *The Origins of Totalitarianism*, 78.

121. Cassin, quoted in Morsink, "World War II and the Universal Declaration," 362.

122. Roosevelt, *Our Rights as Human Beings*, 12.

123. Durkheim, "Individualism and the Intellectuals," 23.

124. Hunt, *Inventing Human Rights*, 27. Like Slaughter, Hunt locates this in the realm of the literary/cultural without making mention of the religious.

125. Durkheim, "Individualism and the Intellectuals," 23.

126. Ibid., 24.

127. Ibid., 22.

128. Commission on Human Rights Drafting Committee, First Session, Eighth Meeting, Summary Records (E/CN.4/AC.1/SR.8), 2.

129. Malik, "The Twin Scourges: Materialism, Human Self-Sufficiency," 208.

130. Lefebvre, *Human Rights as a Way of Life*, 41.

131. Ibid., 47.

132. Durkheim, *Moral Education*, 81. Durkheim ultimately rejected the "family" as an embodiment of this ideal human rights community (75–76). Morsink makes a similar claim under the auspices of what he terms "civic patriotism" (Morsink, *Inherent Human Rights*, 189–93).

133. Lefebvre, *Human Rights as a Way of Life*, 47.

134. Carl Schmitt, *The Concept of the Political*, trans. George Schwab (Chicago: University of Chicago Press, 1996), 26–30; Leo Strauss, "Notes on *The Concept of the Political*," in *The Concept of the Political*, 84–85.

135. Habermas, *The Postnational Constellation: Political Essays*, trans. Max Pensky (Cambridge, Mass.: MIT Press, 2001), 107.

136. Ibid.

137. Ibid., 107–8.

138. Ibid.: "the political culture of a world society lacks the common ethical-political dimension that would be necessary for a corresponding global community—and its identity formation." See also Habermas, "Pre-Political Foundations of the Democratic Constitutional State?" in *The Dialectics of Secularization: On Reason and Religion*, trans. Brian McNeil, C.R.V. (San Francisco: Ignatius Press, 2005), 29–34.

139. Strauss, "Notes on *The Concept of the Political*," 84.

140. Habermas, *The Postnational Constellation*, 184.

141. Lefebvre, *Human Rights as a Way of Life*, 116.

142. Ibid., 122.

143. Roosevelt, quoted in Commission on Human Rights, Second Session, Forty-First Meeting, Summary Records (E/CN.4/SR.41), 9.

Chapter 4. The Legal Personality and a New World Order

1. Malik, "The UN and Essential Human Rights," 96–97.

2. UN Charter; Malik, "The UN and Essential Human Rights," 96.

3. Durkheim typically utilized this term in reference to the community building work of religious ceremony and ritual, but it clearly resonates with the mythopoeic elements of religion as well.

4. Arendt, *The Origins of Totalitarianism*, 293.

5. Roger Cotterrell, *Emile Durkheim: Law in a Moral Domain* (Stanford, Calif.: Stanford University Press, 1999), ix.

6. Ibid.

7. Derrida is a clear example of this approach to law. See also, for example, Fitzpatrick, *The Mythology of Modern Law* and Firzpatrick, *Modernism and the Grounds of Law*, Cambridge Studies in Law and Society (Cambridge: Cambridge University Press, 2001).

8. Cotterrell, *Emile Durkheim*, x.

9. Lyotard, quoted in Fitzpatrick, *The Mythology of Modern Law*, 165.

10. Durkheim, *Division of Labor in Society*, trans. George Simpson (New York: Macmillan, 1933), 64.

11. Ibid., 32.

12. Durkheim evolved in his assessment of the secularity of law from a presumption that modern law is undergoing a process of desacralization to a presumption that law will perhaps always remain implicated with processes of sacralization (Joas, *The Sacredness of the Person*, 57–58).

13. Cotterrell, *Emile Durkheim*, 60.

14. Ibid., 60–61. It is important to realize that Durkheim does consistently frame these distinctions in terms of historical evolution. My argument, and Cotterrell's as well, is that such historicization does not represent a crucial feature of his distinction between the functions of morality and law.

15. Durkheim, *The Elementary Forms of Religious Life*, 421.

16. Durkheim, *Division of Labor in Society*, 64. Since, according to Durkheim, social solidarity is "a completely moral phenomenon[, it] does not lend itself to exact observation nor indeed to measurement." Thus, according to Durkheim, "To proceed to this classification and this comparison, we must substitute for this internal fact which escapes us an external index which symbolizes it and study the former in the light of the latter." In Durkheim's assessment, "This visible symbol is law."

17. Ibid.

18. Cotterrell, *Emile Durkheim*, 60, 58.

19. Ibid.

20. Ibid., 50.

21. Ibid. [italics added].

22. Ibid., 52.

23. Ibid.

24. Ibid. Of course, in light of Durkheim's assessment of the decline of religious sentiment and attachment in modern life, one might be tempted to imagine that law might then serve as a "replacement" for religion. Cotterrell asserts that Durkheim "never goes so far" as to make this claim (52). "What kinds of beliefs can fulfil the social function of established but declining religions in Western societies remains a difficult question. Nevertheless, religion provides an object of attachment. For Durkheim this object can only be social—found in the experience of collective life. And we have seen that law and morality are, for him, the pre-eminent expressions of this collective life—of society itself" (52).

25. Geertz, *The Interpretation of Cultures*, 90.

26. Max Weber, "Politics as a Vocation," *From Max Weber: Essays in Sociology*, ed. H. H. Gerth and C. Wright Mills (New York: Routledge, 1991).

27. See, for example, Taussig, *The Nervous System* (New York: Routledge, 1992) and *The Magic of the State* (New York: Routledge, 1997); Ivan Strenski, *Four Theories of Myth in Twentieth-Century History: Cassirer, Eliade, Lévi-Strauss and Malinowski* (London: Macmillan, 1987); Anthony Giddens, *Capitalism and Modern Social Theory: An Analysis of the Writings of Marx, Durkheim, and Max Weber* (Cambridge: Cambridge University Press, 1973).

28. Morsink, "World War II and the Universal Declaration," 375.

29. Indeed, as both Arendt and Agamben point out, the authority of the Fuhrer ultimately supersedes the sacredness of the *Volksgemeinschaft* (Arendt, *The Origins of Totalitarianism*, 364–88; Agamben, *Homo Sacer*, 166–80). Arendt seems to sense that this infringement of the integrity upon the *Volksgemeinschaft* is an integral feature of the logic of totalitarianism—a feature of the manner in which the Führer, "Being in the center of the movement . . . can act as though he were above it"—but she also repeatedly portrays this infringement as a betrayal or an act of "lying" on the part of Nazi leaders (Arendt, *The Origins of Totalitarianism*, 375, 383). Agamben's novel insights into the logic of sacralization afford him greater clarity upon the manner in which this infringement is ultimately a constitutive element of the biopolitics of the Reich. In any case, the framers of the Declaration consistently approached the Nazification of the law under the Reich as a phenomenon synonymous with the veneration of the *Volksgemeinschaft*.

30. Marcelo Neves, "The Symbolic Force of Human Rights," *Philosophy and Social Criticism* 33, 4 (2007): 417. Also see Lefort, "Democracy and Totalitarianism," in *The Political Forms of Modern Society: Bureaucracy, Democracy, Totalitarianism* (Cambridge, Mass.: MIT Press, 1986).

31. "Verbatim Record of the Thirteenth Meeting of the Drafting Committee of the Commission on Human Rights," *The Eleanor Roosevelt Papers*, vol. 1, ed. Allida Black (Charlottesville: University of Virginia Press, 2007), 572.

32. Arendt, *The Origins of Totalitarianism*, 291.

33. Ibid., 286.

34. Morsink, *Inherent Human Rights*, 148.

35. Ibid.

36. Ibid.

37. Morsink, *The Universal Declaration*, 22.

38. Roosevelt, "Making Human Rights Come Alive," 562–63.

39. See Morsink, *The Universal Declaration of Human Rights*, 44. See also Commission on Human Rights Drafting Committee, First Session, Thirteenth Meeting, Summary Records (E/CN.4/AC.1/SR.13), 12–14.

40. "Verbatim Record of the Thirteenth Meeting of the Drafting Committee of the Commission on Human Rights," *The Eleanor Roosevelt Papers*, 1: 572; Commission on Human Rights Drafting Committee, First Session, Thirteenth Meeting, Summary Records (E/CN.4/AC.1/SR.13), 14.

41. "Verbatim Record of the Thirteenth Meeting of the Drafting Committee of the Commission on Human Rights," *The Eleanor Roosevelt Papers*, 1: 570.

42. Habermas, "The Concept of Human Dignity and the Realistic Utopia of Human Rights," 470.

43. Ibid.

44. Ibid. "Human rights differ from moral rights in that the former are oriented toward institutionalization and call for a shared act of inclusive will formation, whereas morally acting persons regard one another without further mediation as subjects who are embedded from the start in a network of moral rights and duties." Habermas complicates this assertion in the course of this article, but does not disown it.

45. Davies, quoted in Morsink, *The Universal Declaration*, 311.

46. Habermas, "The Concept of Human Dignity and the Realistic Utopia of Human Rights," 469 [italics altered].

47. Arendt, *The Origins of Totalitarianism*, 296. See also Birmingham, *Hannah Arendt and Human Rights* and Parekh, *Hannah Arendt and the Challenge of Modernity*.

48. Arendt, *The Origins of Totalitarianism*, 291–92. Even worse, the main supporters of human rights in this context were charities "who no one, not even the persecuted, took seriously," or "marginal figures" (Parekh, *Hannah Arendt and the Challenge of Modernity*, 25; Arendt, *The Origins of Totalitarianism*, 292).

49. Arendt, *The Origins of Totalitarianism*, 297. See also Parekh, *Hannah Arendt and the Challenge of Modernity*, 12. It is worth noting that Seyla Benhabib has argued that Arendt does not go far enough in her advocacy—that the right to have rights amounts to a call for mere membership within a particular political community (Benhabib, *Dignity in Adversity*). I am not convinced that this reading of Arendt does justice to the depth of the connection Arendt perceives between social life and human flourishing, but, at any rate, I have shown in Chapter 3 that the framers of the Declaration unquestionably fostered a strong predilection toward preexisting social and political communities.

50. Cassin, quoted in "Verbatim Record of the Thirteenth Meeting of the Drafting Committee of the Commission on Human Rights," *The Eleanor Roosevelt Papers*, 1: 572.

51. Ibid.

52. Ibid., 572–73.

53. "World War II and the Universal Declaration," 376.

54. Parekh, *Hannah Arendt and the Challenge of Modernity*, 12.

55. Ibid., 12.

56. Arendt, quoted in ibid., 11.

57. Malik, "Spiritual Implications of Human Rights," 134–35.

58. Ibid., 135.

59. Ibid.

60. Totalitarianism, Arendt asserted, "depended less on the structurelessness of a mass society than on the specific conditions of an atomized and individualized mass" (*The Origins of Totalitarianism*, 318). See also Hayden, "The Relevance of Hannah Arendt's Reflections on Evil," 456.

61. Arendt, *The Origins of Totalitarianism*, 444: "There are no parallels to the life in the concentration camps. . . . [A]ll parallels create confusion and distract attention from what is essential. Forced labor in prisons and penal colonies, banishment, slavery, all seem for a moment to offer helpful comparisons, but on closer examination lead nowhere. . . . Forced labor as a punishment is limited as to time and intensity. The convict retains rights over his body; he is not absolutely tortured and he is not absolutely dominated. Banishment banishes only from one part of the world to another part of the world, also inhabited by human beings; it does not exclude from the human world altogether. Throughout history slavery has been an institution within a social order; slaves were not, like concentration-camp inmates, withdrawn from sight and hence the protection of their fellow-men; as instruments of labor they has a definite price and as property a definite value. The concentration-camp inmate has no price, because he has already been replaced; nobody knows to whom he belongs, because he is never seen. From the point of view of normal society he is absolutely superfluous, although in times of acute labor shortage . . . he is used for work."

62. Cassin, quoted in "Verbatim Record of the Thirteenth Meeting of the Drafting Committee of the Commission on Human Rights," *The Eleanor Roosevelt Papers*, 1: 569.

63. Morsink, *The Universal Declaration*, 43–44. Ultimately, the Commission's depiction of this logic was decidedly circular, despite its clarity on the idea that the legal personality is the key to basic human empowerment. As Cassin put it during the Thirteenth Drafting Committee Meeting, "Slavery has two principal aspects. The first aspect is the destruction of the physical liberty of man. This what we dealt with a few minutes ago in saying that slavery is inconsistent with the dignity of man. But a very important point remains, namely, that slavery is the negation of the legal personality. For thousands of years it was said that if somebody was a slave, it means that he has no right to enter into a contract, he has no right to marry freely, he has no right to inherit or leave inheritance. This is a point which we have not yet examined and I think it is appropriate, since we are studying the fundamental rights of man, to state that not only must everybody be free physically, but to state also that every human being normally possesses rights and obligations, and, therefore, has 'legal personality'" ("Verbatim Record of the Thirteenth

Meeting of the Drafting Committee of the Commission on Human Rights," *The Eleanor Roosevelt Papers*, 1: 569).

64. Cassin, quoted in "Verbatim Record of the Thirteenth Meeting of the Drafting Committee of the Commission on Human Rights," *The Eleanor Roosevelt Papers*, 1: 569.

65. Roosevelt, quoted in Commission on Human Rights Drafting Committee, First Session, Thirteenth Meeting, Summary Records (E/CN.4/AC.1/SR.13), 14.

66. Habermas, "Human Dignity and the Realistic Utopia of Human Rights," 475 [italics omitted].

67. Pavlov, quoted in Morsink, *The Universal Declaration of Human Rights*, 44.

68. See, for example, Joshua Cohen, "Is There a Human Right to Democracy?" in *The Egalitarian Conscience: Essays in Honor of G. A. Cohen* (Oxford: Oxford University Press, 2006).

69. Commission on Human Rights Drafting Committee, First Session, Fifth Meeting, Summary Records (E/CN.4/AC.1/SR.5), 5.

70. Ibid.

71. Neves, "The Symbolic Force of Human Rights," 418 [italics omitted].

72. Ibid.

73. Gerald Neuman, "Human Rights and Constitutional Rights: Harmony and Dissonance," *Stanford Law Review* 55 (2002–2003): 1868. "All constitutional norms and treaty norms claim consensual bases, but fundamental rights norms have another aspect. Positive fundamental rights embodied in a legal system are often conceived as reflections of nonlegal principles that have normative force independent of their embodiment in law, or even superior to the positive legal system. . . . Reference to the assumed content of the suprapositive norms may provide one source of guidance in the interpretation of the legal norms."

74. Carozza, "Human Dignity and Judicial Interpretation of Human Rights: A Reply," 932.

75. Cassin, quoted in Morsink, *The Universal Declaration*, 44–45.

76. Cassin, quoted in Glendon, *A World Made New*, 86. Cassin endeavored to bring home this point in relation to what have become known as the "international rights" of freedom of movement, freedom to seek asylum, and the right to a nationality (ibid.). This aspiration, however, resonates with the broader logic of the Declaration as well.

77. Romulo [delegate for the Philippines], quoted in Sluga, "René Cassin: Les droits de l'homme and the Universality of Human Rights," 113.

78. Glendon, *A World Made New*, 69.

79. Cassin, quoted in ibid., The manner in which the ideological conflict between the U.S. and the Soviet Union shaped this cannot be gainsaid, but this practical/historical conflict does not change the aspiration articulated here by Cassin.

80. Ruti Teitel, *Humanity's Law* (Oxford: Oxford University Press, 2011), 8; Theodor Meron, *The Humanization of International Law* (Leiden: Nijhoff, 2006).

81. Teitel, *Humanity's Law*, 8 [italics added]. See also Charles Olney's review of *Humanity's Law* in *Human Rights Review* 14 (2013): "Humanity law . . . treats human

security as a *collective* responsibility, not something dependent on state sponsors. This recalibrates law by making the recipients of rights, rather than the creators of rules, its primary subjects" (Olney, review of *Humanity's Law*, 421 [italics omitted]).

82. Meron, *The Humanization of International Law*, 7; Teitel, *Humanity's Law*, 9.

83. Teitel, *Humanity's Law*, 45, 47. See also Meron's affirmation of Georges Abi-Saab's claim that contemporary human rights law is marked by "the intent 'to go beyond the inter-State level and to reach for the level of the real (or ultimate) beneficiaries of humanitarian protection. *i.e.* individuals and groups of individuals'" (7–8).

84. Teitel, *Humanity's Law*, 109: "As the humanity law framework in important respects, modifies (without wholly replacing) older norms based on territoriality and the protection of state borders, it produces a transformed understanding of human security, the security of persons and peoples. A humanity-based scheme protects individual and collective rights across state borders, as is necessary for stability in a globalizing politics."

85. Olney, review of *Humanity Law*, 421.

86. Minority treaties are an example of earlier efforts to remedy this. Agamben, of course, locates this situation of withdrawal of legal remedy at the heart of political sovereignty in the west.

87. Birmingham, *Hannah Arendt and Human Rights*, 6.

88. Teitel, *Humanity's Law*, 6: "The shift in the role of law in managing conflict reflects a changed political consciousness—and the change at issue goes to the very values and principles associated with legality itself."

89. Cotterrell, *Emile Durkheim*, 63.

90. Kay Schaffer and Sidonie Smith, *Human Rights and Narrated Lives: The Ethics of Recognition* (New York: Palgrave Macmillan, 2006), 1.

91. Ibid., 2.

92. Lisa Hajjar, "Human Rights," in *Blackwell Companion to Law and Society*, ed. Austin Sarat (New York: Blackwell, 2004), 591. This extension beyond the confines of the nation-state is, admittedly, primarily a conceptual extension, as Asad and many others have pointed out. This fact was and remains a significant limitation upon the universalism of the rule of law, but it should not occlude the unquestionable recalibrations that this document represents for the field of international law, or the palpable shift this particular narrative of human rights has helped engender over the past thirty years.

93. Schaffer and Smith, *Human Rights and Narrated Lives*, 3.

94. Slaughter, quoted in ibid.

95. Ibid., 2.

96. Such observations are far from merely the purview of sociofunctionalists: As Benhabib puts it (by way of Robert Cover), "Laws acquire meaning in that they are interpreted within the context of significations which they themselves cannot control. There can be no rules *without* interpretation; rules can only be followed insofar as they are interpreted; but there are also no rules which can control the varieties of interpretation each rule can be subject to within all different hermeneutical contexts" (Benhabib, *Dignity in Adversity*, 127–28).

97. José Alves, "The Declaration of Human Rights in Postmodernity," *Human Rights Quarterly* 22 (2000): 499. Indeed, Alves believes that human rights are marked by their success in doing this. "If, according to Derrida, justice is an imprecise reference for the application of Law, something that imposes itself but cannot be legally prescribed in the form of rights and duties, the 1948 Declaration, in its shape of manifesto (or 'shaped as a manifesto'), may, at least, represent a legitimate yard stick. For in different degrees, all civilizations have by now been influenced by it. Likewise, bearing in mind Lyotard's concerns, since its 'universalization' by the Vienna Conference, and because of its constant use by 'voiceless minorities,' the Declaration can also be envisaged as a widely accepted point of convergence for all micronarratives and different language games. . . . Therefore, even for the staunchest post-structuralists and postmodern theoreticians, the Universal Declaration of Human Rights opens invaluable paths."

98. Samir Kumar Das, "'People Without Shadows': Ethnographic Reflections on Identity and Justice in Contemporary India," *Peace Prints: South Asian Journal of Peacebuilding* 3, 2 (Winter 2010): 2.

99. Ibid.

100. Cotterrell, *Emile Durkheim*, 51.

101. Hamacher, "The Right Not to Have Rights," 672. As Hamacher puts it, "In the Declaration, the human announces itself *clare et distincte* as juridical essence, as the process and product of an autoenactment and autoverification carried out in universal consensus." The end result of this maneuver is, according to Hamacher, "that human rights are the form in which human essence articulates itself and that this form is the juridical one of rights and their perpetual declaration."

102. Ibid., 674.

103. Cotterrell, *Emile Durkheim*, 60.

Conclusion. Making and Unmaking Myth

1. Tony Evans, "International Human Rights Law as Power/Knowledge," *Human Rights Quarterly* 27 (2005): 1050–51.

2. Ibid., 1053–54.

3. To claim that human rights' philosophical questions are *pragmatically* settled is not to claim that they are resolved; it is merely to claim that human rights have achieved sufficient international traction to render such philosophical matters unnecessary or even counterproductive.

4. Ibid., 1053–54; Adamantia Pollis, "A New Universalism," in *Human Rights: New Perspectives, New Realities,* ed. Adamantia Pollis and Peter Schwab (Boulder, Colo.: Rienner, 2000), 22.

5. Hajjar, "Human Rights," 601.

6. Hitchcock, "The Rise and Fall of Human Rights?" 89.

7. "Press Statement by Eleanor Roosevelt," *The Eleanor Roosevelt Papers*, vol. 2, ed. Allida Black (Charlottesville: University of Virginia Press, 2007), 841.

8. Ignatieff, *Human Rights as Politics and Idolatry*, 53. In his critique of human rights as a form of "idolatry," Ignatieff famously conflates the desire on the part of certain human rights advocates to elevate human rights to the position of "lingua franca of global moral thought" (something the framers clearly endeavored to accomplish) with an advocacy on behalf of particular "metaphysical claims about human nature" (53–54).

9. Charles R. Beitz, *The Idea of Human Rights* (Oxford: Oxford University Press, 2009), 1.

10. Moyn, *The Last Utopia*, 7.

11. Ibid., 68.

12. Indeed, what little purchase human rights were able to achieve in the wake of the creation of the Declaration was largely due, according to Moyn, to the fact that the Soviet Union bowed out of negotiations of the subsequent covenants (ibid., 69).

13. Stanley Cohen, *Denial and Acknowledgement: The Impact of Information About Human Rights Violations* (Jerusalem: Center for Human Rights, Hebrew University of Jerusalem, 1995), 71.

14. Lauren, *The Evolution of International Human Rights*, 297, 303.

15. Moyn, *The Last Utopia*, 5.

16. Morsink, *The Universal Declaration of Human Rights*, xi.

17. Moyn, *The Last Utopia*, 6.

18. Ibid., 12: "The worst consequence of the myth of deep roots [that such narratives] provide is that they distract from the real conditions for the historical developments they claim to explain. If human rights are treated as inborn, or long in preparation, people will not confront the true reasons they have become so powerful today and examine whether those reasons are still persuasive."

19. Jerome Bruner, "The Narrative Construction of Reality," *Critical Inquiry* 18, 1 (1991): 20–21.

20. Derrida, quoted in Giovanna Borradori, *Philosophy in a Time of Terror: Dialogues with Jürgen Habermas and Jacques Derrida* (Chicago: University of Chicago Press, 2003), 132.

21. Ibid., 132–33. See also Judith Butler's assertion that "ethics undermines its own credibility when it does not become critique." Butler, quoted in Jodi Dean, "The Politics of Avoidance: The Limits of Weak Ontology," *Hedgehog Review* 7, 2 (Summer 2005): 60.

22. Jerome J. Shestack, "The Philosophic Foundations of Human Rights," *Human Rights Quarterly* 20, 2 (1998): 217. Doniger grapples with this dynamic of myth by recounting a striking narrative from Jacques Roubaud: "The tale always tells the truth. What the tale says is true because the tale tells it. Some say that the tale tells the truth because what the tale tells is true. Others that the tale doesn't tell the truth because truth is not a tale. But in reality what the tale tells is true of what the tale tells that what the tale tells is true. That is why the tale tells the truth" (Roubaud, quoted in Doniger, *The Implied Spider*, 2–3).

23. Sharon Silwinski has raised this question of the aesthetics of human rights in a series of contexts, though not in the context of mythmaking. See Silwinski, "The

Aesthetics of Human Rights," *Culture, Theory, and Critique* 50, 1 (2009) and *Human Rights in Camera* (Chicago: University of Chicago Press, 2011). See also Lori Allen, "Martyr Bodies in the Media: Human Rights, Aesthetics, and the Politics of Immediation in the Palestinian Intifada," *American Ethnologist* 36, 1 (2009). For a more normative engagement with this question, see Feisal Mohamed, "Poignancy as Human Rights Aesthetic," *Journal of Human Rights* 9 (2010).

24. Habermas, "Human Dignity and the Realistic Utopia of Human Rights," 478 [italics omitted].

25. Asad, *Formations of the Secular*, 148.

26. Ibid., 150.

27. Ibid.

28. Ibid., 129. See also Margaret R. Somers, "Citizenship Imperiled: How Marketzation Creates Social Exclusion, Statelessness, and Rightlessness," in Somers, *Genealogies of Citizenship: Markets, Statelessness, and the Right to Have Rights*, Cambridge Cultural Studies Series (Cambridge: Cambridge University Press, 2008). A number of scholars have endeavored to push human rights pointedly in the direction of critiquing modern capitalism: see, for example Collier, "Durkheim Revisited: Human Rights as the Moral Discourse for the Postcolonial, Post-Cold War World"; Pheng Cheah, "Posit(ion)ing Human Rights in the Current Global Conjecture," *Public Culture* 9 (1997); Kristie M. McClure, "Taking Liberties in Foucault's Triangle: Sovereignty, Discipline, Governmentality, and the Subject of Rights," in *Identities, Politics, and Rights*, ed. Austin Sarat and Thomas R. Kearns (Ann Arbor: University of Michigan Press, 1997).

29. Ibid., 150.

30. Ibid., 151. See also Mutua, "Savages, Victims, and Saviors: The Metaphor of Human Rights." Saba Mahmood has famously explored this matter in relation to the broader issue of secularism in "Secularism, Hermeneutics, and Empire: The Politics of Islamic Reformation," *Public Culture* 18, 2 (2006).

31. Tarik Kochi, "Terror in the Name of Human Rights," *Melbourne Journal of International Law* 7, 1 (2006): 144.

32. Julie Owen, "Human Rights as Civil Religion: The Glue for Global Governance?" in *Criticizing Global Governance*, ed. Markus Lederer and Philipp S. Müller (New York: Palgrave Macmillan, 2005). In *Why I Am Not a Secularist* (Minneapolis: University of Minnesota Press, 1999), William Connolly offers a more expansive argument along these lines. See also Habermas, "Pre-Political Foundations of the Democratic Constitutional State?" 29–34, and Michael Freeman, "The Problem of Secularism in Human Rights," *Human Rights Quarterly* 26, 2 (2004): 375–400.

33. Carozza, quoted in Owen, "Human Rights as Civil Religion: The Glue for Global Governance?" 222.

34. Freeman, "The Problem of Secularism on Human Rights," 376 [italics omitted].

35. Piotr Hoffman highlights the manner in which liberal democratic systems of governance in general demand a conversion that the language of "freedom" tends to obscure; Hoffman, *Freedom, Equality, Power: The Ontological Consequences of the*

Political Philosophies of Hobbes, Locke, and Rousseau (New York: Peter Lang, 1999), 268. This demand for conversion is always potentially coercive, as Mahmood has shown (Mahmood, "Secularism, Hermeneutics, and Empire"). Such issues point to the manner in which, as Elizabeth Shakman Hurd has famously put it, "Secularism Is a Social Construction." Hurd, *The Politics of Secularism in International Relations* (Princeton, N.J.: Princeton University Press, 2008), 134.

36. Zakaria, "The Rise of Illiberal Democracy," *Foreign Affairs* (1997); Reinbold, "Radical Islam and Human Rights Values: A 'Religious-Minded' Critique of Secular Liberty, Equality, and Brotherhood," *Journal of the American Academy of Religion* 78, 2 (2010).

37. Reinbold, "Radical Islam and Human Rights Values," 456.

38. Borradori, *Philosophy in a Time of Terror*, 139.

39. Stephen White, "Weak Ontology: Genealogy and Critical Issues," *Hedgehog Review* 7, 2 (2005): 22–23.

40. Somers, *Genealogies of Citizenship*, 7 [italics omitted].

41. Benjamin Gregg, *Human Rights as Social Construction* (Cambridge: Cambridge University Press, 2012), 5. In his insistence upon a distinction between these dimensions of human rights, Gregg is ultimately not unlike Perry, who draws a dichotomy between a "subjective" and an "objective" logic of sacredness within human rights (Perry, *The Idea of Human Rights*, 28). While I obviously don't dispute Perry's claim that human rights are "ineliminably religious," I have already highlighted the manner in which I dispute his conflation of "religion" with transcendence. His distinction between subjective and objective enters at precisely this point: in *The Idea of Human Rights*, "subjective" sacredness is depicted as a more or less utilitarian conviction that the sacredness of an item derives from the fact that we "attach great value to it" while "objective" sacredness rests upon a conviction that we attach great value to an item *because* we harbor a prior conviction that it is sacred. In Perry's view, only the "objective" form of sacredness is religious, and only from within such an objective frame of reference can one formulate a coherent argument for the sacredness of all human life. As I have argued here, however, the sociofunctionalist approach to myth allows us to perceive the manner in which the Commission's sacralization of human dignity can be understood to be both subjective and objective in Perry's sense of the terms.

BIBLIOGRAPHY

Agamben, Giorgio. *Homo Sacer: Sovereign Power and Bare Life*. Trans. David Heller-Roazen. Stanford, Calif.: Stanford University Press, 1998.

Albanese, Catherine. *Sons of the Fathers: The Civil Religion of the American Revolution*. Philadelphia: Temple University Press, 1977.

Allen, Lori. "Martyr Bodies in the Media: Human Rights, Aesthetics, and the Politics of Immediation in the Palestinian Intifada." *American Ethnologist* 36, 1 (February 2009): 161–80.

Alves, José A. Lindgreen. "The Declaration of Human Rights in Postmodernity." *Human Rights Quarterly* 22 (2000): 478–500.

American Anthropological Association Executive Board. "Statement on Human Rights." *American Anthropologist* 49, 4 (October–December 1947): 539–43.

Arendt, Hannah. *Eichmann in Jerusalem: A Report on the Banality of Evil*. New York: Penguin, 1964.

———. *The Human Condition*. Chicago: University of Chicago Press, 1958.

———. *The Origins of Totalitarianism*. Cleveland: World, 1958.

Asad, Talal. *Formations of the Secular: Christianity, Islam, Modernity*. Stanford, Calif.: Stanford University Press, 2003.

———. *Genealogies of Religion: Disciplines and Reasons of Power in Christianity and Islam*. Baltimore: Johns Hopkins University Press, 1993.

Barthes, Roland. *Mythologies*. Trans. Annette Lavers. New York: Hill and Wang, 1972.

Bataille, Georges. *The Accursed Share: An Essay on General Economy*. Trans. Robert Hurley. New York: Zone, 1988.

Bauman, Zygmunt. *Modernity and the Holocaust*. Ithaca, N.Y.: Cornell University Press, 1989.

Bellah, Robert N. *Beyond Belief: Essays on Religion in a Post-Traditional World*. Berkeley: University of California Press, 1991.

Beitz, Charles R. *The Idea of Human Rights*. Oxford: Oxford University Press, 2009.

Benhabib, Seyla. *Dignity in Adversity: Human Rights in Troubled Times*. Malden, Mass.: Polity, 2011.

Bentham, Jeremy. "Anarchical Fallacies: Being An Examination of The Declaration of Rights Issued During the French Revolution by Jeremy Bentham." In *The Works of Jeremy Bentham*, ed. John Bowring, vol. 2. 489–534. Edinburgh: Simpkin, Marshall, 1843.

Berger, Peter L. "The Desecularization of the World: A Global Overview." In *The Desecularization of the World: Resurgent Religion and World Politics*, ed. Peter Berger, 1–18. Grand Rapids, Mich.: Eerdmans, 1999.

Birmingham, Peg. *Hannah Arendt and Human Rights: The Predicament of Common Responsibility*. Bloomington: Indiana University Press, 2006.

Black, Allida, ed. *The Eleanor Roosevelt Papers*, vol. 1 and 2, Charlottesville: University of Virginia Press, 2007.

Blumenberg, Hans. *The Legitimacy of the Modern Age*. Trans. Robert M. Wallace. Cambridge, Mass.: MIT Press, 1983.

———. *Work on Myth*. Trans. Robert M. Wallace. Cambridge, Mass.: MIT Press, 1985.

Bolle, Kees. "Myth: An Overview." In *Encyclopedia of Religion*, vol. 9, ed. Lindsay Jones. 2nd ed., 6359–71. Detroit: Macmillan Reference, 2005.

Borradori, Giovanna. *Philosophy in a Time of Terror: Dialogues with Jürgen Habermas and Jacques Derrida*. Chicago: University of Chicago Press, 2003.

Bottici, Chiara and Benoît Challand. "Rethinking Political Myth: The Clash of Civilizations as a Self-Fulfilling Prophecy." *European Journal of Social Theory* 9, 3 (2006): 315–36.

Bruner, Jerome. "The Narrative Construction of Reality." *Critical Inquiry* 18, 1 (1991): 1–21.

Bultmann, Rudolf. "New Testament and Mythology." In *Kerygma and Myth*, ed. Hans Werner Bartsch. New York: Harper TorchBooks, 1961.

Carozza, Paolo G. "Human Dignity and Judicial Interpretation of Human Rights: A Reply." *European Journal of International Law* 19, 5 (2008): 931–44.

Casanova, José. *Public Religions in the Modern World*. Chicago: University of Chicago Press, 1994.

———. "The Secular, Secularizations, Secularisms." In *Rethinking Secularism*, ed. Craig Calhoun, Mark Juergensmeyer, and Jonathan VanAntwerpen, 54–74. Oxford: Oxford University Press, 2011.

Cassin, René. *La pensée et l'action*. Ed. François-Joachim Beer. Boulogne-sur-Seine: F. Laclou, 1972.

Cassirer, Ernst. *The Myth of the State*. New Haven, Conn.: Yale University Press, 1974.

Cheah, Pheng. "Posit(ion)ing Human Rights in the Current Global Conjecture." *Public Culture* 9 (1997): 233–66.

Chidester, David. *Savage Systems: Colonialism and Comparative Religion in Southern Africa*. Charlottesville: University of Virginia Press, 1996.

Chidester, David and Edward T. Linenthal. Introduction. In *American Sacred Space*, ed. David Chidester and Edward T. Linenthal, 1–42. Bloomington: Indiana University Press, 2001.

Clinton, William Jefferson. "A Message from the President." *The Universal Declaration of Human Rights at 50*, Special Issue, *Issues in Democracy* 3, 3 (1998): 6–7. U.S. Information Agency. usa.usembassy.de/etexts/crights/ijde1098.pdf.

Cohen, Joshua. "Is There a Human Right to Democracy?" In *The Egalitarian Conscience: Essays in Honor of G. A. Cohen*, ed. Christine Sypnowich, 226–48. Oxford: Oxford University Press, 2006.

Cohen, Stanley. *Denial and Acknowledgement: The Impact of Information About Human Rights Violations*. Jerusalem: Center for Human Rights, Hebrew University of Jerusalem, 1995.

Collier, Jane F. "Durkheim Revisited: Human Rights as the Moral Discourse for the Postcolonial, Post-Cold War World." In *Human Rights: Concepts, Contests, and Contingencies*, ed. Austin Sarat and Thomas R. Kearns, 63–88. Ann Arbor: University of Michigan Press, 2001.

Connolly, William E. *Why I Am Not a Secularist*. Minneapolis: University of Minnesota Press, 1999.

Cotterrell, Roger. *Emile Durkheim: Law in a Moral Domain*. Stanford, Calif: Stanford University Press, 1999.

Das, Samir Kumar. "'People Without Shadows': Ethnographic Reflections on Identity and Justice in Contemporary India." *Peace Prints: South Asian Journal of Peacebuilding* 3, 2 (Winter 2010): 1–10.

Dean, Jodi. "The Politics of Avoidance: The Limits of Weak Ontology." *Hedgehog Review* 7, 2 (Summer 2005): 55–65.

Derrida, Jacques. "Declarations of Independence." *New Political Science* (1986): 7–15.

———. "Force of Law: The 'Mystical Foundation of Authority'," trans. Mary Quaintance. *Cardozo Law Review* 11 (1989–1990): 920–1045.

de Vries, Hent. "Introduction: Before, Around, and Beyond the Theologico-Political." In *Political Theologies: Public Religions in a Post-Secular World*, ed. Hent de Vries and Lawrence E. Sullivan, 1–88. New York: Fordham University Press, 2006.

Doniger, Wendy. *The Implied Spider: Politics and Theology in Myth*. New York: Columbia University Press, 2011.

Donnelly, Jack. *Universal Human Rights in Theory and Practice*. Ithaca, N.Y.: Cornell University Press, 2003.

Douglas, Mary. *Purity and Danger: An Analysis of Concepts of Pollution and Taboo*. London: Routledge, 1966.

Dovey, Kim. *Framing Places: Mediating Power in Built Form*. London: Routledge, 1999.

Durkheim, Émile. *The Division of Labor in Society*. Trans. George Simpson. New York: Macmillan, 1933.

———. *The Elementary Forms of Religious Life*. Trans. Karen E. Fields. New York: Free Press, 1999.

———. *Les formes élémentaires de la vie religieuse*. Paris: Presses Universitaires de France, 1960.

——. "Individualism and the Intellectuals," trans. Steven Lukes. *Political Studies* 71, 1 (1969): 14–30.

——. *Moral Education*. Mineola, N.Y.: Dover, 2002.

Durkheim, Émile and Marcel Mauss. *Primitive Classification*. Trans. Rodney Needham. Chicago: University of Chicago Press, 1967.

Eck, Diana. *Darsan: Seeing the Divine Image in India*. New York: Columbia University Press, 1998.

Eliade, Mircea. *The Myth of the Eternal Return: or, Cosmos and History*. Trans. Willard R. Trask. Princeton, N.J.: Princeton University Press, 1974.

——. *Patterns in Comparative Religion*. Trans. Rosemary Sheed. London: Sheed and Ward, 1958.

——. *The Sacred and the Profane: The Nature of Religion*. London: Harcourt, 1957.

Evans, Tony. "International Human Rights Law as Power/Knowledge." *Human Rights Quarterly* 27 (2005): 1046–68.

Fitzpatrick, Peter. *Modernism and the Grounds of Law*. Cambridge Studies in Law and Society. Cambridge: Cambridge University Press, 2001.

——. *The Mythology of Modern Law*. New York: Routledge, 1992.

Flood, Christopher. *Political Myth*. New York: Routledge, 2002.

Forst, Rainer. "The Justification of Human Rights and the Basic Right to Justification: A Reflexive Approach." *Ethics* 120, 4 (2010): 711–40.

Foucault, Michel. "The Political Technologies of Individuals." In *Technologies of the Self: A Seminar with Michel Foucault*, ed. Luther H. Martin, Huck Gutman, and Patrick H. Hutton, 145–63. Amherst: University of Massachusetts Press, 1998.

Freeman, Michael. "The Problem of Secularism in Human Rights." *Human Rights Quarterly* 26, 2 (2004): 375–400.

Freud, Sigmund. *The Future of an Illusion*. Trans. and ed. James Strachey. New York: Norton, 1961.

——. *The Uncanny*. New York: Penguin, 2003.

Gauchet, Marcel. *The Disenchantment of the World: A Political History of Religion*. Princeton, N.J.: Princeton University Press, 1997.

Geertz, Clifford. *The Interpretation of Cultures: Selected Essays by Clifford Geertz*. New York: Basic, 1975.

Gentile, Emilio. *Politics as Religion*. Trans. George Staunton. Princeton, N.J.: Princeton University Press, 2006.

Giddens, Anthony. *Capitalism and Modern Social Theory: An Analysis of the Writings of Marx, Durkheim, and Max Weber*. Cambridge: Cambridge University Press, 1973.

Glendon, Mary Ann. *A World Made New: Eleanor Roosevelt and the Universal Declaration of Human Rights*. New York: Random House, 2002.

Goodale, Mark. *Surrendering to Utopia: An Anthropology of Human Rights*. Stanford, Calif.: Stanford University Press, 2009.

Gregg, Benjamin. *Human Rights as Social Construction*. Cambridge: Cambridge University Press, 2012.

Gregory, Brad S. *The Unintended Reformation: How a Religious Revolution Secularized Society*. Cambridge, Mass.: Belknap Press of Harvard University Press, 2012.

Gündogdu, Ayten. "'Perplexities of the Rights of Man': Arendt on the Aporias of Human Rights." In *The Aporia of Rights: Explorations in Citizenship in the Era of Human Rights*, ed. Anna Yeatman and Peg Birmingham, 13–35. New York: Bloomsbury, 2014.

Habermas, Jürgen. "The Concept of Human Dignity and the Realistic Utopia of Human Rights." *Metaphilosophy* 41, 4 (July 2010): 464–80.

———. *The Postnational Constellation: Political Essays*. Trans. Max Pensky. Cambridge, Mass.: MIT Press, 2001.

———. "Pre-Political Foundations of the Democratic Constitutional State?" in *The Dialectics of Secularization: On Reason and Religion*. Trans. Brian McNeil, C.R.V. San Francisco: Ignatius Press, 2005.

Hajjar, Lisa. "Human Rights." In *Blackwell Companion to Law and Society*, ed. Austin Sarat, 589–604. New York: Blackwell, 2004.

Hamacher, Werner. "The Right Not to Use Rights: Human Rights and the Structure of Judgments." In *Political Theologies: Public Religions in a Post-Secular World*, ed. Hent de Vries and Lawrence E. Sullivan, 671–90. New York: Fordham University Press, 2006.

Hardt, Michael and Antonio Negri. *Empire*. Cambridge, Mass.: Harvard University Press, 2000.

Hayden, Patrick. "The Relevance of Hannah Arendt's Reflections on Evil: Globalization and Rightlessness." *Human Rights Review* 11 (2010): 451–67.

Hitchcock, William I. "The Rise and Fall of Human Rights? Searching for a Narrative from the Cold War to the 9/11 Era." *Human Rights Quarterly* 34, 1 (February 2015): 80–106.

Hoffman, Piotr. *Freedom, Equality, Power: The Ontological Consequences of the Political Philosophies of Hobbes, Locke, and Rousseau*. New York: Peter Lang, 1999.

Horkheimer, Max and Theodor Adorno. *Dialectic of Enlightenment*. Trans. John Cumming. New York: Continuum, 1999.

Hunt, Lynn. *Inventing Human Rights: A History*. New York: Norton, 2007.

Hurd, Elizabeth Shakman. *The Politics of Secularism in International Relations*. Princeton, N.J.: Princeton University Press, 2008.

Ignatieff, Michael. *Human Rights as Politics and Idolatry*. Ed. Amy Gutmann. Princeton, N.J.: Princeton University Press, 2001.

Joas, Hans. *The Sacredness of the Person: A New Genealogy of Human Rights*. Washington, D.C.: Georgetown University Press, 2013.

Kahn, Paul W. "American Hegemony and International Law: Speaking Law to Power: Popular Sovereignty, Human Rights, and the New International Order." *Chicago Journal of International Law* (Spring 2000): 1–18.

Kochi, Tarik. "Terror in the Name of Human Rights." *Melbourne Journal of International Law* 7, 1 (2006): 127–54.

Lacoue-Labarthe, Philippe, Jean-Luc Nancy, and Brian Holmes. "The Nazi Myth." *Critical Inquiry* 16, 2 (Winter 1990): 291–312.

Lauren, Paul Gordon. *The Evolution of International Human Rights: Visions Seen.* Philadelphia: University of Pennsylvania Press, 2003.

Lefebvre, Alexandre. *Human Rights as a Way of Life: On Bergson's Political Philosophy.* Stanford, Calif: Stanford University Press, 2013.

Lefort, Claude. *The Political Forms of Modern Society: Bureaucracy, Democracy, Totalitarianism.* Cambridge, Mass.: MIT Press, 1986.

Lévi-Strauss, Claude. *Structural Anthropology.* Trans. Claire Jacobson and Brooke Grundfest Schoepf. New York: Basic, 1963.

Lifton, Robert Jay. *The Nazi Doctors: Medical Killing and the Psychology of Genocide.* New York: Basic, 1986.

Lilla, Mark. *The Stillborn God: Religion, Politics, and the Modern West.* New York: Vintage, 2007.

Lincoln, Bruce. *Discourse and the Construction of Society: Comparative Studies of Myth, Ritual, and Classification.* New York: Oxford University Press, 1989.

———. *Holy Terrors: Thinking About Religion After September 11.* Chicago: University of Chicago Press, 2006.

———. *Theorizing Myth: Narrative, Ideology, and Scholarship.* Chicago: University of Chicago Press, 1999.

Little, David. *Essays on Human Rights: Ground to Stand On.* Cambridge: Cambridge University Press, 2015.

———. Foreword to John S. Nurser, *For All Peoples and All Nations: The Ecumenical Church and Human Rights.* Washington, D.C.: Georgetown University Press, 2005.

Lovin, Robin and Frank E. Reynolds, eds. *Cosmogony and Ethical Order: New Essays in Comparative Ethics.* Chicago: University of Chicago Press, 1985.

Lukes, Steven. Introduction to "Individualism and the Intellectuals." *Political Studies* 17, 1 (1969): 14–30.

Lynch, Gordon. *The Sacred in the Modern World.* Oxford: Oxford University Press, 2012.

Mahmood, Saba. "Secularism, Hermeneutics, and Empire: The Politics of Islamic Reformation." *Public Culture* 18, 2 (2006): 323–47.

Mahoney, Jack. *The Challenge of Human Rights: Origin, Development, and Significance.* Oxford: Blackwell, 2007.

Malik, Charles. "The Drafting of the Universal Declaration of Human Rights." *UN Bulletin of Human Rights* 86, 1 (1986).

———. "An International Bill of Human Rights." In *The Challenge of Human Rights: Charles Malik and the Universal Declaration,* ed. Habib C. Malik, 53–60. Oxford: Charles Malik Foundation Center for Lebanese Studies, 2000. Originally a discussion of the report of the Commission on Human Rights (March 14, 1947).

———. "Spiritual Implications of the Universal Declaration." In *The Challenge of Human Rights: Charles Malik and the Universal Declaration,* ed. Habib C. Malik, 134–40.

Oxford: Charles Malik Foundation Center for Lebanese Studies, 2000. Originally an address to the World Council of Churches (April 29, 1949).

———. "Talk on Human Rights." Speech given to the Committee on International, Political and Social Problems of the U.S. Chamber of Commerce, November 1949.

———. "The Twin Scourges: Materialism, Human Self-Sufficiency." In *The Challenge of Human Rights: Charles Malik and the Universal Declaration*, ed. Habib C. Malik, 205–13. Oxford: Charles Malik Foundation Center for Lebanese Studies, 2000. Originally delivered to Round Table on World Affairs in Extension Education of the Carnegie Endowment for International Peace (September 19, 1951).

———. "The UN and Essential Human Rights." In *The Challenge of Human Rights: Charles Malik and the Universal Declaration*, ed. Habib C. Malik, 96–112. Oxford: Charles Malik Foundation Center for Lebanese Studies, 2000. Originally an address at the Conference of Religion for Moral and Spiritual Support of the United Nations (June 16, 1948).

———. "What Are Human Rights?" *The Rotarian* (August 1948).

Malinowski, Bronisław. *Magic, Science and Religion and Other Essays*. London: Souvenir Press, 1974.

———. *Myth in Primitive Psychology*. New York: Norton, 1926.

Marietta, Morgan. *The Politics of Sacred Rhetoric: Absolutist Appeals and Political Persuasions*. Waco, Tex.: Baylor University Press, 2012.

Maritain, Jacques. Introduction to UNESCO, ed., *Human Rights: Comments and Interpretations*. New York: Allan Wingate, 1949.

Marovich, Beatrice. "Interview: Simon Critchley, Atheist Religious Thinker on Utopia and the Fiction of Faith." *Religion Dispatches*, August 20, 2012. http://www.religiondispatches.org/.

Masuzawa, Tomoko. *The Invention of World Religions: Or, How European Universalism Was Preserved in the Language of Pluralism*. Chicago: University of Chicago Press, 2005.

Mazur, Eric Michael and Kate McCarthy, eds. *God in the Details: American Religion in Popular Culture*. London: Routledge, 2011.

McClure, Kristie M. "Taking Liberties in Foucault's Triangle: Sovereignty, Discipline, Governmentality, and the Subject of Rights." In *Identities, Politics, and Rights*, ed. Austin Sarat and Thomas R. Kearns, 149–77. Ann Arbor: University of Michigan Press, 1997.

McCrudden, Christopher. "Human Dignity and Judicial Interpretation of Human Rights." *European Journal of International Law* 19, 4 (2008): 655–724.

Meron, Theodor. *The Humanization of International Law*. Leiden: Nijhoff, 2006.

Mohamed, Feisel G. "Poignancy as a Human Rights Aesthetic." *Journal of Human Rights* 9 (2010): 143–60.

Morsink, Johannes. *Inherent Human Rights: Philosophical Roots of the Universal Declaration*. Philadelphia: University of Pennsylvania Press, 2009.

———. *The Universal Declaration of Human Rights: Origins, Drafting, and Intent.* Philadelphia: University of Pennsylvania Press, 1999.

———. "World War Two and the Universal Declaration." *Human Rights Quarterly* 15, 2 (1993): 357–405.

Moyn, Samuel. *The Last Utopia: Human Rights in History.* Cambridge, Mass.: Belknap Press of Harvard University Press, 2010.

Mutua, Makau. "Savages, Victims and Saviors: The Metaphor of Human Rights." *Harvard International Law Journal* 42 (2001): 201–45.

Neuman, Gerald L. "Human Rights and Constitutional Rights: Harmony and Dissonance." *Stanford Law Review* 55 (2002–2003): 1863–1900.

Neves, Marcelo. "The Symbolic Force of Human Rights." *Philosophy and Social Criticism* 33, 4 (2007): 411–44.

Nongbri, Brent. *Before Religion: A History of a Modern Concept.* New Haven, Conn.: Yale University Press, 2013.

Olney, Charles. Review of *Humanity's Law* by Ruti Teitel. *Human Rights Review* 14 (2013): 421–23.

Orsi, Robert. *The Madonna of 115th Street: Faith and Community in Italian Harlem, 1880–1950.* New Haven, Conn.: Yale University Press, 2010.

Otto, Rudolph. *The Idea of the Holy.* Trans. John W. Harvey. New York: Oxford University Press, 1958.

Owen, Julie. "Human Rights as Civil Religion: The Glue for Global Governance?" In *Criticizing Global Governance*, ed. Markus Lederer and Philipp S. Müller, 221–41. New York: Palgrave Macmillan, 2005.

Parekh, Serena. *Hannah Arendt and the Challenge of Modernity: A Phenomenology of Human Rights.* New York: Routledge, 2008.

Patton, Laurie L. and Wendy Doniger. Introduction. In *Myth and Method*, ed. Laurie Patton and Wendy Doniger, 1–28. Charlottesville: University Press of Virginia, 1996.

Perry, Michael. *The Idea of Human Rights: Four Inquiries.* New York: Oxford University Press, 1998.

Pollis, Adamantia. "A New Universalism." In *Human Rights: New Perspectives, New Realities*, ed. Adamantia Pollis and Peter Schwab, 9–30. Boulder, Colo.: Lynne Rienner, 2000.

Power, Samantha. *A Problem from Hell: America in the Age of Genocide.* New York: Basic, 2002.

Rawls, John. "The Idea of Overlapping Consensus." In Rawls, *Political Liberalism.* New York: Columbia University Press, 1993.

———. "The Idea of Public Reason Revisited." In Rawls, *The Law of Peoples.* 129–80. Cambridge, Mass.: Harvard University Press, 1999.

———. *A Theory of Justice.* Cambridge: Belknap Press of Harvard University Press, 1971.

Reinbold, Jenna. "Political Myth and the Sacred Center of Human Rights: The Universal Declaration and the Narrative of 'Inherent Human Dignity.'" *Human Rights Review* 12, 2 (May 2011): 147–71.

———. "Radical Islam and Human Rights Values: A 'Religious-Minded' Critique of Secular Liberty, Equality, and Brotherhood." *Journal of the American Academy of Religion* 78, 2 (June 2010): 449–76.

———. "Sacred Institutions and Secular Law: The Faltering Voice of Religion in the Courtroom Debate over Same-Sex Marriage." *Journal of Church and State* 56, 2 (2014): 248–68.

Roosevelt, Eleanor. "In Your Hands: A Guide for Community Action for the Tenth Anniversary of the Universal Declaration of Human Rights." New York: Church Peace Union, 1958. *Milestone Documents*. www.milestonedocuments.com.

———. "Making Human Rights Come Alive." In *What I Hope to Leave Behind: The Essential Essays of Eleanor Roosevelt*, ed. Allida M. Black, 559–73. New York: Carlson, 1995. Originally published in *Phi Delta Kappan* 31 (September 1949): 23–33.

———. *Our Rights as Human Beings: A Discussion Guide on the Universal Declaration of Human Rights*. UN Department of Public Information, 1949.

———. "Press Statement by Eleanor Roosevelt," *The Eleanor Roosevelt Papers*, vol. 2, ed. Allida Black, 841–43. Charlottesville: University of Virginia Press, 2007.

———. "The Promise of Human Rights." In *What I Hope to Leave Behind: The Essential Essays of Eleanor Roosevelt*, ed. Allida M. Black, 553–58. New York: Carlson, 1995. Originally published in *Foreign Affairs* 26 (April 1948): 470–77.

Rorty, Richard. *Truth and Progress: Philosophical Papers*. Cambridge: Cambridge University Press, 1998.

Roubaud, Jacques. *The Princess Hoppy, or The Take of Labrador*. Normal, Ill.: Dalkey Archive Press, 1993.

Schaffer, Kay and Sidonie Smith. *Human Rights and Narrated Lives: The Ethics of Recognition*. New York: Palgrave Macmillan, 2006.

Schmitt, Carl. *The Concept of the Political*. Trans. George Schwab. Chicago: University of Chicago Press, 1996.

Schwarz, Elke. "@hannah_arendt: An Arendtian Critique of Online Social Networks." *Millennium: Journal of International Studies* 43 (2014): 165–86.

Segal, Robert A. "Does Myth Have a Future?" In *Myth and Method*, ed. Laurie L. Patton and Wendy Doniger, 82–108. Charlottesville: University Press of Virginia, 1996.

Shestack, Jerome J. "The Philosophic Foundations of Human Rights." *Human Rights Quarterly* 20, 2 (1998): 201–34.

Silwinski, Sharon. "The Aesthetics of Human Rights." *Culture, Theory, and Critique* 50, 1 (2009): 23–39.

———. *Human Rights in Camera*. Chicago: University of Chicago Press, 2011.

Slaughter, Joseph. *Human Rights, Inc.: The World Novel, Narrative Form, and International Law*. New York: Fordham University Press, 2007.

Sluga, Glenda. "René Cassin: Les droits de l'homme and the Universality of Human Rights, 1945–1966." In *Human Rights in the Twentieth Century*, ed. Stefan-Ludwig Hoffmann, 107–24. Cambridge: Cambridge University Press, 2011.

Smith, Jonathan Z. *Imagining Religion: From Babylon to Jonestown*. Chicago: University of Chicago Press, 1988.

———. *To Take Place: Toward and Theory of Ritual*. Chicago: University of Chicago Press, 1992.

Smith, Leslie Dorrough. *Righteous Rhetoric: Sex, Speech, and the Politics of Concerned Women for America*. Oxford: Oxford University Press, 2014.

Somers, Margaret R. *Genealogies of Citizenship: Markets, Statelessness, and the Right to Have Rights*. Cambridge Cultural Social Studies. Cambridge: Cambridge University Press, 2008.

Strauss, Leo. "Notes on *The Concept of the Political*." In Carl Schmidt, *The Concept of the Political*, trans. George Schwab, 83–107. Chicago: University of Chicago Press, 1996.

Strenski, Ivan. *Four Theories of Myth in Twentieth-Century History: Cassirer, Eliade, Lévi-Strauss and Malinowski*. London: Macmillan, 1987.

Sullivan, Winnifred Fallers. *The Impossibility of Religious Freedom*. Princeton, N.J.: Princeton University Press, 2007.

Taussig, Michael. *Defacement: Public Secrecy and the Labor of the Negative*. Stanford, Calif.: Stanford University Press, 1999.

———. *The Magic of the State*. New York: Routledge, 1997.

———. *The Nervous System*. New York: Routledge, 1992.

Taylor, Charles. *A Secular Age*. Cambridge: Belknap Press of Harvard University Press, 2007.

Teitel, Ruti. *Humanity's Law*. Oxford: Oxford University Press, 2011.

Tseng, Pauline. "Beyond Myth and Reality in the Expedition to the Cosmopolitan Utopia: The Parable of Human Rights." *Non-State Actors and International Law* 2, 2 (January 2002): 157–200.

Tylor, E. B. *Primitive Culture: Researches into the Development of Mythology, Philosophy, Religion, Art, and Custom*. London: Bradbury, Evans, 1871.

United Nations. *Yearbook of Human Rights for 1948*. New York: United Nations, 1950.

Walzer, Michael. "On the Role of Symbolism in Political Thought." *Political Science Quarterly* 82, 2 (June 1967): 191–204.

Weber, Max. "Politics as a Vocation." In *From Max Weber: Essays in Sociology*, ed. H. H. Gerth and C. Wright Mills, 77–128. New York: Routledge, 1991.

White, Melanie. "Habit as a Force of Life in Durkheim and Bergson." *Body and Society* 19, 2–3 (2013): 240–62.

White, Stephen K. *Sustaining Affirmation: The Strengths of Weak Ontology in Political Theory*. Princeton, N.J.: Princeton University Press, 2000.

———. "Weak Ontology: Genealogy and Critical Issues." *Hedgehog Review* 7, 2 (Summer 2005): 11–25.

Wingo, Ajume. *Veil Politics in Liberal Democratic States*. Cambridge: Cambridge University Press, 2003.

Wolterstorff, Nicholas. *Justice: Rights and Wrongs*. Princeton, N.J.: Princeton University Press, 2010.

Zakaria, Fareed. "Culture Is Destiny: A Conversation with Lee Kwan." *Foreign Affairs* 73, 2 (March/April 1994): 109–126.

———. "The Rise of Illiberal Democracy." *Foreign Affairs* (November/December 1997): 22–43.

INDEX

Abi-Saab, Georges, 168n83
Adorno, Theodor, 146n32
aesthetics of human rights, 124, 126–27,
170-71n23
Agamben, Giorgio: biopolitics, 48, 49–50,
152nn48, 49, 53, 153n54; human rights
and sacredness/sacralization, 50, 153n56;
human rights under Nazism, 47, 48–49;
Nazification of law, 99–100, 164n29;
sacredness/sacralization, 48, 149n18,
150n29, 152n49; state sovereignty, 49–50,
152nn48, 53, 153n54
Albanese, Catherine, 147n42
Allen, Lori, 170n23
Alves, José, A. Lindgreen, 169n97
American Anthropological Association, 63
American Declaration of Independence. *See*
Declaration of Independence
Arendt, Hannah: common responsibility,
78–79; human rights, 47, 50, 104–5, 122–23;
moral community, 83, 84, 85; nation-states,
101; Nazification of law, 99–100, 164n29;
right to have rights, 104–6, 112, 165n49;
slavery analogy, 107, 166n61; social identity,
81–82, 85, 161nn100, 103; state sovereignty
and human rights, 46, 47, 49–50, 65; totalitarianism, 46, 81–85, 164n29; universal
access to human rights, 104–5, 165n48
Aristotle, 81, 161n100
Article 1, 58, 134, 150n30, 161n95
Article 6 (Right to Recognition as a Person
before the Law), 99, 102–3, 134
Article 7 (Equal Protection and Nondiscrimi-
nation), 99, 108, 134
Article 8 (Right to Effective Legal Remedy),
99, 108, 134
Article 9 (Arbitrary Arrest, Detention or
Exile), 99, 134

Article 10 (Fair and Public Hearings), 99,
108, 135
Article 11 (Right to be Presumed Innocent
until Proven Guilty/Right to Public Trial),
99, 108, 135
Article 12 (Freedom from Arbitrary Interfer-
ence), 99, 135
Article 16 (Right to Marriage and Family),
70, 135
Article 19 (Right to Freedom of Opinion and
Expression), 136, 154n75
Article 20 (Right to Peaceful Assembly and
Association), 136, 154n75
Article 22 (Right to Social Security/Social,
Economic and Cultural Rights), 136,
150n30
Article 23 (Right to Work and to Join Trade
Unions), 136, 150n30
Article 26 (Right to Education), 76–78, 137
Article 28 (Right to a Social and International
Order in which the Rights and Freedoms
set out in the Declaration can be Realized),
109, 137
Article 29 (concerning Rights, Freedoms and
Duties), 70–71, 75, 138, 158n47
Asad, Talal: aesthetics of human rights,
126–27; inherent human dignity, 125–26;
nation-state interrelationship with rule
of law, 168n92; sacredness/sacralization,
43; secularism/secularity, 26, 40, 41, 60,
149n14; state sovereignty and human
rights, 65
Azkoul, Karim, 39, 53

Barthes, Roland, 143n4, 145n26
Bataille, Georges, 44
Beitz, Charles R., 170n9
Bellah, Robert N., 7

Benhabib, Seyla, 165n49, 168n96
Bentham, Jeremy, 147n58
Berger, Peter L., 42
Bergson, Henri, 68, 74, 88–89, 90
biological/racial logic of *Volksgemeinschaft*,
　49, 82, 152n52
biopolitics, 45, 47–51, 152nn48, 49, 52, 53,
　164n29
Birmingham, Peg, 112, 140nn14, 16, 153n55,
　165n47
Blumenberg, Hans, 30–31, 32
bodily/human integrity, 49, 50, 53, 62, 125
Bolle, Kees, 143n3
Bottici, Chiara, 29–30
Bruner, Jerome, 170n19
Bultmann, Rudolf, 32
Butler, Judith, 170n21

Campbell, Joseph, 25
Carozza, Paolo G., 66, 127
Casanova, José, 20
Cassin, René: Enlightenment legacy, 59;
　extrajudicial logic of human rights, 110–11,
　167nn76, 79; leadership of Commission, 18;
　legal personality, 102–3, 105–6; nation-
　states, 90; organic state, 80; right to have
　rights, 108; rule of law, 100; slavery analogy,
　107, 166n63; social identity, 75–76, 77;
　universalism of human rights, 61
Cassirer, Ernst, 27–28, 152n50
Challand, Benoît, 29–30
Chang, Peng Chun, 18, 73–75, 76, 87, 120,
　142n5. *See also* educational logic; human
　family
Cheah, Pheng, 171n28
Chidester, David, 41–43, 149nn14, 18
Christianity, 7, 28, 57–59, 63–64, 65, 143n.54,
　144n.14
Clinton, William Jefferson, 1–2, 18
coercion/power within law/legal systems, 5,
　90–91, 98, 115, 126, 128, 143n54
Cohen, Joshua, 167n68
Cohen, Stanley, 170n13
Collier, Jane F., 150n24
Commission on Human Rights (Human
　Rights Commission), 3, 17, 18, 142n5. *See
　also* Universal Declaration of Human Rights
concentration camps, 48, 51, 84, 153n56,
　166n61. *See also* Holocaust; Nazism; World
　War II

Connolly, William E., 171n32
conversion, human rights as, 87, 90, 127–28,
　160n81, 171n35, 172n35
cosmogony, 151n35
cosmopolitanism of human rights. *See* moral
　community; social identity
Cotterrell, Roger, 94, 96–97, 98, 113, 116,
　163n14, 164n24
Critchley, Simon, 141n23
cultural relativist critique of human rights,
　62–64

Das, Samir Kumar, 169nn98-99
Davies, Ernest, 104
the Declaration. *See* Universal Declaration of
　Human Rights
Declaration of Independence, United States,
　6, 9, 47, 124
Declaration of the Rights of Man and of the
　Citizen, French, 6, 9, 45, 47, 58, 65, 105,
　123, 124, 151n34
Dean, Jodi, 170n21
Derrida, Jacques, 6–7, 38, 96, 123, 129,
　140n22, 141n24, 169n97
de Vries, Hent, 80
Doniger, Wendy, 17, 27, 32, 33, 142n47,
　170n22
Donnelly, Jack, 2, 5, 148n6
Douglas, Mary, 150n32
Dovey, Kim, 28
Durkheim, Émile: coercion/power within
　law/legal systems, 98, 115, 126; dualism of
　sacred and profane, 150nn28–29; human
　dignity as sacred, 43, 150n24; human
　rights, 9, 73, 86, 88, 90; legal theory, 94,
　95–99, 104, 113, 115, 116, 163nn12, 14, 16,
　164n24; moral community, 67, 69, 76–77,
　85, 89, 94, 158n39; myth, 8, 11, 26–27, 67,
　69, 142n37, 145n26; nation-states, 88, 90;
　public opinion, 74; religious logic, 8–10,
　41, 67–68, 69, 74, 77, 85, 86; sacredness/
　sacralization, 41, 43, 149n14, 150nn24,
　28, 29; social identity, 14–15, 67, 81, 85,
　162nn119, 132; sociofunctionalism, 8,
　10–11, 66–67

Eck, Diane, 26,
educational logic: of human family, 76;
　within human rights, 22, 37, 73–76, 80,
　159n55; moral community and, 80; of

Nazism, 78, 83; social identity and, 37, 75, 77–78, 83. *See also* Article 26; Article 28
Eichmann, Adolf, 84
Eliade, Mircea, 25, 41, 144n12, 149n18, 150n28
enforcement of human rights: description of, 3, 34–35, 87; rule of law and, 101, 103–4; unenforceable declaration versus binding covenant and, 2–6, 11, 15, 19–20, 34–35, 90, 159n58. *See also* extrajudicial logic of human rights; law/legal systems; rule of law
Enlightenment, legacy of, 23, 26, 36, 47, 58–59, 62–64, 124, 155n90
Eurocentrism, 19, 58, 63, 66, 144n14. *See also* Enlightenment; international (global) community
Evans, Tony, 117–18
extrajudicial logic of human rights: description of, 3–7, 34, 93, 114, 140n22, 169n97; in international community, 5–6, 110–11, 167nn76, 79; religious logic of, 7. *See also* rule of law

family, human. *See* human family
Fields, Karen E., 74
Fitzpatrick, Peter, 6, 140n22, 142n43
Flood, Christopher, 141n30, 146nn29, 33, 37, 147n42
Forst, Rainer, 140n18
Foucault, Michel, 47, 115
foundational arguments, 38–39, 148n6
Freeman, Michael, 127
French Declaration of the Rights of Man and of the Citizen. *See* Declaration of the Rights of Man and of the Citizen
Freud, Sigmund, 115, 144n14

Gauchet, Marcel, 63-64
Geertz, Clifford, 8, 10, 141n31, 142n36, 146n36
Gentile, Emilio, 157n9
Giddens, Anthony, 164n27
Glendon, Mary Ann, 5, 21, 54, 66, 71, 110, 142n5
global (international) community. *See* international (global) community; nation-states
Goodale, Mark, 156n1
Gramsci, Antonio, 5, 6, 145n26
Gregg, Benjamin, 172n41

Gregory, Brad S., 64
Gündogdu, Ayten, 140n14

Habermas, Jürgen, 89, 90, 103–4, 108–9, 143n54, 165n44
Hajjar, Lisa, 118, 168n92
Hamacher, Werner, 44, 45, 151n34, 169n101
Hardt, Michael, 157n19
Hayden, Patrick, 162n117
Hegel, G. W. F., 47, 144n14
Himmler, Heinrich, 47
Hitchcock, William I., 142n49
Hitler, Adolf, 46, 78, 80, 164n29. *See also* Nazism; *Volksgemeinschaft*
Hoffman, Piotr, 128, 172n35
Holmes, Brian, 146n30, 152n50
Holocaust, 13–14, 44–46, 48–51, 55, 84, 107–8, 114, 125, 153n56, 166n61. *See also* Nazism; *Volksgemeinschaft*; World War II
Horkheimer, Max, 146n32
human/bodily integrity, 49, 50, 53, 62, 125
human dignity, concept of, 43, 59–60, 68, 87, 150n24. *See also* inherent human dignity; sacredness/sacralization of human dignity
human family: educational logic of, 76; moral community and, 72, 74–75, 78–79, 89, 101; religious logic of, 77; rule of law and, 104, 116; social identity and, 67, 71–72, 75–76, 79–80, 86, 88, 89–91, 158n54
human labor, myth as. *See* myth as human labor
human rights: aesthetics of, 124, 126–27, 170n170; biopolitics interrelationship with, 47, 50; bodily/human integrity and, 53, 62, 125; as conversion, 77, 87, 90, 127–28, 128, 160n81, 171n35, 172n35; educational logic in, 22, 37, 73–76, 76, 80, 159n55; foundational arguments for, 39; globalization of, 2; inherent human dignity as prescription for, 36–39, 52, 53, 57, 59–60; in international community, 2–4, 7, 13, 15–18, 117–18; in law/legal systems, 79–80, 79–80, 79–80, 103, 103, 160n92, 165n44; literary/cultural support for, 86, 162n124; moral logic of, 9–10, 16–18, 103, 165n44; nation-states interrelationship with, 46, 49–50, 65, 77, 88, 101, 113–14, 160n82; under Nazi totalitarianism, 47, 48–49, 152n45; pragmatic versus philosophical approaches to, 4–6; religious logic interrelationship with,

human rights (*continued*)
  8–10, 20, 86; sacredness/sacralization of,
  39–41, 44, 45, 50, 66, 148n9, 153n56; secular logic of, 7, 8–9, 105, 127, 130; slavery
  analogy and, 107–8, 166n61, 166n63; universalism in narrative of, 2, 4, 7, 18, 19, 29,
  34, 37, 40, 61. *See also* extrajudicial logic of
  human rights
Human Rights Commission. *See* Commission on Human Rights
Hunt, Lynn, 5, 86, 162n124
Hurd, Elizabeth Shakman, 171n35

Ignatieff, Michael, 2, 4, 66, 72, 118, 155n77,
  157n18, 170n8
immanent frame, the, 19–20, 63–64
index of human worth, 55–56, 60–61,
  62, 65, 99, 124. *See also* inherent human
  dignity
individual/s: biopolitics and, 45, 47–51,
  152nn48, 49, 52, 53, 164n29; law/legal
  systems interrelationship with, 113;
  nation-states interrelationship with, 101–2;
  rule of law and, 100–101, 111–13, 168n83;
  state sovereignty interrelationship with,
  46–48, 53, 55, 65; under totalitarianism,
  107, 166n60
individualism, cultural relativist critique of
  human rights and, 62–63, 64
inherent human dignity: description, 13,
  36–37, 44, 51–52, 125–26, 128–29, 150n30,
  153n63; conceptions versus concept of
  human dignity and, 59–60; human rights
  as prescribed by, 36–39, 52, 53, 57, 59–60;
  index of human worth and, 55–56, 60–61,
  62, 65, 99, 124; within international
  community, 39, 50, 56, 57, 90; in law/legal
  systems, 79–80, 160n92; legal personality
  interrelationship with, 104, 105; rule of
  law interrelationship with, 11, 98–99, 104,
  108–11, 114–16, 168nn83, 84, 169n101;
  secular logic of, 63; within social identity,
  69–70, 71, 73, 79, 86; state sovereignty
  conflicts with, 52–55, 154nn66, 75,
  158n54; universalism of, 39, 50, 53, 59,
  66, 90; World War II abuses context
  for, 44–46, 99, 150n33, 151n35. *See also*
  human dignity; individualism; sacredness/
  sacralization of human dignity
integrity, bodily/human, 49, 50, 53, 62, 125

international (global) community: the
  Declaration interrelationship with, 18, 34,
  39; Eurocentrism within, 19, 58, 63, 66,
  144n14; extrajudicial logic of human rights
  within, 5–6, 110–11, 167n76, 167n79; indi-
  vidual/s within, 70, 106, 113–15, 168n92;
  inherent human dignity within, 39, 50, 56,
  57, 90; laws of, 2–3, 19, 20, 34, 46, 51, 54,
  76, 80, 93, 100, 168nn83, 84; moral logic
  of, 9, 17–18; rule of law interrelationship
  with, 109–11, 113–15, 167nn76, 79, 181,
  83, 168n92; secular logic of, 27, 58–59, 66.
  See also nation-states

Joas, Hans, 32, 157n33, 163n12
Jonas, Hans, 32

Kahn, Paul W., 135n60
Kaminsky, Leonid, 52
Kant, Immanuel, 64, 72, 73, 143n54
Kochi, Tarik, 171n31
Koretsky, Vladimir, and topics: declaration
  versus covenant, 34–35; individual/s as
  embedded in society, 70; inherent human
  dignity in conflict with state sovereignty,
  52, 53, 55, 154n66, 154n75; legal personality, 103; rule of law, 109

Lacoue-Labarthe, Philippe, 146n30, 152n50
Lauren, Paul Gordon, 120–21, 142n44,
  135n58
law/legal systems: coercion/power within, 5,
  90–91, 98, 115, 126, 143n54; human rights
  within, 79–80, 103, 160n92, 165n44; indi-
  vidual/s interrelationship with, 113; inherent human dignity within, 79–80, 160n92;
  of international community, 2–3, 19, 20,
  34, 46, 51, 54, 76, 80, 93, 100, 168nn83,
  84; legal rights within, 99, 160n92; in
  moral community, 96, 98, 115; moral logic
  interrelationship with, 94–99, 114, 116,
  163n14, 168n96; moral rights within, 103,
  165n44; of nation-states, 2–3, 47, 54, 102,
  105, 111, 153n54; Nazification of, 99–100,
  114, 164n29; religious logic interrelationship with, 93, 95–98, 100, 163nn3, 12, 16,
  164n24; right to have rights within, 104–6,
  108, 112, 165n49; sacredness/sacraliza-
  tion of, 163n12; secular logic of, 6, 7, 20,
  163n12; social identity interrelationship

with, 100, 113; universalism of, 104–5,
165n48. *See also* enforcement of human
rights; rule of law
Lefebvre, Alexandre, 73, 74, 77, 87–89, 90,
128, 160n82
Lefort, Claude, 164n30
legal personality, 102–5, 104, 105, 108–10,
112–16, 166n63. *See also* law/legal systems;
rule of law
legal positivism, 6, 7, 19–20, 54, 92–93, 96,
104, 109–10, 160n92, 167n73
legal rights, 99, 160n92. *See also* Articles
6-12; enforcement of human rights; extrajudicial logic of human rights; law/legal
systems; legal personality
Lévi-Strauss, Claude, 41–42, 145n26, 149n18
Lincoln, Bruce, 25, 26–27, 28, 29, 145n26
Linenthal, Edward T., 41–43, 149nn14, 18
Little, David, 140nn16, 18, 141n33, 155n89
Lovin, Robin, 151n35
Lukes, Steven, 150n24
Lynch, Gordon, 33, 149n21
Lyotard, Jean-François, 94–95, 169n97

Mahmood, Saba, 128, 172n35
Mahoney, Jack, 155n90, 156n99
Malik, Charles, and topics: educational logic
of human rights, 87; Enlightenment legacy,
59; extrajudicial logic of human rights, 4,
87; human family, 158n54; index of human
worth, 55–56; individual/s as embedded
in society, 71, 106–7, 158n47; inherent
human dignity, 51–52, 54–56, 57, 60,
153n63, 158n54; leadership of Commis-
sion, 18, 142n5; moral logic of human
rights, 3–4; slavery analogy, 107; social
identity, 71, 106, 158nn47, 54; universal-
ism, 61, 156n98; values, right scale of, 38,
54–55
Malinowski, Bronisław, 7, 141n28
Marietta, Morgan, 43, 149n21
Maritain, Jacques, 60
Masuzawa, Tomoko, 144n13
Mauss, Marcel, 145n26
Mazur, Eric Michael, 141n26
McCarthy, Kate, 141n26
McClure, Kristie M., 171n28
McCrudden, Christopher, 59, 155n85
Mehta, Hansa, 70
Meron, Theodor, 111, 168n83

Mohamed, Feisel G., 170n23
moral community: description of, 69, 94,
143n54, 155n90, 157n33, 158n39; educational logic and, 80; foundational arguments and, 148n6; human dignity within,
68, 87; human family and, 72, 74–75, 89,
101; law/legal systems and, 96, 98, 101,
115; myth and, 67; religious logic of, 9–11,
67–69, 77, 85, 88–89; rule of law and, 101;
sacredness/sacralization of human dignity
in, 68, 87, 92, 93; totalitarianism ramifications on, 81–85. *See also* human family;
social identity
moral logic of human rights: description of,
3–4, 5, 9–11, 15, 16–18, 20, 103, 165n44;
law/legal systems interrelationship with,
94–99, 114, 116, 163n14, 168n96; in rule
of law, 104, 114, 116; sacredness/sacral-
ization and, 11, 20, 43; secular logic of,
40, 43; unenforceable declaration versus
binding covenant and, 34. *See also* moral
community
Morsink, Johannes: common responsibility,
79, 160n90; human rights, 56–57, 79,
162n132; inherent human dignity, 13,
58, 154n75; legal rights, 99, 160n92;
moral community, 72, 78, 101, 155n90,
162n132; Nazification of law, 99–100;
World War II abuses, 54, 99–100, 150n33,
153n57
Moyn, Samuel, 16–18, 65, 119, 120, 121–23,
170nn12, 18
Mutua, Makau, 156n1, 171n30
myth as human labor, 16-17, 23-24, 26-27,
31-34, 146n30
mythopoeic narratives: description and
purpose of, 7–9, 11–12, 18–19, 23, 26–28,
120, 122, 129, 141n28, 142n37, 145n26,
146n35; human labor and, 23–24, 26, 27,
31, 34, 146n30; of Nazism, 49, 152nn50-
51; sacred versus secular, 22–23; versus
ideology, 10, 26, 28, 32, 146n33; in sociofunctionalism, 7–8, 11, 17, 32, 66–67,
118, 123, 129; of *Volksgemeinschaft*, 49,
152n51. *See also* myth
myth: description of, 67, 69, 124; as continuum of narratives, 17, 142n47; as human
labor, 16–17, 23–24, 27, 32, 145n145;
sacred versus secular, 22-23, 27–31,
146n37. *See also* mythopoeic narratives

Nancy, Jean-Luc, 146n30, 152n50
nation-states: in the Declaration, 72; human
   rights interrelationship with, 46, 49–50,
   65, 77, 88, 101, 113–14, 160n82, 162n132;
   individual/s interrelationship with, 101–2;
   law/legal systems of, 2–3, 47, 54, 102,
   105, 111, 153n54; as moral community,
   101; rule of law interrelationship with,
   101, 109–15, 167n73, 168n92; secular
   logic of, 66. See also international (global)
   community
natural law, 20, 58-59, 143n54, 155n90
Nazism: biopolitics and, 47–50, 164n29;
   concentration camps under, 48, 51, 84,
   153n56, 166n61; educational logic of, 78,
   83; human rights under, 47, 48–49; law/
   legal systems of, 99–100, 114, 164n29;
   mythopoeic narrative of, 49, 152n50;
   slavery analogy and, 107–8, 166n.61; social
   identity under, 80–85. See also Holocaust;
   totalitarianism; Volksgemeinschaft; World
   War II
Negri, Antonio, 157n19
Neuman, Gerald L., 167n73
Neves, Marcelo, 109
Nongbri, Brent, 26, 144n13
Nussbaum, Martha, 125

Olney, Charles, 111–12, 167n81
organic state, 47, 80. See also
   Volksgemeinschaft
Orsi, Robert, 26
Otto, Rudolph, 144n7, 145n23
Owen, Julie, 127

Parekh, Serena, 106, 152n45, 165n48
Patton, Laurie L., 33
Pavlov, Alexie, 55, 109
Perry, Michael, 40, 148n9, 172n41
philosophical approach to human rights theory, 4–5, 39, 57, 64, 117–19, 124, 169n3
Plato, 47, 59, 81, 146n30
Platonic-Christian tradition, 57–58
political consciousness, 112–13, 115, 119,
   168n88
political landscape of the Declaration:
   description of, 1, 6, 7, 141n24; enforcement in context of, 3–6, 11, 15, 19–20,
   34–35; international (global) community and, 3, 50, 51, 76; unenforceable

declaration versus binding covenant and,
   2–6, 11, 15, 19–20, 34–35, 90, 159n58
political myth: description of, 7–8, 12–13,
   15–16, 23–31; demystification of, 16, 18,
   19, 121–23, 128–29, 170n18, 170n21;
   sacredness/sacralization within, 28–31,
   146n37
Pollis, Adamantia, 118
Power, Samantha, 160n89
power/coercion within law/legal systems, 5,
   90–91, 98, 115, 126, 128, 143n54
pragmatic approach to human rights theory,
   4–7, 17–18, 117, 130, 140n18, 155n77,
   169n3
Preamble of the Declaration: drafts and text
   of, 52–53, 133–34, 148n3, 154n67. See also
   Universal Declaration of Human Rights
Pritchard, Richard, 74
profanation: dualism of sacred and profane
   and, 29, 43-45, 67, 150nn28–29, 150n32
public opinion: in creation of social identity,
   3, 74–75, 159n58, 160nn81, 82; religious
   logic of, 74–77

Qutb, Sayyid, 128

Rawls, John, 29, 64, 72, 73, 146n38
religious logic of human rights: description of, 6–12, 19–20, 67–68, 69, 86, 118,
   143n52; extrajudicial logic and, 7; of
   human family, 77; immanent frame and,
   19–20, 63–64; inherent human dignity
   and, 57–58; law/legal systems interrelationship with, 93, 95–98, 100, 163n3,
   163nn12, 16, 164n24; moral community
   and, 9–11, 67–69, 77, 85, 88–89; political
   context for, 23; versus secular logic, 20, 27,
   30; social identity interrelationship with,
   67, 93, 95–98, 163nn3, 12, 16, 164n24; in
   sociofunctionalism, 10–11, 23, 24, 66, 85,
   142n37, 144n12; theory of, 9, 12, 25, 40,
   118, 144n14
Reynolds, Frank E., 151n35
right to have rights, the 104–6, 108, 112, 130,
   165n49
Romulo, Carlos, 110
Roosevelt, Eleanor: educational logic of
   human rights, 22, 73–74, 76, 83, 159n55;
   extrajudicial logic of human rights, 4;
   inherent human dignity, 56; leadership of

Commission, 18, 142n5; legacy of Declaration, 118; legal personality, 102–3; moral community, 73, 85; moral logic of human rights, 22; public opinion, 74, 90, 159n58, 160n81; slavery analogy, 107; unenforceable declaration versus binding covenant, 159n58; universalism, 59, 66

Rorty, Richard, 140n16, 148n2

Roubaud, Jacques, 170n22

rule of law: as term of use, 104; description of, 14–15, 92–94, 100–101, 119, 142n43; coercion/power within, 115, 126, 128; enforcement of human rights and, 101, 103–4; the human family and, 104, 116; individual/s and, 100–101, 111–12, 111–13, 168n83; inherent human dignity interrelationship with, 11, 98–99, 104, 108–11, 114–16, 168nn83–84, 169n101; international community interrelationship with, 109–11, 113–15, 167nn76, 79, 81, 83, 168n92; legal personality and, 102–5, 108–10, 112–16, 166n63; moral community and, 101; moral logic of, 104, 114, 116; nation-states interrelationship with, 101, 109–15, 167n73, 168n92; Nazification of law interrelationship with, 99–100, 112, 164n29; political consciousness and, 112–13, 115, 119, 168n88; right to have rights and, 106, 130; universalism of, 100–102, 104, 109, 115, 116, 168n92. *See also* Articles 6-12; enforcement of human rights; extrajudicial logic of human rights; law/legal systems; legal personality.

sacredness/sacralization: description of, 43; biopolitics interrelationship with, 45, 48, 152nn48–49; dualism of sacred and profane and, 29,43-45, 67, 150nn28, 29, 32; of human rights, 39–41, 44, 45, 50, 66, 148n9, 153n56, 172n41; myth and, 22–23, 28–31, 146n37; profanation dualism with, 29, 43–45, 67, 150n32; secularism/secularity interrelationship with, 20, 26, 27, 30, 40, 41, 60, 149n14; situational approach to, 41–43, 48, 49, 51, 149n18, 150n29; in sociofunctionalism, 41, 149n14; substantial approach to, 41, 149n14, 149n18; the orization of, 42, 149n21; universalism of, 40–41; of *Volksgemeinschaft*, 13, 48–49, 80,

82, 100, 164n29. *See also* inherent human dignity; profanation

sacredness/sacralization of human dignity: description of, 13–14, 124, 130, 172n41; historical context for, 43, 57–58, 150n24; human rights interrelationship with, 39–42, 44, 45, 60, 66, 148n9; legal personality interrelationship with, 105; moral community and, 68, 87, 92, 93; preexistence of, 56–57, 155n85; religious logic and, 57; rule of law interrelationship with, 11, 98–99, 109–10. *See also* human dignity; inherent human dignity; sacredness/ sacralization

Saint-Lot, Emile, 34

Santa Cruz, Hernán, 11

Schaffer, Kay, 113

Schmitt, Carl, 89

Schwarz, Elke, 161n102

secularism/secularity: description of, 11, 13, 20, 23, 60, 118, 170n8; extrajudicial logic and, 20; human rights interrelationship with, 7, 8–9, 105, 127, 130; immanent frame and, 19–20, 63–64; inherent human dignity in logic of, 63; of international community, 27, 58–59, 66; of law/legal systems, 6, 7, 20, 163n12; of moral logic, 40, 43; mythopoeic narratives' boundary effacement with, 10, 26, 28, 32, 146n33; religious logic interrelationship with, 20, 26, 27, 30; sacredness/sacralization interrelationship with, 20, 26, 27, 30, 40, 41, 60, 149n14

Silwinski, Sharon, 170n23

situational approach to the sacred, 41–43, 48, 49, 51, 149n18, 150n29

Slaughter, Joseph, 2–3, 5–6, 19–20, 27, 38–39, 114, 162n123

slavery analogy, 107–8, 166nn61, 63

Sluga, Glenda, 143n51

Smith, Jonathan Z., 12, 25, 31, 32, 142n37, 145n25, 149n18

Smith, Leslie Dorrough, 147n42

Smith, Sidonie, 113

social identity: description of, 14, 67, 81–82, 161nn100, 103; common responsibility and, 78–79, 160n90; educational logic and, 37, 75, 77–78, 83; human family and, 67, 71–72, 75–76, 79–80, 86, 88, 89–91, 158n54; individual/s as embedded in,

social identity (*continued*)
  69–71, 106–7, 113, 158n47, 162n119;
  inherent human dignity context for, 69–70,
  71, 73, 79, 86; law/legal systems interrelationship with, 93, 95–98, 100, 113, 163nn3,
  12, 16, 164n24; mythopoeic narratives
  context for, 32; public opinion and, 3,
  74–75, 159n58, 160nn81, 82; religious
  logic interrelationship with, 67, 93, 95–98,
  163nn3, 12, 16, 164n24; under totalitarianism, 80–85. *See also* human family; moral
  community
sociofunctionalism: mythopoeic narratives
  in, 7–8, 11, 17, 32, 66–67, 118, 123, 129;
  religion in, 10–11, 23, 24, 66–67, 85,
  142n37, 144n12; sacredness/sacralization
  in, 41, 149n14
Somers, Margaret, 130
sovereign state. *See* state sovereignty
state sovereignty: biopolitics interrelationship with, 49–50, 152n53, 153n54; human
  rights interrelationship with, 46, 49–50,
  65, 77, 88; individual/s interrelationship
  with, 46–48, 53, 55, 65; inherent human
  dignity conflicts with, 52–55, 154nn66, 75,
  158n54. See also *Volksgemeinschaft*
Strauss, Leo, 89, 90
Strenski, Ivan, 164n27
substantial approach to the sacred, 41,
  149nn14, 18
Sullivan, Winnifred Fallers, 145n20

Taussig, Michael, 44, 150n32
Taylor, Charles, 32, 63, 143n53
Teitel, Ruti, 111–12, 168nn84, 88
Third Reich. *See* Nazism; World War II
totalitarianism, 46, 48, 81–85, 107, 152n45,
  164n29, 166n60
Tseng, Pauline, 4–5
Tylor, E. B., 144n6

United Nations Charter of 1945, 2, 51, 92,
  154n67
Universal Declaration of Human Rights (the
  Declaration): abstentions from final vote,
  19, 53, 139n3, 154n75, 159n55; legacy of,
  2, 3–4, 6, 15, 19, 57, 92, 114, 118, 169n97;
  text of, 133–38; votes on, 1, 3, 19, 53, 61,

139n3, 154n75. *See also* Articles; Commission on Human Rights; enforcement of
  human rights; extrajudicial logic of human
  rights; human rights; moral community;
  mythopoeic narratives; philosophical
  approach to human rights theory; political
  myth; pragmatic approach to human
  rights theory; Preamble of the Declaration;
  religious logic; rule of law; secularism/
  secularity; universalism
universal human rights. *See* human rights
universalism: of the Declaration, 1–2, 5, 9,
  13, 18, 29, 53–54, 59–61, 66, 156n98; in
  human rights narrative, 2, 4, 7, 18, 19, 29,
  34, 37, 40, 61; of inherent human dignity,
  39–41, 50, 53, 59, 66, 90; of rule of law,
  100–102, 109, 115, 116, 168n92
utilitarianism, 17, 37–38, 50, 55–56, 72–74,
  151n34

Volksgemeinschaft (organic state): description of, 46; biological/racial logic of, 49,
  82, 152n52; biopolitics and, 49, 152n52;
  historical context for, 47; integrity, bodily/
  human and, 49, 50; moral community and,
  85; mythopoeic narrative of, 49, 152n51;
  references to, 50, 51; sacredness/sacral-
  ization of, 13, 48–49, 80, 82, 100, 164n29;
  state sovereignty context for, 64. *See also*
  Nazism; totalitarianism
Vyshinsky, Andrei, 102

Weber, Max, 98
White, Melanie, 157n31, 160nn76–78
White, Stephen K., 33, 34, 74, 129
Wingo, Ajume, 147n42
Wolterstorff, Nicholas, 148n1
World War II: cosmogony and, 151n35;
  Holocaust during, 13–14, 44–46, 48–50,
  55, 107–8, 114, 125; inherent human
  dignity context for abuses during, 44–46,
  99, 150n33, 151n35; references to abuses
  during, 50, 51, 53–54, 85, 153n57. *See also*
  Nazism; totalitarianism; *Volksgemeinschaft*

Yew, Lee Kuan, 62, 63, 64, 125

Zakaria, Fareed, 156n1, 172n36

ACKNOWLEDGMENTS

A number of years ago, I found myself walking outside into a frigid March morning in upstate New York to meet the people who would eventually become my colleagues in the Colgate University Department of Religion. At the time, I didn't actually know that they would become my colleagues—and, given the bitter weather of that particular spring, I might have balked just a bit if I had known then that the post-doc for which I was interviewing would eventually grow into a visiting and then a tenure-track professorship. What I did know as I headed into the chill of downtown Hamilton was that I felt immediately at home in the company of my guide, Christopher Vecsey, who gave me an enthusiastic tour of the environs and who, in the wake of that first tour, has never failed to convey a similar level of warmth and enthusiasm in the face of my various questions, ideas, and dilemmas.

As I was soon to discover, Chris's congeniality was a quality endemic to Colgate's Department of Religion; since beginning my employment, I have never lacked for a friendly word of support or gesture of encouragement. Ultimately, the time that I have spent at Colgate converges so neatly with my development as a scholar that I find it difficult to separate these aspects of my life. If that doesn't qualify as a true intellectual home, I don't know what does. In addition to my gratitude to Chris, then, I offer my thanks to those other Religion Department colleagues who have played an invaluable role in my ongoing presence and intellectual growth at Colgate: Harvey Sindima, Steven Kepnes, Clarice Martin, Georgia Frank, Eliza Kent, and John Carter. I offer my particular thanks to two department members who have been inordinately generous with their attention and input: Lesleigh Cushing Stahlberg, who is not only a cherished collaborator but also a model to me as a teacher, friend, and mother, and Benjamin Stahlberg, an irreplaceable colleague and friend who has been an astute and good-humored reader of earlier iterations of these chapters.

I have been fortunate to have been supported in a variety of ways by the broader Colgate community as well as by my own department. I offer my thanks to Alexander Karn for his many words of advice and encouragement over the past few years, and to the Colgate University Research Council for its generosity in funding many elements of the research and editing of this book.

In the distant background of this project are Richard Hecht, Giles Gunn, Lisa Hajjar, and Eve Darian-Smith. Giles will always have my particular gratitude for (perhaps without even remembering it) having taken the time one random day to send me a letter expressing his enthusiasm for my project and insisting that I publish it. In the much more immediate background, I offer my thanks to Peter Agree, an enthusiastic and generous editor and one of the nicest people I have never actually met. Thank you, Peter, for all of your help. I also wish to thank Alison Anderson for her careful, thoughtful, and timely management of the copyediting over the course of many months.This is a better book for having received her scrutiny and input.

I am deeply grateful to my parents for their unflagging love and encouragement—particularly to my father, Michael Reinbold, who offered without hesitation to give me a hefty portion of his time and his attention to detail as I put the finishing touches on this manuscript. I am most grateful, though, to my immediate family. I am astounded to realize how much time has passed since I offered a humble thanks to my soon-to-be-husband for his willingness to weather at least two New York winters so that I might pursue my academic career. Today, I have no words to express my gratitude to him for all that he has done to enable me to do the work that has led to this book. As if that weren't enough, he has given me the two most precious gifts that I have ever received. This book is dedicated to Joe, Isaac, and Eleanor.